*Puppet Theatre in Performance*

# PUPPET THEATRE IN PERFORMANCE

## Nancy H. Cole

### Everything You Need to Know About How to Produce Puppet Plays

WILLIAM MORROW AND COMPANY, INC.

NEW YORK        1978

*For Kimberley, Jennifer,*
*and Jason*

Library of Congress Cataloging in Publication Data

Cole, Nancy H.
  Puppet theatre in performance.
  Bibliography: p.
  Includes index.
  SUMMARY: A compendium of information on setting up a puppet theatre and putting on plays.
  1.  Puppets and puppet-plays. [1.  Puppets and puppet-plays]  I.  Title.
PN1972.C597  791.5′3  78-5968
ISBN 0-698-03318-0

Printed in the United States of America.
First Edition      1   2   3   4   5   6   7   8   9   10

Designed by Lesley Achitoff

# The Perfectibility of Puppet Theatre

by Lowell Swortzell

Heinrich von Kleist, that brilliant nineteenth-century novelist, playwright, and essayist whose work only now is appreciated fully for its modern viewpoint, recognized the perfectibility of puppets in a series of newspaper articles published in 1810. His discovery came by accident and by second hand, the result of noticing a leading dancer of the day in regular attendance in the marketplace where public performances were played upon a marionette stage. Kleist was surprised by the reply when he asked the gentleman why he took so much pleasure in these shows, for the dancer said he came in order to improve himself and to learn from the puppets. What knowledge, Kleist pondered, could a dancer, indeed could anybody, acquire from puppets? After all, weren't they momentary amusements to please the mingling masses, and nothing more? The dancer, leading Kleist to observe the small stage as never before, pointed to the grace of the dancing puppets whose movements proved to be so real that their execution seemed to require a web of strings and many nimble-fingered operators. Yet, to his astonishment, Kleist counted only the usual number of strings and puppeteers at work. The dancer explained that not every movement was controlled by strings, or by operators either, inasmuch as some limbs moved from the puppet's center of gravity, swinging freely as pendulums do in line, curve, and rhythm. It was this free movement that gave the puppets their most lifelike action and made them true dancers.

The center of gravity, Kleist now realized, was the key to operating the dancing puppets. But to discover it, he also recognized, the manipulator had to find his own center and to undergo the same movement himself. In other words, the puppeteer had to dance and to discover the extent of freedom in his own swinging arms and thereby to duplicate this exact experience in the puppets who, in turn, communicated it to the audience. Finding mystery in this creative process, he saw it as the pathway to the performer's soul. For now he perceived that puppeteers not only knew the expressiveness of every limb of their dolls but also were masters of their own limbs, able to transfer truths discovered in themselves to the creatures they enhanced with life. Thinking that in this regard they could be compared to God, Kleist suddenly elevated puppets and puppeteers to a higher art than their marketplace popularity previously had suggested.

In spite of its title, "On the Marionette Theatre," Kleist's essay is really a treatise on human consciousness. Nonetheless, it has benefited the field of puppetry by opening readers' eyes in much the fashion the author reports his were made to see puppets as pure performers and to appreciate puppeteers as actual artists.

## A Philosophic Art

Kleist, of course, was not the first to compare the relationship between puppet and man to that between man and God. Both Plato and Aristotle found the same analogy irresistible, but unfortunately in employing it neither revealed any information about actual puppet practices of their time. Nor did Marcus Aurelius and Apuleius in their comments, although we know far more about Roman puppets in general than we do about those of the Greeks. Few of us in the twentieth century have escaped Carlo Collodi's popular treatment of this same classic parallel in Pinocchio's arduous transformation from wooden puppet to real live boy.

Perhaps puppetry as an art of the highest order was not recognized before Kleist simply because it had been around so long, taken for granted for centuries by those masses mingling in public places, waiting to be amused. Its lengthy history, however, is proof of the high value the general populace has placed upon the puppet theatre from ancient times until now.

## Prehistoric Origins

Today a number of museums depict this history in their exhibitions of puppets past to present. Sergei Obraztsov's collection in his own puppet theatre in Moscow, The International Marionette Museum in Lyons, and the puppet museums in Munich and Zurich are four of the best. Here we see such early examples as primitive dolls and figurines with moving parts which were first activated by hand, water, and weights, and finally by strings. The Medieval church discovered the dynamics of depicting Christian saints and martyrs that moved—an image of Christ, for instance, with rising arms could not fail to impress parishioners. Our present use of the Christmas crèche, those miniature mangers with the familiar Bethlehem Nativity figures, descends from this same tradition of theatricalization of religious subjects. We also find on view the full-fledged puppets of antiquity, with India, China, and Greece each seeming to have developed puppets independently of one another at more or less the same earliest times. As folk art, these puppets were used by wandering storytellers to illustrate their tales or to entertain leaders of tribes and heads of primitive states.

## A Folk Art

Some puppets were cut out of leather and supported by rods, as were the first shadow puppets found in China, India, and Turkey. In Java shadow puppets became more intricate in design. In China they related the folklore and history of the people. In Sicily, centuries later, they incorporated rod and string techniques, and reenacted episodes from the heroic tale of *Orlando Furioso*. Twentieth-century descendants in Sicily and in the United States still popularize this epic theatre, employing armored knights each weighing about eighty pounds and standing between four and five feet tall. When they go into combat, as without fail they do at every performance, heads come off at the thrust of a sword, bodies topple, and the battlefield fills with slaughtered villains and conquering heroes. Viewers examining these puppets at close range following performances often find it impossible to believe the mighty warriors are not life-sized, so real has been their derring-do of attacks and counterattacks. The folk tradition of Sicily is emphatically preserved in the spirited text and spectacular performance of this national art.

## A Popular Art

The popular tradition of puppetry is nowhere better represented than in the British Punch-and-Judy show, which has its wellspring in Italian *commedia dell'arte* where Pulcinella inspired the hooknosed master of self-confidence and vulgarity, Mr. Punch. This wooden-headed clown carries a slapstick which also links his heritage to the court jester, and, like jester and fool, he can say whatever he pleases, be as rude, loud, and impossible as he likes, and get away with it. We tolerate and enjoy his bad behavior because he fulfills our desire to say and do what society, and our better judgment, forbid us. Punch can throw his crying baby out the window, hit his best friend over the head, beat his wife, Judy, until she is senseless (and sometimes dead), and then, just as he is about to be punished, outwit the Devil himself and run away, victorious and free. His is a cruel, head-banging world filled with biting dogs, kicking horses, gullible doctors, angry policemen, and the ever-present Hangman, but it is also one that has made generations appreciate all the more that they dwell in slightly tamer and saner surroundings where the slap of a stick does not yet accompany every word.

## A Refined Art

Puppetry also can be a most sophisticated art, as demonstrated by the Bunraku of Japan. This intricate and highly specialized theatre, consisting of large, brilliantly costumed figures, dates back to the end of the sixteenth century. Three operators are required to move each puppet: one to guide the feet, one to control the left arm, and the master puppeteer who looks after the weight, the head and face, and the right arm. All three wear black-hooded outfits and appear onstage throughout the performance. Such is the strong illusion created by the puppets that audiences disregard the operators, who gradually seem to disappear. These beautiful doll-puppets inspired dramatists to write a repertory especially for them to perform, and to enhance this special repertory, a style of acting was perfected in which the puppets seem to open their mouths, move their fingers, close their eyes, even shift their eyebrows. More than once in Japan's theatrical history, living actors have become jealous of their expressiveness and sought to imitate them.

## Values of Puppetry

Yes, as museums and any number of published histories can document, puppetry always has been popular in its many manifestations, but perhaps at no other time has it been more important than it is today. One reason, of course, is that most of the needs served by puppets in the past still must be met: the continuation of the folk tradition, the enrichment of literature, the glorification of history, the cultural contribution to a national identity, and the intensification of human awareness. These eternal values must be redefined and newly established by each generation. Each age also seems to discover original uses for puppets, and ours is no exception. In an era mesmerized by television, tapes, cassettes, and mechanized amusements, we recognize as perhaps never before the importance of "live" theatre. For many youngsters puppet performances are not only the first "live" shows they see but also the *only* live shows they experience for years at a time. Increasingly mobile and accessible, puppet theatres perform today throughout the country, reaching small towns and large cities alike. Here they continue to communicate the liveliness and humor of long ago; a good Punch-and-Judy show gains as many laughs now before inner-city children in parks and playgrounds or before rural youngsters at a country fair as its counterpart did in London's streets and at village crossings a century ago. Here they also reflect the concerns and consciousness of contemporary life with a directness and immediacy that most young people find exciting and memorable. For this reason puppetry is also earning a permanent place in schools and hospitals, not just as entertainment but as a recognized component of education and rehabilitation which has demonstrated outstanding effectiveness.

Puppets continue to transport us into unfamiliar worlds of beauty and adventure, as the Bunraku theatre did on its last visit to the United States, and as several Sicilian companies do each year by playing on American college campuses before new audiences. Because puppet shows amplify our knowledge of the world and its people, we need both to receive foreign companies as cultural representatives and to send forth our own as goodwill ambassadors. Several groups proved to be articulate spokesmen for the United States when they played before audiences in India and Latin America. Unofficial ties between the Soviet and American people never have been so strong as during the visit of the Obraztsov company here or when American delegations are received at the Obraztsov theatre in Moscow. Puppets can bring countries together in new understanding simply by sharing their talents.

## The Impact of Puppets

Why are puppet theatres effective both at home and abroad?

By improvising situations and dramatizing current life, they make the most of the moment. Often the best-liked puppeteers are those most up-to-date, most aware of the politics, the economy, and the major complaints of their audience. Even in countries where tradition dictates the content of plays and where spectators demand reenactment of religious epics, audiences still expect satirical observations and topical overtones as part of performances. Like Punch before him, a contemporary puppet can make comments most people cannot, can ridicule a president, mock a priest, correct a teacher—and be applauded instead of arrested, excommunicated, or expelled.

Audiences often succumb to the point of view of puppets and follow their advice simply because empathy is complete and identification strong. Puppets, after all, are people we believe in. If Oliver J. Dragon of *Kukla, Fran and Ollie* fame were to run for president of the United States, he very likely would get my vote even though I am familiar with his many foibles and idiosyncrasies and have no idea whether he is a Democrat, Republican, or independent. Yet he is so much an individual in whose enthusiasms I can believe and in whose company I can rejoice, that I can vow allegiance in his behalf. Indeed, he is more real to me than many actual candidates for whom I have voted but who did not possess his charismatic hold of my attention, confidence, or support. Perhaps like Kleist's discovery of "the center of gravity," another secret of puppets is their ability to be more human in the course of a short performance than most human beings manage to be throughout an entire lifetime.

## A Living Art

Puppets, to be certain, are much more alive when performing in the theatre than on television. (Even Oliver J. Dragon "in person" makes more of an impact than when viewed on camera.) Like Broadway actors, puppets, to be at their best, require live audiences to respond to, interact with, and to reward according to the rhythms, tensions, and energy of the performance. What is lost in close-ups and subtlety of facial expressions is far more than compensated for in the stimulation between spectators and performers, the dynamics of people and puppets in direct communication.

This rapport always has supplied the basis of puppets' spontaneity and improvisation, essential elements of performing now almost lost in movie and television studios and in pretaped programing. The thrill of audience participation achieves no greater success than when an audience of children speak to a puppet hero or villain in unison, a concert of voices cheering and booing but controlled completely by the small figures onstage who know exactly how long to engage in the practice and how far to allow the excitement to build. Puppet theatre, as much as any performing art, can be adapted to other mediums, but like ballet, opera, musical comedy, and serious drama, it is most effective in its own playhouse, the place for which it was intended. Puppet performances in theatres are events because both spectators and performers by virtue of their presence wish it so, and the auditorium and stage contribute the necessary equipment to make it so.

A large audience awaits such theatres today. Already resident companies occupy theatres in Washington, D.C., New York City, Detroit, and other large cities. Their patrons no longer consist exclusively of children, for after two hundred years Americans are undergoing a belated recognition that puppets entertain all ages, even adults! The nationwide popularity of the Muppets of *Sesame Street* throughout the 1970s extends far beyond their daytime programing for children to guest spots on late-night talk shows and to their own general-audience half-hour series in prime time. The Muppets have converted thousands from an attitude of "kid stuff" into regular viewers who enthusiastically quote lines and jokes from shows to colleagues at the office or place of business, much as their children exchange responses to *Sesame Street* at school. Fans of the Muppets, along with those of *Kukla, Fran and Ollie* of a generation earlier, provide the proof of an American audience composed of convinced network executives, school superintendents, and entire families selecting post-supper viewing. Puppetry, through television, has become a fixed part of American life.

## An Educational Art

Puppets are taking over entire classrooms to become teachers as well as entertainers. With their demonstrated ability to hold audience attention, puppets sometimes can communicate subjects to students more effectively than regular teachers, a fact learned by educators, priests, and storytellers centuries ago when first creating these earliest "visual aids." Nowadays puppet companies work in close harmony with school systems, to develop special shows according to curriculum requirements or to commemorate events such as the Bicentennial, Science Week, nutrition campaigns, or to mark holiday celebrations. Issues within schools and communities, depicted by puppets in dramatic situations, often become clearer than when discussed by local officers, social workers, and medical advisers. Puppets have thus helped to combat drugs, encourage birth control, explain alcoholism, as well as teach young children about safety, language skills, and dental hygiene. A variety of educational puppet shows are developed each year with the financial support of local and federal agencies, foundations, and private business. Such subsidies allow the field of educational puppetry to expand more rapidly than puppetry intended purely as entertainment. But if professional standards are maintained in school presentations (at present they often are not, unfortunately), educational puppetry can enlarge the potential audience for all puppetry.

Teachers who involve classrooms in puppet theatre production can meet almost every student interest in one common artistic endeavor that encompasses carpentry of the stage; sewing of costumes; painting of scenery; playwriting; directing; acting; operating the puppets; stage managing; supervising lights, sound, music; writing publicity releases; and selling tickets. A puppet show can extend beyond the classroom to become a schoolwide community event. When excellence is achieved, shows are often invited to perform at other schools, as well as in hospitals and geriatric centers, thereby introducing pupils to the discipline as well as pleasure that comes from trouping, day to day and week to week.

To prepare teachers and puppeteers to make the most effective uses of puppetry in education, as well as to elevate standards of classroom performance, courses and special workshops are now offered throughout the country. Universities and colleges have established credit courses and even degree programs specializing in puppetry. I am proud to count among them my own department, The Program in Educational Theatre at New York University, where for the last ten years such distinguished puppeteers as Nancy H. Cole, Caroly Wilcox of the Muppets, and George Latshaw have instructed and inspired students to impressive achievements, and where we now have the first Ph.D. dissertations being researched and written in the ever-growing field of educational puppetry.

## A Therapeutic Art

Puppet therapy, a recent development, significantly expands this world even more. Its use is now recognized by numerous hospitals where doctors often are eager to include trained puppeteers as staff specialists to work with emotionally disturbed children and adults, with the brain-damaged, physically handicapped, deaf, blind, and nonambulatory patients. Examples abound of children never before able to speak for themselves who suddenly discover voices for their puppets, of youngsters never before able to concentrate who eagerly spend long periods in conversations with puppets, of patients never before willing to admit emotional problems who in role playing recognize themselves in puppets and puppet plays. As in the regular classroom, the puppet show given in the special school or hospital provides everyone with a specific task and reward—the opportunity of achieving success in performance. Recognition won through artistic accomplishment is important, nay, essential, to the development of every child, and through puppetry it is available to all children. No matter so-called handicaps, a way can be found to give a puppet life and in so doing, as Kleist promised, receive some in return.

## A Theatre Art

Many books contend that puppetry depends upon far more than puppets for artistic success; in fact, say some, it only begins and not ends with puppets. Yet most authors spend the bulk of their texts discussing the creation of puppets and then hurriedly provide brief comments on the considerable remainder of a practice which incorporates all the elements of theatrical production. Puppeteers, likewise, sometimes seem to put their major effort into construction of figures, with little attention given to the dramatic vehicle that is to receive them. This is not true of great puppeteers, of course. "I have always been more theatre-oriented than craft-oriented," Burr Tillstrom has said, significantly insisting he has placed least emphasis upon the making of his puppets and most upon their story and performance.[1] Considering himself primarily a storyteller and an actor, Tillstrom calls for good puppets *and* settings, costuming, and music to "complement" the performance as they do in every theatrical production.

Tillstrom's advice pinpoints a major problem in puppetry today. While both professional puppets and puppeteers flourish as never before, we are still without sufficient companies whose plays, shows, and entertainments together can be said to constitute an American puppet theatre, in the way that we can identify Russian, Czechoslovakian, Austrian, and German puppet theatres and know that we are talking about individual companies whose collective styles represent their countries much as Broadway may be said to portray the American theatre or the West End England's theatrical achievement. If puppeteers become responsible to the performers they have already created by bringing about productions to keep them steadily employed, such a theatre can emerge. Once it does, dramatists may be attracted to write especially for puppets, as happened in Japan, or in Spain, where playwright-poet Federico García Lorca put into his puppet plays his most extravagant fantasies, his richest sense of the grotesque, and his greatest demand for spectacle, knowing that no other theatre could meet the cost of supplying his imagination with gold coaches, fountains, and a world that shimmers on cue with tiny fairy lights.

Equally important, puppeteers themselves will create for such a theatre, improvising on the spot and returning to puppetry that essential spontaneity now in danger of being lost. And when the best of costumes, sets, music, and performance techniques consistently "complement" these productions,

---

[1] Quoted in Hanford, Robert Ten Eyck, *The Complete Book of Puppets and Puppetry* (New York: Drake Publishers, 1976), p. 153.

we will have the true American puppet theatre for which we already possess the audience, the performers, and, God knows, the talent.

## Summary

Such a theatre is envisioned in this book in which Nancy H. Cole, like Kleist's dancer, stands at our side and makes the reader comprehend, perhaps for the first time, the importance not just of puppets but of puppets in performance. Hers is a total theatre in which every element of production is given full attention. Here we encounter puppeteers learning to act in order that their puppets may perform with control, form, and technique. They search for the "inner self" that allows them to share knowledge, emotions, and motivations. Her insistence that a puppeteer define what puppets want every minute they are onstage extends Kleist's "center of gravity" concept to the mind, even to the psyche, of both puppet and operator. Their duality becomes unified through established objectives and mutual belief in what they are doing. Together they discover movements, voices, gestures, and those unique qualities of style that always come from within rather than from imitation of other puppets or puppeteers. She reminds us that puppets can perform actions people cannot, fantastic, abstract, grotesque movements that go far beyond human limitations but which, to be believable, must be based in weight distribution and proper proportion. They, too, originate in the center of gravity and stem from the puppet's "inner life."

The playwrights of this theatre are urged to discard every nonessential word and to create dialogue and scenes that are verbal but, more important, are constantly visual. Then the directors take over to block the play and to conduct rehearsals, employing the same techniques and disciplines found in the living theatre. Puppetry *is* living theatre, we should know by now! Even properties and "makeup" become fundamental as this complete theatre goes into performance.

From the midst of this wide-ranging operation, we look more closely at the stage, its performing characters, their movements and costumes; we listen to their dialogue and follow their action, and we come to believe in their reality. In the company of this modern-day Kleist, we also become conscious that puppet theatre, unlike any other, can be the complete expression of an individual. By necessity, all other theatres depend upon the collaborative talents of many to create a single work of art. But the puppet theatre can be the creation and statement of the "inner self" of one person, even if he or she is assisted by other operators and technicians. Sensing that it can be the most personal of theatre, and the most ideal, we can recognize the puppet theatre as a metaphor for the perfectibility of all theatre.

The Program in Educational Theatre
New York University
*July 1977*

## *Acknowledgments*

So many people have contributed to this book through their gift of information and ideas, but most of all by their encouragement. My heartfelt thanks go to Marilyn Phillips for deciphering and typing the original manuscript and to Leta Westmoreland for reading it in its roughest state.

I would especially like to thank the following people, knowing I will omit many others inadvertently. I hope they will understand that in the long course toward completion of this book, I have lost track of how many have been gracious of their time and knowledge. My special gratitude, then, to Dr. Frank Ballard, Arlyn and Luman Coad, James Henson, George Latshaw, Lewis Mahlmann, Marjorie McPharlin, Prof. Sergei Obraztsov, Margo Rose, and Dr. Lowell Swortzell.

# Contents

# *Introduction*

Despite a flowering of puppet theatre in the 1930s and 1940s fostered by individual artists such as Tony Sarg and Remo Bufano and teams such as Romain and Ellen Proctor and Margo and Rufus Rose, the United States has never really developed a tradition of puppetry as a theatre art. You have just read in Dr. Swortzell's Preface some of the long and rich heritage of the art of the puppet. Why is it that an art which has both nurtured and inspired playwrights has, if not fallen to disrepute, at least failed to come of age in the United States? Without the puppet theatre he possessed at his grandmother's house as a boy, Goethe might never have given us *Faust*; much of Maurice Maeterlinck's most poignant writing was intended to be performed by puppets; García Lorca's fascination with the puppet has already been mentioned. On a contemporary note, Edward Albee once told me that the Grandmother in *The American Dream* was inspired by my treasured friend, Burr Tillstrom's incorrigible Beulah Witch.

Surely the television success of the Kuklapolitans and now of the Muppets has brought an awareness of the art of the puppet to the American public, but this awareness has done little to alter the preconceived notion of the potential American audience for live puppet theatre. Despite the existence in this country of individual brilliance in certain companies and puppeteers, the popular assumption still exists that puppets are "just for children" and that a puppet show will be a brief, possibly amusing, but certainly trivial form of entertainment. Curiously, if an audience is told that an act they are about to see "has appeared on television," they are impressed and eager to receive it, as though appearance on television automatically guaranteed some sort of fascination, but they seldom realize until they experience it that there is a unique quality both for the performer and for the audience in the intimacy and immediacy of live puppet theatre. Dr. Swortzell has already pointed out that seeing Burr Tillstrom work on television was a delight, but seeing him work "live" is something quite different and special.

How, then, are we to awaken the general public to the potential for education, imaginative involvement, and sheer entertainment that puppet theatre has to offer? Clearly one cannot expect to market a product for long if it is not a quality product. It is safe to assume that while quality exists and always has existed in live puppet theatre in the United States, there has not been *enough* quality reaching *enough* people to establish a tradition of appreciation for the art form. Clearly the answer lies in education—of the artists who will perform and thence, by the excellence of their performances, of their audiences. Puppetry is definitely on the rise; more and more colleges and universities are offering courses in the art of puppetry and several even have degree programs. Though our few permanent puppet theatres struggle constantly to keep their doors open, they do exist, and more are forming. With all this interest and effort on the part of educators and performers, we have lacked a text that treated puppetry as a theatre art; a text for those teachers, students, and aspiring beginning puppeteers learning on their own who seek to study puppetry not just as an arts-and-crafts hobby, but who are willing to work ceaselessly, perfecting, discovering, and reaching out to their audiences. We hope this book will fill that need and, accordingly, contribute in a small way to the maturity of puppet theatre in the United States.

This book differs markedly from other puppet books that precede it. It is not basically a how-to-make-a-puppet book. The craft material that is included is either not normally found in other books or is offered as part of an overview of the many methods of construction. Were we to detail all those methods here, we would need volumes, and there are more important and less widely treated aspects of the art of the puppet that need our attention. Though material on remaking purchased or previously constructed puppets is included in order to get the fledgling puppeteer up on his or her feet and working faster, craft material has been pared to the minimum; what is offered here is a manual of production techniques in the art of puppet theatre.

In order for a "puppet show" to become puppet theatre it must satisfy all of the criteria by which we test the success of live theatre, for puppet theatre is a style of the theatre as a whole, not a totally different art form. Just as in live theatre, puppetry represents a synthesis of many arts: acting, directing, writing, and design, to keep the list to a minimum. As in live theatre, and distinguishing it from the purely visual arts of painting and design that may be viewed and judged by a later age, puppet theatre must communicate at the moment of its performance; and communicate it must, for puppetry is not a "closet art," and those who play with puppets in a precious manner only to please themselves are missing the whole point. Puppet theatre may be an elaborate production requiring the cooperative efforts of many artists, or it may be a solo effort by one who has become a legitimate Jack-of-all-trades. Like live theatre, the success of puppet theatre depends upon capturing the poetic faith of the audience, obtaining their "willing suspension of disbelief." [1] For however brief a time, however simple the stage, the set of puppets, or the technical effects, the ability of the puppeteer to lead his audience to set aside their disbelief and enter into the world of his performance is the definition of his excellence.

Everything in the puppet theatre is pared toward greater simplicity. The emphasis is always upon the visual; this is a theatre of action, with a minimum or even an absence of dialogue. The resulting directness and appeal reaches that which is most emotionally basic in all of us and has been referred to by Professor Sergei Obraztsov of the Central State Puppet Theatre in Moscow as the "use of metaphor to convey the quintessential life." Obraztsov went on, in his remarkable address to the 1976 Congress of UNIMA (Union Internationale des Marionnettes), to refer to the use of both simplicity and folk art in puppet theatre, likening the resultant performance and its effect upon the audience to Teilhard de Chardin's "touching of the naked ground."

It is this closeness to "the ground of our being" that makes the puppet always a cousin to the mime, whether he performs with dialogue or not. He is the complete mask. He appears to live, and yet he has no life after the performance. We can talk to him, love him, hate him, participate in whatever his schemes; and since the puppet is not alive to reprimand us after the performance—nor can he "tell on us"—we are utterly free to enter into his world. Since he cannot step out of character, drop his mask, and disappoint us, for he *is* the mask, he can, when in the hands of a skilled artist, provoke a powerful empathy with which he can delight, instruct, and even heal. His appeal is ageless in the historical sense, and the age of his audience is limited only by the choice of subject matter, the approach, and the skill of the puppeteers. The home of the puppet is in abstraction (not to the point of being abstruse), never a realistic photograph of life. If the puppeteer will leave alone any material better suited to live actors than to puppets and perform only that which puppets can do better, the scope of his poetry is unlimited. Artistry, however, does not arrive overnight; it is clearly a case of Stanislavski's "my life in art, not art in my life."

In order to help you arrive at the synthesis of the arts that is puppet theatre, this text treats each aspect of theatre separately and guides the student to shape the component parts toward puppet theatre's unique demands. Whatever your strongest interest is, please read the text in order

---

[1] Samuel Taylor Coleridge, *Biographia Literaria* (New York: The Macmillan Company, 1926), Chapter 14.

instead of skipping to the chapter you need most. For instance, even if you have no interest in acting with puppets, our approach to later chapters will be much clearer if you will read through the exercises and study of this discipline first, the rest following in order, each complementing the other.

Many of you will wonder why the early chapters concentrate on the hand puppet. No, we do not believe him to be superior to, but of equal importance with other forms of puppets. Most people begin with hand puppets and work most easily with them, and they require the least construction. Moreover, most of the techniques taught for the hand puppet are applied later in the chapters on the marionette and the rod and shadow puppets.

It is our hope that this text will deepen your respect for puppet theatre. We hope to save you from lost hours of trial and error by offering hints we have discovered in construction and production of our own shows. At no time, however, does this book propose to be *the one method*. It is a good, solid working method, but there are others, and you will probably develop your own, which will combine aspects of many methods. Our aim is to supply a framework for development as an artist in the puppet theatre. There is no rule set that cannot be broken, except possibly the demand for discipline and for devotion. With those two qualities, you cannot but move forward, and as each of you who read this text performs work of greater strength, conviction, and beauty, our beloved small-theatre art will move that much closer to its rightful place of respect before the audience of our American people. Puppet theatre offers a small but important gateway to international understanding. As the general quality of puppet theatre in America improves, more and finer ambassadors from our puppet companies will comfortably join the frequent excellence found in the puppet theatres of Eastern and Western Europe.

The only way a puppeteer becomes proficient in our style of working is by spending many, many hours working at it. You must spend literally days in front of the mirror, watching your characters act and react, listen, think, and do all those tiny little things that a person does, because you have to keep working until the puppet is a living thing that you believe in.

This puppet now has a personality and you work until you can think and act directly through him or her. Once a puppeteer has reached this point, it now is just a matter of time—usually years—until he is good enough to be a principal in our group.

There are so many mechanics involved in puppeteering that all of those mechanics have to be totally automatic before you can give a real performance. It always seems strange, because no one believes this—particularly new puppeteers. It is only after they look back, years later, that they realize how bad they were.

—Jim Henson,
creator of the Muppets
*New York City*
*May 3, 1977*

# 1
## Acting with Puppets

When, as a producer of puppet plays, you accept the statement that puppetry represents a style of the theatre, you are immediately committing yourself to a large but gratifying assignment. It is now up to you to master all the theatre skills of writing, acting, directing, and design. You must be able to synthesize these skills and focus them upon the ideas you want to project, and you must do so in such a way that you form a bond of communication with your audience.

Now, don't get discouraged and take up needlepoint instead. There are ways to master each of the skills you need, shortcuts and "tricks of the trade." Some of the skills you may find yourself assigning to someone else. Many puppeteers do not make their own puppets, though it usually works out better if you do, because they are then "part of you" from the very start. If you are lucky enough to team up with someone else whose natural talents fill in where you feel a need for help and with whom you can really share ideas, great. But even if you are starting off alone with a puppet or two that you have made or purchased, you can become a skilled puppeteer. You will need time, devotion, and a willingness to practice and make mistakes. Think about it; would you expect to learn any other art without the same commitment?

So that the list of skills you need will feel more conquerable, let us treat them in the order of need. Thus, as you acquire one facility, you will naturally be led on to the next arena of challenge, and soon you will find yourself a master of, if not all you survey, at least of a company of "actors" who delight an audience and return you much joy. There is very little more satisfying than that electric feeling that is conveyed to a performer by a captivated audience. Let us get on with your training so that you can feel it, too.

Our first target will be acting with puppets, and you can master it even if you feel you cannot act on stage as a live actor. Most people find themselves much freer hidden behind a puppet stage. Don't forget: the puppet is a mask! Soon you will discover the fun of having the puppets do and say things that you never would. Though puppets have a long history of use in satire and political propaganda, there is no record of the puppeteer being hanged. The *puppet* said it, not the puppeteer, so how could the latter be blamed?

In order to begin acting with a puppet, you must get him on your hands and start him moving. Look at your puppets lying there. Not very interesting, are they? They aren't dolls to be displayed attractively on shelves. In order to be interesting, they must have you to give them life. And that life, in order to communicate with your audience, must be ordered by technique. As in any art, you will constantly work for a balance of technique and inner life. Because most people's first question is "How do you work a puppet?" rather than "For goodness sake, what is 'inner life'?" we will begin with technique, and you will see how the inner life of the puppet evolves from your newfound skills.

Webster's dictionary defines technique as "The method or the details of procedure essential to expertness of execution." Just so, you must be able to make your puppet do *exactly* what you want him to do; and you will learn to master your puppet through control and flexibility of your own hands and body. The expertness of your technique will enable you to focus your audience's attention where you want it and to select that which you want your audience to see.

Along about now in a puppetry class some student always protests, "But why can't I just *feel* it, just move the puppet and let it 'happen'?" The answer to that, Virginia, is that despite the validity of improvisation, feeling without form is rarely communicative in the theatre. By mastering technique, you are placing yourself in control of your instrument, the puppet. You are also sure, then, that you can handle any sudden inspiration that does come up and communicate it. As with playing the piano, it is necessary to play the scales before the sonata. This does not mean that there is a hard-and-fast set of rules never to be broken; it means that for the foundation of your work, you must master certain basics; then you can set about breaking "rules." Consider the truth behind most improvisational theatre. Almost never is it totally impromptu. Usually an idea is carefully worked out, including a resolution, and only the dialogue is left open. Even when a suggestion is tossed from the audience, the troupe will usually turn it toward an idea previously worked out. The rare, totally new "improv" most often comes out like an attempt at something that didn't quite make it. Once in a while, it is true, pure improvisation is brilliant. But you cannot, as a performer, afford to hope for "once in a while." You have got to be right there, in control and reaching that audience every time.

I do not mean that you will become so preoccupied with technique that you will perform like the pianist who is all precision and no feeling. We see the technique-only performance more often with marionettes than with hand puppets, but it is a great loss when any puppeteer becomes so "hooked" on technique that he stifles freshness and feeling. What happens then is a kind of sleight of hand, an emptiness that doesn't move the audience or create the empathy that is so much the special gift of the puppet.

I am asking you to develop such a sound technique that you can depend upon it and forget about it; then you can turn your attention to what your puppet wants and feels. It is your belief in what your puppet is doing that allows him to feel and want and care. It is this undercurrent of the puppet's own desires that is meant by "inner life." It can exist without technique, but under those circumstances seldom will it be conveyed to the audience. Again, it may happen once in a while, but in order to achieve a dependable performance you must strive for a balance of technique and inspiration. You can, of course, approach the creation of puppet work from either standpoint—inner life *or* technique—but here, for the purposes of instruction and for the discipline and development of your early work, it is best to begin with technique. Be patient. It takes time. If you don't skip any of the exercises, however foolish they may seem, you will be more than repaid for your tolerance. You are learning to play the scales.

> *Note:* The exercises given here will be for the hand puppet, but most of what works for him applies to other forms of puppets as well, and it is a good idea for every puppeteer to learn how to work hand puppets. Contrary to popular belief, they are *not* the easiest puppets to work—at least to work well. If your specialty is rod puppets, after completing the work in this chapter refer to Chapter 12, if marionettes, to Chapter 13, for some specific help with these two types.

This first group of exercises is just for your hands, in order to develop flexibility and control, and to help you to isolate the movement of each finger.

*1.* Using just the right hand, hold it up as if to take an oath. Now, make slow circles upward with the thumb and third finger, curling the fourth and little finger toward the palm as below:

Work to keep the index finger still and straight and to bring the third finger downward into line with the thumb. Try it four or five times. Now, reverse, and circle the fingers downward, again slowly and with as accurate a circle as you can manage. Stop and repeat the exercise with the left hand. Don't force for perfection or practice more than ten times with

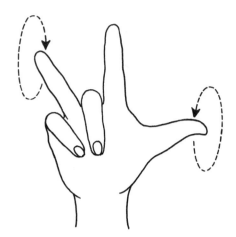

*Exercise making circles with thumb and third finger*

each hand. Like any exercise, if you are unused to it, it will make your muscles stiff. Instead, repeat it daily, and you will be surprised how supple your hands become.

2. This exercise is similar, done first with one hand and then with the other, while the hand is in an upright, "puppet" position. Now, imagining that your third finger and thumb are puppet arms, you are going to do calisthenics. Touch the tip of your thumb to the tip of your third finger. Open both fingers straight out and really reach with both fingers. Like this:

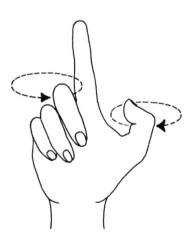

*Figure eight exercise*

Try to keep that middle finger straight.

*Note:* Most people prefer to use the thumb and third finger for puppet arms. If you prefer to use your little finger and thumb, do the above exercises using those digits.

*3.* Touching your "toes." Letting the fourth and fifth fingers move freely, but keeping the index finger straight, touch your third finger as close to the base of your palm as you can manage. Keep your arm up and straight while you do this. Repeat with the other hand.

*4.* The "wave." Sit with your feet flat on the floor and put your hands down on your thighs, relaxed, with the fingers together. Now raise just your knuckle joints, hold, and lower to flat hand. Repeat several times to get the feel of just one set of joints working at once. Now raise the knuckles and middle joints, and finally raise the third joints, and as you do so, reach up and outward with the fingertips. Repeat several times. After you think you have mastered the exercise, lift your hands off your thighs, and try the exercise in midair. Really reach with the fingers. Gradually increase the speed with which you do the exercise until it becomes one fluid motion, like a wave, but don't lose the reach from the fingertips. This is teaching you to complete a movement, as in dance. You will find it very useful exercise later to reduce tension before a performance and loosen yourself up.

For the second group of exercises, you will need a hollow rubber ball (three inches in diameter) with a hole cut in it to accommodate your index finger and a glove in which your hand moves easily. Put on the glove and the ball and you have your first "working puppet." (Many people get so fond of these glove-and-ball puppets that they never let them leave their repertoire.) You are about to learn basic puppet movements.

*1.* The walk. First, walk across the room yourself. Notice that as your weight shifts from one foot to the other, your shoulders move. Feel the movement of your body; exaggerate it. Your puppet has got to capture that same kind of movement, or he will seem to swoop or glide instead of walk. Try this (no one ever believes it will work, but it does).

Turn your own body in the direction your puppet is going to walk, being very careful to hold your arm straight, with a direct line from the tip of your index finger to your elbow. Otherwise, your puppet will look either bent over or pregnant. Keeping the puppet in one place, turn him at right angles to you, facing the imaginary audience. Turn him again to face as you face. Now, turn him to face away from you. This is a partial turn to keep your arm straight. Lastly, turn him to face the "audience" again. Repeat slowly and definitely until you have mastered the progression. Just as slowly, start to walk forward as you repeat the exercise.

It is important that at first you keep the movements very definite. Watch that your elbow doesn't bounce up and down. Before you walk into a wall, turn around and go the other way. Now, start to slur the movements and *watch* your puppet. Notice him begin to develop a bouncy little walk. Stay with this walk until you really feel comfortable with it. You will use it in every puppet play you produce.

2. The bow. It may not seem logical, but the bow is crucial to every puppet production, not because your puppets will always be impersonating princes and princesses, but because the movement forms the basis for a puppet picking up an object. It is done this way. Arm up, rubber-ball head erect, the puppet bows forward. You and he are both facing the "audience," or he may be facing you. Relax your hand and drop it forward from the wrist. Raise it up again. Imagine a string attached to the back of your hand pulling him up.

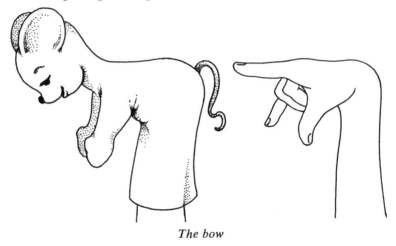

*The bow*

Watch what happens when the puppet wants to pick up an object. For the object you need something easy to handle, at least three inches across; individual cereal boxes work very well. Hold the cereal box (or whatever object you have handy) in your other hand on a level about six inches below your wrist in the glove body. Have your puppet turn and "see" the box. Now make him bow. Next, holding him quite close to the object, lower him straight down so that your puppet arms can easily grab the box. Raise him up, holding the box but still bent over. Straighten him up. Be very precise in your actions. Now put the object down again, simply reversing the procedure.

This all may feel very elementary and obvious to you. But think of the last amateur puppet show you saw. (If you haven't seen one lately, now

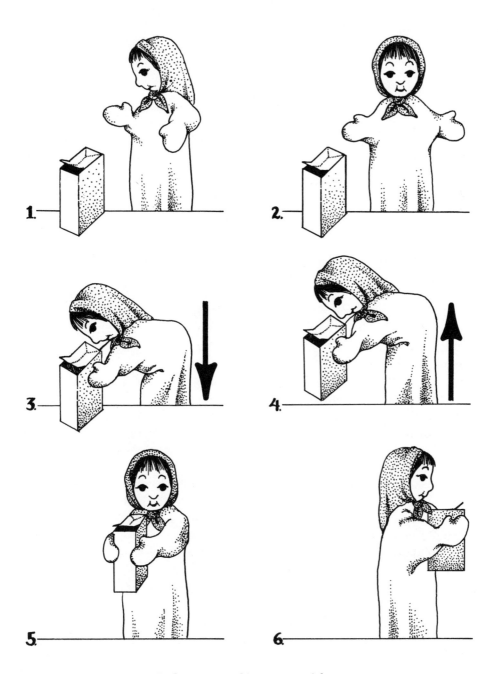

*Picking up an object; sequential*

is the time to find one and refresh your memory.) Think how many times the puppets picked things up while lying on their stomachs.

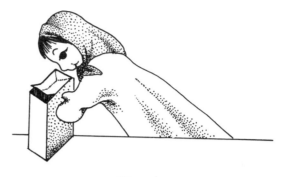

*Wrong!*

A useful variation is sometimes called "spotting an object." Your puppet walks in, sees the object, then turns and looks directly at the audience, then back to the object—all of this before he picks the object up. What is accomplished is that your audience's attention is drawn not only to the object but to what the puppet is going to do. He can also "take," or look directly at the audience, after he has picked the thing up. This sequence of action constitutes "telling them you are going to do it, doing it, and then telling them you have done it," which is one of the backbones of puppetry. The audience loves the direct contact when the puppet looks right at them. You have probably watched a mime establish rapport with the audience the same way. As you work, you will learn to use the puppet "take" to capture attention and to focus importance on an action.

You have had no need for staging in your early puppet exercises, but now you are going to have to provide yourself with the bare rudiments in order to learn further. There is no need to rush out and hire a contractor to build you a splendid performing facility; there are many ways around the problem at this point in your work. One obvious solution is to use whatever child's stage you have or can acquire and adapt. You can borrow a stage, but the owner may not wish it changed, and you may find yourself working with a construction that hampers you. Puppet stages, unfortunately, are not as standard as the wheel. The variations are numberless and sometimes exceedingly odd. Do not underestimate the possibilities of a refrigerator carton. Even a doorway can be temporarily utilized. As for building yourself a stage or having someone else build it, wait. Find out what you need, look at lots of other people's stages, and determine your own special needs before you make that investment. Before you do anything else you need to decide which of two ways you want to work: behind a scrim at eye level, or above the head in the European manner. There are advantages and disadvantages to both systems.

*Fractional rendering of a scrim stage. Note: Light source is in front of the curtain masking the puppeteer.*

The scrim stage is very good for one-person shows, especially if they involve much small, detailed movement. (Burr Tillstrom uses a variation of the scrim stage for the Kuklapolitans.) You can see what your puppets are doing, and to a degree, you can see your audience. It is generally less tiring to work with a scrim, and the stage is small and portable. But consider the limitations. Hold your arms up so that your upper arms are perpendicular to the floor. That's about the level at which you would be working. Now, pretend you have a puppet on each hand. Suppose the puppet on your right hand wants to exit left. Can't do it, can you? So, you're limited to having a puppet always enter and exit from the same side. Now, suppose you have two operators. One cannot pass in front of the other to exit the other side. Move your hands forward and back. Do you see that when you move forward, your puppet is beginning to lie down? The scrim unavoidably limits you to a very linear plane of movement. Therefore, you might, despite the usefulness and comfort of the scrim, consider the advantages of working overhead.

If you now raise your arms above your head and imagine an area about five feet wide and four feet deep to play in, you'll begin to get the idea of overhead staging. The playboard, that shelf about six inches deep that comprises the puppets' "floor," instead of being level with your chest as in the scrim stage, will now be just above your head. Some operators like to work sitting on swivel stools in order to lower the sight lines for the audience and to prevent members of the company from having to crouch or wear built-up shoes. We have never found the cumbersome stools flexible enough, but you may like them. Others perform on their knees!

With the overhead manner of staging, one operator can pass another, you have considerable depth to vary the theatre picture, and you can even play a scene with your back to the audience. Look at the diagrams in Chapter 9 showing a finished stage of this type. So much for the advantages, which, considerable as they are, for some people do not outweigh the fact that this is a much more tiring way to work. As in a sport, however, muscles get used to it.

Being a much larger structure, an overhead stage is generally more cumbersome and difficult to build. The one described in this book, designed by Al H. Morrison, is, however, incredibly flexible and, like a giant erector set, is assembled, except for lights and curtains, out of three specially constructed cases. Before you opt for the easier method of staging we hope you will consider the great adaptability to many types of productions that the overhead stage offers. At any rate, for the time being you will have to make a choice about your rudimentary stage in order to determine the height at which you will work. You can, of course, after working one way, try out the other. And that is another good reason for not building a full stage yet. Have you made your temporary choice?

Fine. Here's what you will need. You must have a playboard, mentioned above, placed at whichever of the two heights you have chosen. This floor for your puppets can be plywood, and it should have a piece of molding secured to the audience side of it, because puppets will put objects or "properties" on it, and you don't want props falling into the audience. The width of the shelf is determined by your doorway, refrigerator carton, or existing stage. Less than three feet isn't going to allow you much room, but you really don't need more than that yet. If you are using a doorway and can't face nailing into its molding, you'll have to support your playboard securely at the same height at either side of the door.

Second, you need a "prop shelf," which is simply a shelf like the playboard and placed about level with your knees. It's there for you to rest props on when not in use, so that you can get them easily with one hand while the other is working a puppet. The third requirement is a row of cup hooks, attached to the prop shelf if it is high enough, or above it on another small piece of wood reaching all the way across your stage. On this row of hooks you will hang your puppets upside down and facing you when they are not onstage. This way you can get at them easily, even without someone to help you in a one-person show. Some puppeteers lay all their puppets on a table behind them and dispense with the hooks, but it is a much less convenient way of working and you then *have* to have help to get at the puppets.

That's really all you need right now. Other things, like lights and curtains and sound equipment, come later. For now, keep it very simple, and we'll go back to learning how to act with puppets.

Your third group of exercises extends what you have done before. Now that you have a floor for your puppets and some kind of definition to your proscenium—the space in which you perform—you are ready to consider entrances and exits, the further exploration of an object, and your first pantomime.

*1.* Entrances and exits. Take your glove-and-ball puppet "offstage." Get him ready to enter by establishing where on the glove his imaginary feet are. Imagine legs and feet and establish the point on the glove for yourself, measuring against the playboard. Your puppet has got to stay at that level from the time of his entrance to his exit (unless he's picking up something), or he will look as though he is growing or sinking through the floor. All right, now, walk your puppet to the center of the playboard. Be sure that he can't be seen before he enters, and even more important, make sure that he goes all the way off before he drops down. How many puppets have you seen that appeared to drop through the floor before making their exits? This may be a fine exit (or entrance) for a ghost or spirit, but it can destroy an audience's concentration if people-puppets disappear this way.

It may be that you do wish to establish a "hole in the ground." If you have a puppet fall down through a certain spot behind the playboard, fine. Your audience now imagines that there is a hole in the ground at that point. But please, remember that the hole *is* there. Your audience will continue to believe whatever you establish for them, and if the next character doesn't fall in the hole, they will wonder why. It is also very important to keep the hole (or pond or whatever you have chosen) in the same spot. Block it off with masking tape on the inside of the playboard if you have to, but *do* remember where it is!

Now that you feel comfortable entering, walking, and exiting, it is time to extend your earlier object-handling exercise. Go back and find your cereal box or whatever other object you worked with before. In the first exercise, you simply noticed it and picked it up. Still using your rubber-ball-and-glove puppet, you are going to explore the object and learn that your puppet has a sense of touch. Impose a "condition" upon the object: suppose it to be hot, cold, or slippery. Any condition will do, but be sure to impose only one. Concentrating very hard, go through the early picking-up-the-object exercise, having your puppet constantly aware of the condition you have imposed. How does he move if the object is slippery? What changes in the speed of his movements occur if the object is hot? How do they differ if it is cold? Invent as many separate conditions for the object as you can, and watch your puppet react to them. Do you feel your puppet beginning to take over, almost as though he were thinking for himself? Good. That means you are concentrating. And that is the birth of an inner life for your puppet.

2. Pantomime. Let us take this exercise one step further and compose your first pantomime. Your puppet enters and discovers the object, reacting to its condition. Suppose that he wants to pick up the object. Let him try. See if he accomplishes his mission and exits with it, or if he gives up and exits alone in defeat.

It is very important that you do not at this stage use your voice. All of your concentration, which is the most important talent for you to develop, should be focused on the puppet and what he *does*. In the puppet theatre, actions speak *much* louder than words, and they must be very clear in order to speak. Clarity takes practice and, above all, acute concentration. Do not make the mistake of thinking about the effect your puppet is about to create; if you do that, your actions will appear empty and phony. Concentrate on *what your puppet wants to do*, watch him, and find out whether or not he achieves his goal. Voice will come later. You have plenty of time.

But it can become dull doing exercises repeatedly, and it is important to awaken your sense of puppetry as theatre. It is time to communicate. Find yourself a noncritical friend and invite him or her to watch your little pantomime. Ask your friend to describe to you what your puppet did. How close does the description come to what your puppet *thought* he was doing? Go back over your work and see where you can clarify it. (Please don't become overzealous here and invite all of the neighborhood children. One adult will be all you can handle now. Children's reactions are priceless but complicated; they are not able to provide the critique you need right now. From them you are likely to get, "What do you mean, that's a puppet show? *Now,* what happens?") At this stage, you do not need to be discouraged. Nor should you be discouraged if your friend doesn't understand everything your puppet was doing. Try it again. Clarify it.

You will find it ever so much better the second and third times.

Do you begin to see how important it is to determine what your puppet *wants* every moment that he is on stage? He must care terribly whether he achieves his goal or not. This means the goal has to be worth achieving, at least in his terms. You will find yourself "dropping out" more and more as your puppet thinks and cares on his own; you are projecting through your puppet. Your puppet is now important; you are simply the vehicle through which he becomes alive. The stronger the puppet's desire is to achieve a goal or objective, the stronger your concentration must be, and will be. The curious result of this interaction between you and your puppet and of your forgetting about yourself is that it virtually eliminates the possibility of "playing down" to your audience. No puppeteer who is concentrating on his puppet's well-defined objectives can fall into that trap. No matter what he does, the audience will care and watch and return.

If what the puppet wants is so important, how do we determine it? It was easy enough in your little pantomime; you were pretty much told what to want. Suppose, however, that you are developing a pantomime of your own, as you soon will be. How do you determine your puppet's objectives? First, you must decide his overall goal. What does he want most? Now, find out what stands in the way of his getting it. (It could very well be "who" stands in his way, and you are almost ready to introduce a second puppet.) Then you must determine whether or not he will achieve his goal. As you progress, there may be "side trips" of smaller objectives on the way to obtaining his central goal or "superobjective." Exploring them will develop texture in your play and make it richer. Just be sure that whatever side trips your puppet makes relate to his overall goal.

The more you know about your puppet character, the easier it will be to establish his objectives. Look at your simple glove-and-ball puppet. Is he old or young, masculine or feminine? What is the state of his health? Is he/she/it tall, thin, short, or fat? Impose some of these characteristics and circumstances upon your little puppet and walk him across your stage. Find out how the walk changes with the differences in his character. One of the reasons for staying with your simple puppet thus far is that it is virtually neutral, and you can superimpose almost any attributes upon it. Later you will build or buy puppets with specific characters in mind. Their looks will help you to convey what they are, but you will play them much better if you take the trouble now to learn how to convey with a neutral puppet every attribute of character you can imagine. Fool with it, think about it, play it out. All of this work is turning you into a puppeteer instead of "somebody who works puppets."

You are ready now to make up your own pantomime. Get rid of that cereal box or whatever object you have been using, and choose something fresh. Make it unbreakable (a cardinal rule of puppet props) and large enough to be identified by the audience (rule number two for properties, which are often much larger in proportion to puppets than they would be in proportion to people). Be specific about what you want your puppet to do. Let him try to do it, and see if he accomplishes it. Try your panto-mime out on a friend. Don't use voice. It is a temptation right now, but you must learn to make your movements convey your meaning. Let your friend check you out and describe what you have done. Was your pan-tomime clear to your friend? Remember, you are not performing for yourself; you must be clear to your audience. Find out what you could exaggerate or simplify in order to make your pantomime clear. Work at "reaching" your audience. This is what is known as "projection," and there is no way to learn it except by playing before an audience until an acute sense of "when you are getting across" comes naturally to you. It will. Again, give yourself time.

*3.* Working two puppets. If you are satisfied with your work thus far, you are ready to develop a costar for your first puppet. This is a diffi-cult step because it involves splitting your concentration between two hands (and two distinct puppet personalities with conflicting objectives). If you have a willing friend who will volunteer to work your second puppet for now, that will make it easier for you, but it will not necessarily speed your development as a puppeteer. Sooner or later you have got to learn to work two puppets at once, so why not now? Just be sure that you can work in peace and quiet with no one to criticize or distract you. This is *not* the time to let your own children or anyone else's "help" you.

Start very simply. Work up a pantomime in which your new puppet tries to stop the first puppet from achieving his goal. It is very important to make the goal visual. If your puppet wants to "achieve" or "be kind" or "be successful," you are going to have a horrible time trying to convey it. Puppets do not deal well with internal, mental objectives. We must be able to *see* what they want to do. Now, introduce your second character. (If it is too much for you to handle right now, don't detail his character. Leave that for the next step unless you feel comfortable in figuring out just who he is and why. It is enough for him to be "the bad guy.") Feel the tension increase as the conflict between the two characters does. Make the objectives really strong on both their parts so that they each have a reason to put up a good fight (not necessarily physical battle). Be sure that one or the other of your puppets wins. The moment of win or lose will constitute the end of your pantomime. Anything that happens after that is only tidying up ("falling action").

Are you getting a feeling of the importance of beginning, middle, and end? The beginning, when you introduce your first character with an objective and your second character with an opposing goal; the middle, when the characters come to grips with the situation; and the end, when the situation is resolved. If you understand this much, you are already becoming a playwright for the puppet stage. On these beginnings, all the rest you will create will be based.

If you feel ready, and you probably do by now, assign definite characters to your two puppets, rehearse your pantomime, and perform it for a few friends. This time you might get brave and invite three or four children. But don't overwhelm yourself. You don't yet need any more than five people watching you. Listen for when they respond to your puppets. You will use that response and learn to play with it as you continue to work. Your pantomime may seem too short to you, but it is probably just right. Puppet work is always short, even when it is fully developed. Puppets are small, and they demand tremendous concentration from the audience. Like chamber music, they pack a large amount of selected artistry into a short time span. There seems, in fact, to be a magic about twenty-minute segments. The audience needs a break after each, and usually is not able to take more than three such segments in a full professional performance.

Remember, too, to take *your* time. It is natural to feel rushed because there is an audience out there, and you are eager to please. But what you present will be clearer and better appreciated if you keep reminding yourself to *slow down* and make each movement and objective clear. If you feel ready, answer your audience, but only if what they say has something to do with your show or helps it along. It is a very special puppet talent to play with audience reaction, but it is also your right to ignore a reaction if it is irrelevant.

When you have finished your performance and your friends have disappeared, sit down quietly and evaluate your show. Which of your friends' comments helped? Which irritated you? Decide what you want to change and what you want to keep even if someone didn't like it. Remember, you are the artist. Don't forget to give yourself credit. There is always room for improvement, but you are the one who is going to guide your work. It is not a bad idea to keep a notebook with your feelings about a show. Often the least useful memories are hard to forget, but comments that can really help you or your own feelings about changes to be made can be quickly forgotten. Above all, don't forget that no artist makes progress without making mistakes. Acknowledging mistakes, evaluating them, and deciding some of them weren't mistakes is, after all, the mark of creative growth.

Review your work thus far. Your actions should be becoming more and more specific. Thinking out and being specific is a hard, boring task, but you should by now have felt the pleasure successful groundwork provides when performance time comes. You know now that an audience doesn't *have* to watch you, and you have learned some ways to keep their attention. You are growing sick of these early pantomimes. You might try putting several pantomimes together into a real program for another small audience of guests, perhaps "after dinner." You will begin to feel like a puppeteer. Also, no matter how hard you try, there will probably be several things that just aren't working. That is why we must discuss "sneaky tricks that help a lot."

You have already discovered the "take" to the audience. Think over your work so far. Is there anywhere, without overusing it, that you could use the take to point up an action or to make your plot clearer? And remember about "telling them you are going to do it, doing it, and telling them you've done it"? Can you employ this technique in any of your pantomimes? Somehow, there is magic in a sequence of three, as in the 1-2-3 sequence we just spoke of. If your puppet does something, repeats it with a little larger movement and more emphasis, and repeats it yet again with still larger emphasis, an audience is captivated. No one seems to know why three works. But it does. Try it. The trick is to make your actions build; they must grow larger each time and not simply be a repetition. It is a great technique for building suspense. Four never seems to work. Try it. You'll find out.

Think back over your pantomime work. Are your puppets touching each other almost constantly? A very common trap for beginning puppeteers is the feeling that in order for one puppet to make contact with another, they must keep touching each other. The result is something like a frenetic pat-a-cake and is extremely irritating to the audience. Let one puppet touch another only when he has a reason to do so. Then there will be meaning to his gesture. If it is really difficult for you to keep your puppets from constant meaningless touching or, worse, hitting, *make* yourself play your whole pantomime with your puppets twelve inches apart, except when the action demands they approach closer. Really practice until you can prevent the puppets from "overtouching." Be sure that you get this skill now in the beginning of your work, or it will hamper you later.

Two very important considerations are "eye contact" and "focus." When you are using one puppet and an object, be sure that *his* eyes, not yours, are in line with the object at which he is supposed to be looking. He will appear blind if he is gazing above the object he is about to deal with. The same premise applies, but with even more importance, to two puppets working together in a scene. Be sure that they look into each other's eyes. Find the spot and angle of the heads at which this looks natural. You can illustrate the negative of this very easily by talking to someone while looking up at the ceiling; very quickly you will have a most irritated person on your hands, who is likely to walk away or assume that something is quite wrong with you. Puppets who gaze at the ceiling or the floor or anywhere other than into the other puppet's eyes make audiences nervous. Eye contact is one of the prime ways of establishing life within your puppets for your audience. "Focus" is related to eye contact, in that where your puppets look, your audience will look. It is very important for any puppets onstage to look at the puppet character who is the center of attention and, later in your work, at the one who is talking. This is your way of guiding your audience's attention from one puppet to the other.

Should you find that your audience is inattentive, or if they begin giving you too many noisy suggestions, you can always simply freeze the movement on stage. Hold the puppets in the exact position where you have them. Then make one sudden movement. You will find your audience completely quieted in order to find out what happens next. Don't be afraid that your puppets will look dead while you freeze them. An audience somehow just accepts this "freeze" and settles down. Don't stifle interaction with your audience or their responses to the puppets; but if their response becomes too noisy or irrelevant, just freeze the action, settle your audience down, and get on with the show.

Now that you have these sneaky tricks well in hand, and if you have followed the exercise work thus far and evaluated your efforts, you are ready to incorporate voice. Some puppeteers always use pantomime; for most, use of voice is a strong desire. It gives you another whole area of flexibility within which to create.

# 2

## The Puppet Speaks

Every puppeteer, even if he thinks he will only want to do pantomime, should know how and when to use his voice. As a puppeteer you never know what you will be called upon to do, and if you can handle your voice, you can use it or not, at will. Successful puppet voices expand and clarify a puppet's character and are an integral part of his believable personality. A puppet identified with a certain voice cannot be imagined with a different one. Unfortunately, successful puppet voices are comparatively few, and there are many misconceptions among beginning puppeteers about how to arrive at them. Let us begin by clearing away some of the fog.

One of the first questions asked is if ventriloquism is necessary. Emphatically, no. Ventriloquism has its place and is a fascinating feat, but it is not necessary in puppet work. If you are concentrating on your puppet and have adequate sound equipment with speakers reasonably placed (we will treat these technical aspects later), voices will seem to your audience to come naturally from the puppets. This illusion is a function of your concentration, aided by "projection" and "focus."

It is now time for you to apply the same intense concentration that you gave to your exercises in basic movement to the use of your voice, and this concentration will enable you to keep your puppet's voice consistent and to convince the audience it is "his." You will become more and more aware of "projecting" the puppet's personality from your hand. "Focus," remember, means getting the audience to look where you want them to look, and the cardinal rule of focus in the use of voice with puppet is: be sure that the puppet who moves is the one who is speaking. In beginning work, absolutely freeze any other puppet on the stage. Later you will learn what small gestures you can give to the nonspeaking puppets to keep them "alive." You must learn to guide your audience's attention to the speaking puppet. Have any other puppet on stage look at your puppet while he speaks. Since the voice does not obviously originate in the puppet, as it does in the live actor on the stage, the audience needs a clue, and the clue is movement.

Many beginning puppeteers feel the movement clue must be given by moving mouths. The sock puppet such as a Muppet, which is virtually all mouth, can be very effective, and you may well want to use them, alone or in combination with other types. You do not need to animate the mouths of more traditionally constructed heads; in fact, by installing a moving mouth you will invariably call attention to the "trick" of technique and it will absorb all of the audience's attention. This type of moving mouth is usually noisy, distracting, and artificial. Someday you may have an ad agency requiring you to build such puppets for a TV commercial, but as a general rule, unless it's a puppet to whom the mouth is all-important, forget about moving mouths as trick technique. If your concentration is sharp and you bring the puppet alive, you won't need such a crutch.

At this point someone always insists that what they want to do is move their puppets to a prerecorded taped dialogue. More about tape later, but at this early stage, the answer is *don't*. You may be afraid to use your voice, but please, give yourself a *chance* to find the many voices that you have hidden away inside you. If you will trust yourself and forge ahead into this next unit of work, you will learn how much more alive a puppet is whose operator is speaking for him than is a puppet that is moving to a taped dialogue. Also, the taped dialogues are usually very dull, allowing no room for fun with movement. Often nothing happens but talk. If you will develop your work now, you will be able later to cast and record a good acting tape, if that is the way you choose to perform. For now, for the purposes of learning, let your puppets speak.

But, you say, how can I keep from getting the puppet voices mixed up? If a deep-voiced dragon suddenly speaks with the voice of a little-boy hero, it could be very embarrassing for you and confusing for the audience. If you will sharpen your concentration, you will arrive at the point where this sort of mix-up won't happen. All right, you say reluctantly, how do we go about it?

First, you must know your puppet character very well. Review everything you know about him: is he young, old, in good health, ill-tempered, a cat, a cow, or a teapot? Everything you know about him will affect his speech. Choose your favorite puppet and try to find a voice for him. Remember your very first pantomime? Try it now, letting your puppet speak. He may sound very odd to you at first. Instinctively you know that the voice is not "his." Try another (do find a quiet room with no one around to "help"). By the time you have tried out four or five voices, one is likely to "fit" and feel right to you. Stay with it. Play out your pantomime, and try to let the voice out. Your voice may be tight at first, because of nerves, but they will go away. Most people find one voice that pleases them for their

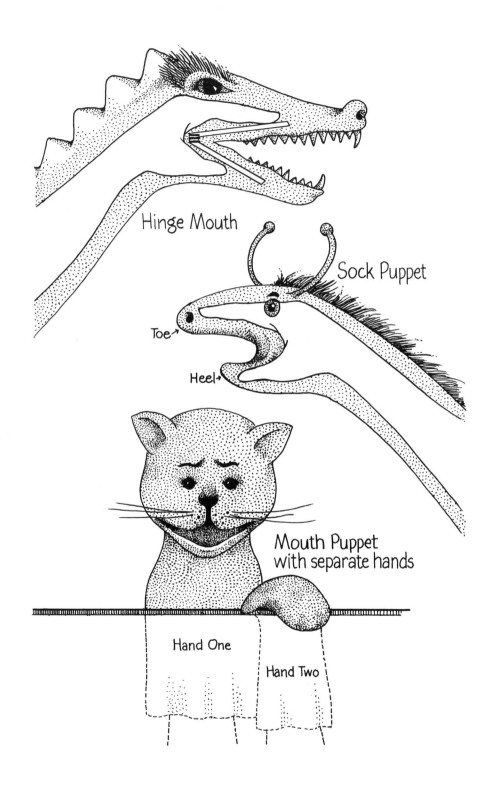

Hinge Mouth

Sock Puppet

Toe→

Heel→

Mouth Puppet
with separate hands

Hand One

Hand Two

very first puppet and then get "stuck" trying to find the next voice, usually believing they can't do it, which, of course, isn't true. What all this means is that the average person, without the advantage of voice and speech training, is ruled by his voice. As he did with moving the puppet, he must learn now to be the one in control of voice too, and to do this he must understand certain things about his own voice and about voice and speech in general. Again, there are exercises. Yes, they can be boring, or you can look upon them as the gateway to what you really want to do. There just isn't any short, easy route. So let's get started.

First, make a tape of your own voice. Read anything. Now, play it back. Do you like what you hear? Analyze your voice for regionalisms, for nasality. Is your voice too high-pitched? Does it sound tight in the throat? Play your tape again and listen carefully. This is often a painful process, especially if you have never heard yourself on tape before. Don't be alarmed. That really is what other people hear when you speak, but you *can* and will improve it. Half the battle is in really hearing yourself. First, get over the shock, and then resolve to do something about it. But what?

One thing you can do right away is learn to breathe. Doesn't that sound silly? You have always known how to breathe, but very probably you do not breathe for most effective voice projection. Try holding a lighted candle before your mouth and quietly speak the numbers from one to ten across the flame. Can you sustain the tone and not put out the candle?

Your "bellows muscle," called the diaphragm, is located just below your rib cage. Many people don't use the diaphragm and instead speak entirely with breath from the chest. They are always surprised at how much fuller their voices sound and how much farther their voices carry when supported by breath from the diaphragm. Put your hand on your diaphragm. Take a deep breath and try to fill the whole cavity. Use numbers, if you like, and speak them distinctly and one on each breath, pushing the diaphragm in with your hand on each spoken word, then taking a deep breath and speaking the next number. Rest. It is very important in early breath work that you do not overdo it, which can cause you to faint. You are not used to so much oxygen. Gradually you can increase the amount you practice, but be consistent and try to practice daily.

Another useful exercise is to use vowel sounds like *meen, mine, moan* and imagine yourself throwing the sounds on one breath across the room so that they bounce against the opposite wall. Be sure to sound the differences between vowel sounds. Despite all the fun that's been made of "How now brown cow," it's still a good way to isolate a pure vowel sound and to practice breath support. Try to say all the words clearly on one breath. And don't laugh! Lie down on the floor and quietly observe your breathing. Begin to speak on the outgoing breaths. One of the least fun but best exercises is reciting, "Is this the face that launched a thousand ships and burned the topless towers of Ilium?" absolutely evenly and on one breath with pitch rising. Include it in your practice work until you can get through the whole sentence and not feel "out of breath."

Why are you going through all this? Because you are learning to make your voice your instrument, so that it will serve you and your puppets. You will, if you take your work seriously, never stop working on breath control. You will need a lot of voice to carry to the last row, and no amount of excellent amplification can replace a good voice; it can only help it along. Without adequate breath support you won't be heard and at best the ends of many sentences will be lost. Think of your breath as a carrier for your voice. Voiced consonants such as z and d must be heard even at the ends of sentences in order for you to be understood. And you must have enough breath to voice them. Try this:

> All the world's a stage| |
> And all the men and women| | merely players| |
> They have their exits and their entrances,| |
> And one man in his time| | plays many parts,| |
> His acts being seven ages.| |

> Wm. Shakespeare, *As You Like It*
> Act II, Scene VII

Be sure to sound the underlined voiced consonants. If you don't have enough breath, try giving yourself a breath at the | | marks. Try again.

Do you know what "placement" is? When you listen to your tape of your voice, can you put your hand on the part of your face or neck where most of your voice seems to come from or is "placed"? Is it nasal? Is your throat tight? Do you tend to swallow words, especially the ends of sentences and let them disappear down the back of your throat? Listen to yourself very carefully. Now try to think, with your eyes closed, of your voice rising on a breath from the diaphragm and easily emerging from the throat, going through the mouth, and being formed by the lips. Focus your energy on the diaphragm and then on the lips and tongue forming sounds that are speech. Your breath and the sound emanating from your throat constitute voice; the formation given to voice by the lips and tongue makes you able to form speech. Try to place your speech as far forward in the mouth as you can. Be conscious of lips and teeth and tip of the tongue. A good exercise to sharpen your control of speech is this:

lllll--rrrr(rolled)--t-d......s-z-nnnn (on one breath)

It works.

Listen again to your tapes. Try to isolate the sounds you made in the above exercises. Does *l* clearly sound *el*? Say the sound. At the finish of the sound is your tongue lightly placed just behind the teeth? If not, you may have a "baby-talk *l*" which sounds like "*eh-o.*" Once you are conscious of it, you can cure it. Listen to yourself say words like *middle* and *little.*

Another troublesome sound for many people is *ing.* Say *happening.* If the final sound for you comes out *een,* you are probably pronouncing all words that end in *ing* in this way. Make a change *now.* If you learn to catch yourself in everyday speech, you will have a far easier time onstage.

These may sound like picky requirements, but when you speak for your puppets you want them to be believable and to be understood. If you are not intelligible, your audience will soon become restless, and if the peculiarities of your pronunciation call attention to themselves, they will jar the listener's ear and even shatter his belief in your puppet world. Especially in period shows or ones involving fantasy in far-off lands, you want to watch regionalisms, baby talk, and modern slang. If you wish to give a lisp or some other peculiarity of speech to a puppet character, you must simply be consistent. Be sure that character *always* speaks in the special way. Try, also, not to make a character's speech peculiarity (or dialect) so marked that he cannot be understood. If you keep in mind that your first purpose always is to be understood, you will succeed.

When you are hidden behind a puppet stage, you must always make your enunciation of words extra-explicit. The more you learn of breath control and of how to really *use* your lips and tongue until you feel that you must look foolish, the more readily you will project what you want to say to your audience, with or without sound equipment. Enunciate. Enunciate.

Can you overdo it? Unfortunately, you can overdo almost anything. Here is where your tape recorder comes in handy again. Record a sample passage and play it back. It may sound great, or the words may sound "chewed." If what you hear is chewed, relax and re-record. If what you hear now sounds pedantic and affected, turn off the tape recorder and have a good talk with yourself. Pedantic or affected speech will send your audience scurrying to the box office for its money back. "But," you say, "you said, 'enunciate.' " You are absolutely correct. Sounds must be clear to be intelligible, but they must be said in the cadence and pronunciation of everyday life. If you are isolating words that are normally elided or pornounced in a run-on fashion, you are producing a word-by-word effect which is, in a word, awful. You must learn to enunciate the *meaning* of what your character says, but you must never get "hung up" on word-by-word "prettiness" of speech if you want to keep an audience.

If you are having difficulty isolating just what good voice and speech is, buy (or borrow from the library) some recordings by respected artists:

Stratford recordings of Shakespeare, *anything* by Charles Laughton (who worked ceaselessly throughout his life on his voice and speech and was perhaps the most versatile of all actors in that area), anything from the Old Vic. Trained actors and actresses usually rely on the British and American theatre standards of speech, which differ only in some dialectal differences and pronunciations. Train your ear. Listen to Lily Tomlin. Hear her wonderful nasal character voice. Then hear her "straight" voice, very pleasant and trained. Start getting critical of the voices you hear on TV. Listen to the news. Newscasters usually have the best American Standard trained speech and a relaxed delivery. Can you match it? Oh, of course you can. Relax, listen, practice, and enjoy yourself. You're only beginning to discover what you can do!

Your best friend through all of this voice work is relaxation. Maybe you have never realized how tense you are, or perhaps you feel tense in a new way because you are attempting something different. That is all right. No one else is around. And you have every right to take your time in mastering a complex new skill. You will need to learn relaxation exercises that work for you, whether they be hatha-yoga or simply stretching to the ceiling and bouncing like a rag doll to the floor. You will need to learn to relax so that you can work in rehearsal, and you will need to learn to relax in performance so that all you have worked on can be permitted to play. Do whatever works for you in allover body relaxation; and then go back to the "wave" you learned in Chapter 1 to relax your hands. You are learning to control your voice, but your voice must supplement the work of your hands, and your hands must stay supple. The wave is a good exercise to repeat directly before performance and has the effect of casting off unnecessary nervousness and centering your attention on what has to be performed.

You have noticed even with the work you have done thus far on breath and relaxation that your voice has lowered in pitch. Tension can raise the voice as much as an octave. (Listen to yourself when you are angry. Doesn't your voice rise as well as become louder?) You will find a lovely side benefit from your voice work for puppets: your own natural speaking voice will become more pleasant!

Do you wonder what to do about a witch's voice? One that must seem "tight" or shrill. You must learn to do these voices, still keeping the throat relaxed, or you will pay the price of a sore throat. Sometimes you will be able to "place" these voices in the nasal area and keep a relaxed throat. Whatever you do, *you must not strain your throat.* Your voices must be comfortable for you or you won't be able to sustain them through a whole show, first performance nerves notwithstanding.

Perhaps you have discovered that you have some sort of regional dialect. What are you going to do about it? There are two solutions. You can decide you are stuck with it and that, therefore, all of your characters are going to have voices of perhaps different pitch but sounding pretty much alike because of the dialect; or you can decide that the dialect may be charming in some instances but not useful *all* the time and you determine to train your voice to a good American Theatre Standard. You listen a lot, you work hard, and you covet the flexible, interesting voice that can "do so many voices," because you have learned that you are not a victim of dialect, that with work your voice can be as versatile as anyone else's. Don't let anyone discourage you. It will take time and patience, but you can do it, using frequent tapings of yourself as teacher. It is equally hard to admit when you are making progress and when you sound dreadful. Keep the old tapes. Play back the first one. See how far you've come?

Try to see a local puppet show and really listen to the voices. Are they clear, understandable, distinct from each other; and do they really fit the characters? One of the great traps to fall into is the sugar-sweet voice that talks down to the audience and thereby annoys both adults and children. The sugar-sweet voice results when the puppeteer has some mistaken idea of what a child wants to hear. You won't ever use this irritating voice if you go carefully back to basics and find the voice through the puppet's character. The delicate interweaving of technique and inner life is just as true of voice as it is of movement.

It would be much simpler right now for you to decide that "it's only for kids, so what does it matter?" or, if you are playing an adult show, that "after all it's only puppets." In both conclusions you sell both yourself and your medium short. An audience *does* know, though they may not know *why* they are bored or restless. It is always easier to find an excuse, to stop practicing, sharpening, perfecting; and there is usually someone in every audience who will tell you they like even your worst performance. If, however, you have developed a sense of self-criticism, you will *know* when you are good. It is a joy to please an audience—an even greater joy to know you deserve their praise. Whatever work you put in on your voice will pay off later in the easy dexterity and actual fun that you will have playing your puppet voices. If you lack a coach, there are several good basic books on voice and speech mentioned in the Bibliography; making one a constant companion in these early stages will help you to train your own voice so that it will be flexible enough to do several different voices in one show without a great deal of difficulty.

When performing different character voices, there are only so many things you can change about your voice, but each one of them separately and in combination with the other factors will help you develop a wide range of distinctly different character voices. You can vary pitch, rate, intonation, rhythm, and quality, and you can throw in a dialect if you feel like it. That's about all, but it isn't as limiting as it sounds. As you work with your voice, you will become much more subtle in varying its pitch. You will not simply be able to produce a "high" voice and a "deep" voice, but you will find many comfortable variations in between. The "rate" of speech, or how fast you talk, can help a great deal in differentiating characters. If one puppet speaks quickly in a high voice and is companioned by a character who speaks slowly in a low voice, the difference is unmistakable. Think about intonation. Perhaps a character may have a peculiarly nasal voice, or try to create a character who almost always ends his sentences on a higher note than he began. Intonation, or the pattern of melody in speech, is fun to play with, and you can make it your servant. Monotonous speech is a deadly bore in daily life; on stage it is guaranteed to put your audience to sleep. "Rhythm" takes a little time to the point where you no longer have to think about it. You can get some sense of rhythm in speech by listening to people around you in a restaurant or theatre lobby. Just as each person develops a rhythm of movement, so does he form a rhythm of speech. Sometimes it is so obvious that you can almost clap out beats; other times it is much more subtle. Don't be discouraged if you don't hear it at first, or if exactly what rhythm of speech is eludes you for awhile. It will come, along with the other components of voice and speech, the last of which to isolate and use is "quality." Think of a rasping voice as compared with that of a dulcet princess. Try both voices. Now, keep the rate and change the pitch; keep the dulcet tone and change the pitch. Thus, you have isolated "quality." Be careful not to confuse quality with volume, i.e., loud versus soft.

Thus, even without the use of dialects (which can be fun, especially when you want to set off one character from all the others), you have discovered five variables in your voice that you can use in developing your characters' voices. Five may not seem like a great number, but think of it in terms of permutations and combinations. In other words, you do not have to vary just pitch, but can combine a pitch change with a change in rate and quality. Intonation and pitch will change a character *without* altering the rate and quality. Alter all four variables and you have a completely different voice character. This gets to be a game of "how many different ways can I use my voice." It is a constructive game to play in order to find out what you can do, but such changes are rarely necessary in a show. Usually, changing only one of the variables of voice and speech will be sufficient, along with skillful movement, to convince your audience that the character has a voice of his own.

You are probably still skeptical about being able to do two, let alone several, voices without mixing them up, and the only way to prove to you that the process is not only possible but fun is to get you on your feet, doing it. After discovering certain abilities within your own range of voice and speech, you will, we hope, be able rather easily to find a voice for your second puppet. When you have it, work up a simple skit, either your first pantomime with words added, or a new, short (no more than three minutes) skit that has a beginning, a middle, and an end. The more intensely one of your characters wants to do something the other equally intensely wants to prevent, the more dramatic action you will develop and the sharper your concentration will be. Now is the time to thank yourself for doing all that early pantomime work to awaken your powers of concentration, because the strength of your concentration is ultimately what keeps the voice belonging to the right puppets. Short practice periods are advised, because the necessary concentration makes the work quite tiring. Even when you work up to performance, playing several puppets with live voices, you are likely to feel exhilarated but very tired afterward. Rest by thinking about something totally else. The more you work, the easier the intense concentration will become. Soon, while you are working you will hear absolutely nothing but the puppets' voices, no matter what is going on around you. Sometimes the puppets will even surprise you and do or say something that you didn't expect! It's all right. They are taking over, that's all. Immediately, you are in control again, just a little startled. What has happened is that your belief is growing, and you are letting yourself become an artist.

You are ready, now, to perform your skit. It is important that you keep yourself stimulated by an audience, but that you not bite off too much too soon. You have not had enough work with story or script yet to put together a whole show without disappointing yourself. It is better to stay for a little longer with a small group of friends for critics; or perhaps you are ready for your first show in the local library or to entertain at a birthday party. For the time being, stay with short skits, and don't let up on evaluating your performances yourself, so that you can improve them. Don't let go what you have learned in the basics of movement as you now add the dimension of voice. As you work, try to find when emphasis in movement can clarify what is being said. Try to time your movement with your character's speech; they are both part of the same character.

You may wish to work with another beginning puppeteer. Whether you work alone or with someone else is simply a function of your personality and/or the availability of another puppeteer. If you are lucky enough to find someone with whom to work and you spark each other's imaginations, great. Just don't feel hampered if you have to work alone. You will be limited in the number of characters you can handle, but a one-person show can be very rewarding in other ways: your total control of timing and the intensity that you can give to a really unified performance can be most exciting. At this stage in your training it is not important whether you work alone or with someone else; what matters is how thoroughly you incorporate the basics of movement and voice into your growing technique and how completely you develop the inner life of your characters.

As soon as a puppeteer begins to use voice, the question of whether to write out all the dialogue arises. Even though writing out your skit may give you a sense of security, the answer is *don't*. One of the reasons for working with pantomime first is to school you in the fact that puppet theatre is a theatre of action, not words. Fully scripting even the brief skits you are doing will trap you into using much more dialogue than you need. Learn to throw out any words that aren't necessary, and to keep on throwing out until you have kept only the fewest words necessary. You will also find that if you fully script your skits, your dialogue is likely to sound "read," and you want very much to preserve the spontaneity you have been learning. Later on we will devote two chapters to building scripts, and there will be times when a full script, written out, cannot be avoided— because of the number of people involved or the difficulty of cuing lights and music—but that is in the future. For now, content yourself with this very workable "script," which you can post backstage on your playboard. It contains every "reminder" you should need and will suffice for even a complicated one-person show. List characters in order of appearance, with any props they use in the middle column next to their name.

| *Left* (hand, yours) | *Props* | *Right* |
|---|---|---|
| Boy | Broom | Ghost |
| (continuing line | | → (exit) |
| means he's on | | Frog |
| all the time) | | → (exit) |
| | Basket | Ghost back |
| *Curtain* | | |

We have now covered all necessary aspects of voice, and it is simply up to you to put them into practice, but there are a few technical questions which may arise as you work toward putting together a show for a real audience. No doubt you have wondered about amplification and whether or not your voice will be strong enough to carry, particularly since you are hidden behind a puppet stage. All of your breath work will help you, and you will develop a sense of projection and the ability to adjust your volume to fill a given hall. As you grow in your work, however, so will the size of the place in which you perform; though you will want to keep it intimate even then, you will doubtless need some sort of amplification.

In putting together a sound system, you can save yourself a lot of grief by keeping it simple and by seeking professional audio advice to begin with. Make sure that your system, when assembled, is complete and does not need to plug into part of the sound system in the hall where you will play. It has got to plug into a regular two-prong electrical outlet so that you can play on any stage or in any hall or home or school. There is little worse than arriving in a hall, setting up, and finding that the jack you had expected to plug into "their" speaker is not compatible. You will be offered chances to "plug into our system"; do this *only* if the quality of sound will be much improved by doing so and *only* if you have checked out the system ahead of time to be *sure* that it is compatible with yours.

You do not need the most sophisticated sound system in the world, but there are certain requirements that must be met. If you use more than one microphone, they must be of matched impedance. And do suspend your mikes from the playboard or wear them in telephone-operator fashion or on a chest support hung around your neck, rather than placing them on stands, where you will hit them during performance and make horrendous noises. Fastening mikes to the playboard has the disadvantage of making the playboard resonant, but it does make it possible for several puppeteers to use one or two mikes. If you wear your mike, take care in positioning it so that it moves with you and picks up your voice. Inexpensive mikes are quite directional, and care must be taken in placing them for maximum pickup. You may find that you can run your mike directly into a tape recorder that has an amplifier and public address facility. In a home you may not need an additional speaker. In almost any hall, you will need to run your mikes through a mixer, then through your tape recorder (functioning as amplifier) and probably into at least one additional speaker placed in front of the stage. A good audio-visual dealer can help you assemble a system compatible with your needs and budget.

It is worth searching to find a tape recorder that has a quiet on-off switch, since you will no doubt be playing recorded music on tape and then simply leaving the machine on as amplifier for voice. Unless you get into very sophisticated and costly equipment, you are unlikely to be able to do "voice over," that is, speaking over the recorded music while tape is playing. You can, however, effectively use two tape recorders, one for voice and one just for music tapes. It is somewhat difficult to find good portable (and when they tell you it is portable, do not take their word for it; *lift* it, and find out if it is portable for *you*) reel-to-reel recorders since cassettes have become so popular. Some puppeteers use a cassette recorder for their music, but cassette tape is very hard to cue, since you cannot put any visual cue (such as white leader tape) into the tape, and you cannot edit it at all without extreme difficulty. A cassette is, admittedly, very light and portable, but the disadvantages far outweigh the convenience. As of this writing, Sony, Wollensak, and Teac make acceptable reel-to-reel units. Watch out for used equipment. If you know what you're buying, fine, but otherwise you can end up with someone else's lemon. It's just like the used car game!

One pitfall to avoid if at all possible is allowing one person to do the voice for a puppet on tape and another to manipulate the puppet. Even if such a two-person effort is accomplished live, it almost never works, simply because it is so difficult to synchronize voice and movement when two persons are involved. Also, of course, this method will leave you almost no room for improvisation. There may be times when you *have* to pair people on one puppet (live or on tape). At this stage of your work, however, when you are playing by yourself or with one other person, do avoid complicating the issue and speak for your own puppet(s)!

You are now nearly ready to develop a whole show. You have movement pretty well under control, you can handle more than one puppet at a time, your voices are steadily improving, and your skits are sparking ideas for longer programs or reminding you of whole stories you would like to adapt. It is quite possible, however, that in working with the puppets you have previously made or bought, you have encountered problems in getting them to do what you want, problems in their construction or design. Therefore, before we deal with the scripting of an entire production, we will take time out to deal with "first aid" and getting your puppets into shape so that they will work their best for you.

# 3

## But My Puppets Won't Do What I Want Them To

Although this book is not intended to be a how-to-make-a-puppet book (there are already many good volumes on that subject, many noted in the Bibliography) it is appropriate to devote some space to helping you re-model a hand puppet that you have either bought or made so that it will move as you need it to. It's also time to give you an overview of several different methods of construction and the "feeling" that is produced by each material or "medium" you might use. Once you understand some of the principles of building a puppet for movement, you will be able to alter existing puppets or begin constructing your own with the aid of the more detailed step-by-step instructions given in a how-to book, if necessary.

In no way is the material presented here intended to stunt your imagi-nation in the use of materials or in the manner of construction. If you want a hammer to become a puppet conversing with a pair of pliers, why not? Found objects can become puppets, and whole books have been devoted to the construction of "junk" puppets out of almost every con-ceivable material. By all means experiment. Keep on trying new products and inventing ingenious ways to make your puppets work; no method is wrong, so long as it works. What is given here is a vocabulary of standard methods, so that you will be aware of certain existing techniques, be able to pick and choose what suits you, and add to them the richness of your own special talents and discoveries. Knowing some tried and true methods of construction and the properties of a number of favored mediums can save you many hours of trial and error. If, after reading this chapter, you want to make out of eight slinkies a puppet that self-destructs to the sound of a steam whistle, go ahead! But when and if you *do* want to con-struct or modify a traditional glove puppet at least you will know how. After all, why try and reinvent the wheel?

First, let us see what "first aid" can be applied to the purchased puppet with which many students begin or with the first puppet you have made that doesn't move quite right. What a waste if, after all the work you have done on acting and voice, your puppets still won't move well! If you've followed the exercises given and your puppets won't move as you wish, the fault must be in their construction. Does the puppet fit your hand closely enough to give you control, but not too tightly, allowing freedom of movement? If not, then the puppet must be altered, for he is not a doll, and as you have learned, his life comes first from movement; his construction must aid, not hamper, your expression of his inner life.

Take a look at the troubled puppet. See if it has a simple "glove" base. This is *very* important, because it allows easy entry and exit of your hand. If you have a puppet that is dressed in a complicated costume and that costume forms the puppet body, you will almost always find your hand getting caught on entry in the intricacies of the dress. If this is the case, you can line the puppet. Enlarge the diagram for a simple glove body given in Illustration 8 to fit your puppet and your hand and insert it within your puppet in the following manner: turn the body of the puppet inside out, leaving the neck exposed. Now, cut and sew your new inner body or lining in muslin or any tightly woven fabric that will really hold the seams. Cotton is best; it will absorb perspiration. Sew the seams on a machine, not by hand, or they will be likely to pull out. Do not turn the inner body; leave the raw seams on the inside so that you have a completely smooth puppet to work in. Take the glove you have made and fit the neck to the puppet's neck and sew, or attach with white glue, being careful to keep the neck hole open. Then sew the wrist openings to the inner wrists of your puppet, turning the raw seams inward. You may find that the glove you made has shorter "arms" than that of your purchased puppet. This is all right. Just let the extra fullness blouse. You need the inner glove to fit you, and the extra fullness will give the illusion of longer arms than your puppet actually has. It is always better to have the glove as loose as possible while still offering you control.

It is absolutely impossible to make one puppet fit everyone. If you are planning to use your puppets in one-person performances, you will have no size problems. Simply fit the puppets to *you*. If you are building for several operators or a show that may be worked by a series of different people, size can cause difficulties. In general, it is better to fit the puppets a little loose, for even in the case of a really large size discrepancy, it is much easier to take a few tucks in the glove or to pad a neck with foam rubber than it is to enlarge glove, neck, and sleeves.

It is not necessary that your fingers fit down inside the hands, though this is possible and can give a gentle "pad" hand effect with a mitten shape. If your finger is in the hand the arms may appear too short. Some puppeteers like to sew together a cuff of three-quarter- to one-and-one-half-

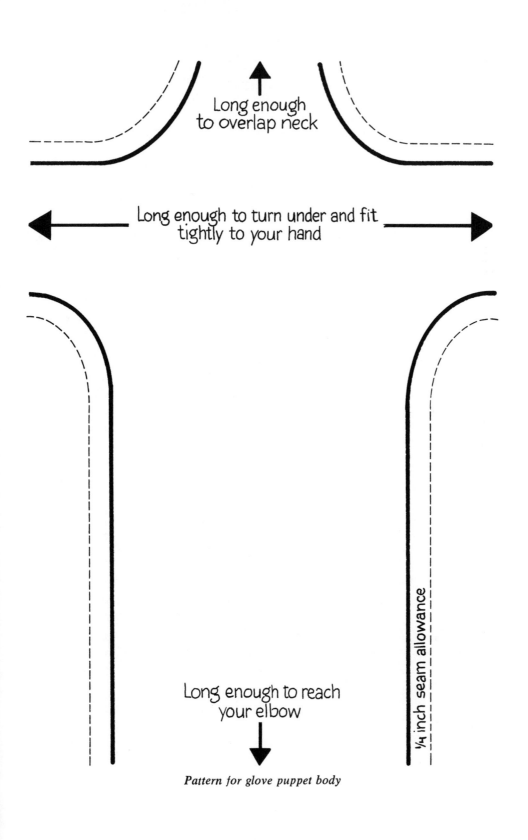

Long enough
to overlap neck

Long enough to turn under and fit
tightly to your hand

Long enough to reach
your elbow

¼ inch seam allowance

*Pattern for glove puppet body*

inch elastic just fitting their finger ends and sew it to the wrist end of the hand and insert it within the inner glove. These cuffs can offer gentle finite control, but you will frequently find yourself changing them to fit different operators.

Look at the glove pattern in Illustration 8. Notice how the underarm slopes and is not cut in at a sharp angle. This construction allows freedom of movement and keeps the underarm from pulling apart. If the puppet with which you are working has square-cut underarms, it would be a good idea to insert gussets, simply ripping the underarm seams for an inch or two and patching in a square (sewing by hand). You can do this before or after installing the inner glove, as long as you do not sew the lining and the puppet together at the bottom of the glove. Any nearly matching fabric will do; the area is rarely seen by the audience, and unless you use a wildly contrasting fabric, they will never notice the addition, and you will greatly benefit from enlargement of the glove.

Before you turn your puppet right side out, check to see if it has a neck tube (if you have had to turn it in order to put in the insertion, turn it inside out again). The puppet's neck needs to fit your index finger quite closely for controlled manipulation. If there is no neck tube, the head will wobble around hopelessly. Neck tubes are very easy to make. Just take a piece of light cardboard and roll it, trying to avoid creases, to a size a little larger than your index finger. It will go up into the puppet's head and should extend below the head to fit comfortably just above the second joint of your index finger. You will attach it into the head (body turned inside out) with white glue, being careful that the tube does not fall into the head, as it is then almost impossible to retrieve. If the neck is much wider than your neck tube, you can take strips of muslin, paint them with white glue, and wrap them around the tube until it fits the neck opening. This is a time-consuming and rather messy process, but it works. Now, just let the thing dry thoroughly before you turn it, to avoid danger of sticking the inner body to itself.

When you can turn the puppet right side out, hem under the lower edge of the lining, but do not attach it to the outer dress, unless it is a male body with supposedly close-fitting pants. It helps to run a light wire through the lower hem of the inner glove. This keeps the glove open for easy entry. Lastly, attach a metal drapery ring to the center back of the hem of the glove. From this ring your puppet can hang on a cup hook back-stage, ready for you to put him on your hand.

If your puppet has legs, you may want to remove them. Attaching rods to the feet for specific control is possible but tricky, and if the puppet is a main character, you are then stuck with them for the whole show. If the puppet would look silly if you removed the legs, leave them, and learn to toss them believably as he walks. He will be able to toss his feet over the playboard and sit down. If you keep his feet just below the playboard when he walks, he will look more lifelike. Generally, hand puppets with legs have limited appeal, and should only be used when the legs are necessary to the movements demanded by the story. You can give an illusion of legs, even on a male body, by sewing a crease down the center front of the lower glove. It also helps greatly if the lower glove is of a dark, plain fabric. Felt and drapery fabric (samples!) are very useful.

Take one more look at your purchased puppet, or one you have made. Now that it is lined, put it on your hand and notice where the glove ends on your arm. Most commercial puppets have very short gloves, and these require you to sew on an extension of black fabric, which should extend to the inside of your elbow joint. Just slip-stitch it firmly to the bottom of the inner glove. Do use a dull finish fabric.

Now, you should have a workable puppet. If you have read the above and find that the neck is not adaptable or the whole puppet too tight or stiff, you may be better off to start over, buy another puppet with the requirements in mind, or give up and start making your own figures.

Not all puppeteers make their own puppets, but most do, because it is so rewarding to be part of the building of a character right from the start —and, of course, if you have made the puppet, you can control his construction so that he fits you and is built for movement. Another considerable advantage is that your puppets will all be in the same style and in better proportion to each other than an assembly of any puppets you can purchase, unless they are all made by the same company or puppeteer. Seeing puppets that are out of proportion to each other can be extremely jarring for your audience.

In the beginning many puppeteers are as afraid of construction as they are of using their voices. You may have thought you couldn't draw, but you will probably be quite surprised at your success in making a puppet head. There are a number of standard methods of construction, all valid, and the important thing is that you choose a material that you like to work with and from which you get the feeling that you want in your finished puppets. Let's go over some of the processes for constructing heads and the qualities each medium or material gives to the finished puppet. Choose a medium that fits the style in which you want to work, and try to be consistent within a given show. You may want to experiment with several different methods of construction; you may want a cloth animal and plastic-wood people. Unless, however, you have a special point to make, do stick to one method of construction for each show, especially among related characters. Don't expect your audience to adjust to a grab bag of styles in design, consruction, and feeling.

Cloth heads give a very soft look, great for children's shows with funny animals; or, if made of felt, they can be very ethereal and take light beautifully. Sewing felt heads by hand, painstakingly slip-stitching, gives a very finished effect, but if you choose to work on a sewing machine, try Lewis Mahlmann's approach. (See the Bibliography for how to order his pattern.) The machine method produces a bolder head, especially if the features are mostly glued- or sewn-on felt. With a little experience, you will be able to draft patterns yourself, as soon as you have discovered how stuffing alters the shape of the original flat piece. As with all types of heads, it is important that they not be too small—at least three to four inches, better four to five inches, from chin to top of head is needed. One of the disadvantages of commercial puppets is that the heads are often much too small.

Sew firmly at the nose, as this is a point of strain. Stuff the head quite tightly, using long-staple cotton. Use sterile cotton if you want it to pack really firmly. Do not use dacron stuffing or kapok, as neither will pack firmly enough to give form. You will find that you can sculpt quite a bit of contour into these heads, but you must be careful to reinforce with extra stitches at the nose and under the chin. If you do not put in a piece resembling two triangles joined at their bases as an under-chin piece, the chin will be unavoidably pointed. For extra durability, when the head is complete you can apply a drop of colorless nail polish to the bridge of the nose and under the chin. This will slightly discolor the fabric but becomes almost unnoticeable and is worth the sacrifice for its strength. The features can be painted on with fine, stiff oil painting brushes and acrylic paint, or they can be appliquéd. Painted faces on felt can appear very lifelike, and we will discuss the manner of applying color in the chapter on costume and makeup.

Now you need hands. The hand has but three fingers and a thumb. Four fingers tend to look like a rake and give a busy effect, whereas three fingers are visually pleasing and usually are quite unnoticed by an audience unless exposed to very close viewing. Even up close the effect is acceptable, and unless you wish for some reason to be superrealistic, omitting one middle digit is recommended.

The proportion of the hand to the face is probably a bit larger than you may have envisioned. Place your own hand, heel against chin, to your face. Your fingertips will about reach your eyebrows. The same proportion of hand to face applies to the puppet. The puppet hand must be at least as big or larger in proportion to the face as the human. Remember, when using the hand puppet, you must convey *everything* with the hands and face. Do not be afraid to exaggerate!!

Both machine- and hand-sewn hands are stuffed and have a piece of wire in the shape of the hand inserted in them. These hands can be used with many types of head construction. For the machine hand, put the wire in first and then stuff, not too firmly, so that you can bend the hand into contours. For the hand-sewn variety, be patient. You can make a pair of hands in about two hours if you're quick with a needle. If that discourages you, forget it, and use some other method, though the result of hand sewing is quite beautiful, if you care to take the time. For hand-made puppet hands you will sew together the two identical pieces. Begin, right sides together, at the little finger side near the wrist and sew up to the top of the little finger. Now, lay the wire shape between the two halves and begin to stuff as you sew, so that the stuffing goes up to the very tip of the finger. Just keep sewing and stuffing until you reach the base of the wrist at the thumb side. You now have a delicate hand that can be shaped almost any way you like; the only ones that match its quality are carved of wood, and they can't be reshaped. Some latex compounds show potential and are worth exploring. Several puppeteers claim excellent results. The compounds are all a little different from each other in handling and results, and their availability varies widely throughout the country. You may well want to try what is obtainable in your area hobby shops, and you may find a latex suitable for heads as well as hands. Some of the compounds are poured into molds; others form on wire bases dipped in the latex solution or can be built up in layers on a positive base. One advantage to a latex form is its flexibility after it is finished.

At the other extreme from cloth in texture and feeling, carved wood heads can be very expressive, giving much play to light and shadow, but you have to like working with wood and be able to put up with the heavy heads this method will produce. Wood carving is an art in itself, and if you can do it, great. Carved wood heads are rarely seen now, but they can be extremely beautiful, and in the marionette, where the extra weight is an advantage, they are practical as well.

Two other mediums: papier-mâché and celastic are similar in construction and produce similar heads. In both cases, you first mold a head in clay (Plasticine, not water clay). We will discuss methods of molding after examining the mediums that use it. The first medium, papier mâché, is usually composed of strips of paper dipped in wheat paste; it is applied in at least three layers on a clay mold. The difficulty is that in working with a positive clay head and applying layers on top of it, you lose a lot of detail. You can make a negative mold of plaster of Paris, halving it or making it in sections, as your head design demands. Then remove the papier mâché from the mold, having used Vaseline as a separating agent, let the sections dry, then rejoin them with glue into a finished head. Either method of using papier mâché produces a reasonaby durable head and has the advantage of being cheap and quite easy to produce.

The celastic head is similar, but the final product is more durable; it also costs more and is a little more difficult to work as it involves the use of acetone, the debatable toxicity of which may or may not scare you off. You can use either a positive or negative mold (clay positive or plaster negative) as with papier mâché. The difference begins after modeling the clay or making the mold. Coat the clay with thin aluminum foil, torn in pieces. Then apply *torn* strips of celastic in varying sizes to fit the contours of the face in two layers. Use only the "fine" celastic. You have to blend the edges in with your fingers, and just about any rubber or poly glove will dissolve in the acetone (your best bet is surgical gloves obtainable at the drugstore). When you have the head coated with celastic, it must dry thoroughly (until it is no longer cold). You can then split the head with a mat knife, usually in just halves if the face is not too complicated, and carefully rejoin it with strips of celastic. The head made from a negative mold must be detached from the plaster mold with a separating agent; the advantage is a head that is far smoother than one built up on a positive clay mold; the disadvantage is that it is very difficult to fit the bits of celastic down into the mold and make them stay put. Whether from a positive or negative mold, the joined celastic head needs to be well sanded; then plastic spackle, sometimes mixed with a bit of white glue for durability, is applied to fill in cracks and smooth out the contours. It is a longer process, but the result is more durable and more controllable than papier mâché, since the layers are thinner and the plastic very strong.

There are several other traditional ways to make heads, and you may well discover compounds or methods of your own. Remember, what is given here is meant to give you an overview of possibilities and to send you on to craft books for detailed step-by-step processes if you need them, which is likely to be the case with plastic wood. Heads made of it can be beautiful, durable, and sculpted in any way you choose, but it is a pesky medium, and you really have to love it to get results. A head is formed of Plasticine, and a plaster mold of that head is made in halves or as many pieces as will allow removal of the finished shell. The plaster mold is then filled with flattened patties of plastic wood. It is best to work under water, since plastic wood contains acetone and dries very quickly. You can dry the filled mold under water, the cavities being filled with BBs or some other small weights. Shrinkage must be allowed for, and it can be up to about 40 percent. One just has to learn how much larger to make the heads than the end result desired. The dried halves (or several parts, if it is a complicated mold) are fitted together, "glued" with more plastic wood and the head is bound round with string and left to dry. Then it is sanded thoroughly and painted with acrylics.

Or you can go the Muppet route and make heads of foam rubber, if you like, covering the foam with jersey or flocking them. Half-inch foam can be easily cut and joined with contact cement to make flexible and very expressive faces. These heads are capable of wonderful facial expressions. They are almost all face, with rods sometimes attached to the hands. (See Chapter 12, "The Rod Puppet.")

Which brings us to a point of ethics. The Muppet type of puppet has become almost generic, and there is nothing wrong with using Henson's principles of movement and construction, but it is hoped that as you work, building puppets and acting with them, you will develop more and more a style of your own. What you do yourself is always going to be better than what you copy from someone else. Perhaps Jim Henson, creator of the Muppets, has best expressed the ethics of "doing your own thing" and not copying someone else's work, however much you may admire it.

A number of people have asked me, from time to time, how I feel about the various puppeteers around the country who have based the look of their puppets on the Muppets. There are indeed many people who are doing things quite derivative of our style of puppetry. This brings up some larger questions relating to the ethics of our profession. . . .

With our Sesame Street characters we are able to legally stop anyone who specifically does one or more of our characters—for example, we have stopped individuals performing "Big Bird" at shopping centers and in circuses. These can be quite damaging and embarrassing to us because their costumes are generally poor reproductions of our Big Bird. We have also stopped companies from selling their products with unauthorized versions of our characters. We are successful in these matters since these characters are all protected by various copyrights and trademarks.

A much thornier problem is how, or if, to try to prevent someone from using puppet concepts which we essentially originated, but which are not protected by specific copyrights and trademarks. We see, frequently, puppets which have the overall "Muppet look," but which do not look like our individual Muppet characters. We feel that the people creating these puppets should create, as we did, their own concepts and not use ours. I think perhaps a parallel can be drawn with the schools of painting, where you have painters that are basing their work on similar ideas, but each interprets these in his or her own unique style. What it boils down to, regardless of the legalities or the ethics of it all, is what I tell young puppeteers who come to me for advice. I describe how I tried various ways of coming up with characters until I had my own style of working. I tell them that they will really be much better off if they find their own unique style of puppetry—to copy us will only result in their work being "like the Muppets" and probably not as good.

It seems to me that each of us expressing our own originality is the essence of our art and professionalism.[1]

Whatever method of construction you have chosen, the first thing you must do is overcome any fear of designing and building puppets, and the surest cure is to model a head in Plasticine that pleases you (yes, just for the experience even if you have chosen felt as a medium). Why? Because many people who swear they can't draw find that they are quite successful at modeling. Some people like to make preliminary renderings of what their puppet will be; others do not. Some like to know exactly what the puppet is going to be before they start; others are content to let the puppet evolve. In order to find out how you work, and to learn some tricks of modeling not usually found in how-to books, go and get yourself two or three pounds of Plasticine, and let's begin.

At first the clay will seem discouragingly hard, but as you warm it with your hands, it becomes more yielding. Make a basic oval shape, if your head is to be human, or the very basic shape of whatever animal or thing you envision for this puppet. Plop the shape on a wide-based bottle and form a neck around the bottle neck. Or you can make a simple armature with a dowel inserted in a five- by five-inch wood base. It is generally better to add on features with "sausages" and lumps of clay than to start digging in and carving away.

Your head will look very lumpy. Now, start smoothing out contours, having spotted the proportions of the face and where the features will be. You may want to add on above the eye and carve some away to recess the eye cavity. Bulging eyes rarely work, unless there is some character reason for the puppet to have them. Now, pick up the whole head, bottle and all, and rotate it under a strong light. Does the expression change as you turn the head? It must. Exaggerate and simplify the features some more. You will never clarify by complicating and adding detail. Simplify. Some of the most beautiful heads may have eyes but the merest suggestion of a nose and no mouth at all. Try to express as much as you can with as few details as possible. Test your head in light again. See if you have formed a head which looks flat in profile. If so, you are not letting light in. You are making a linear face, as you would draw one. Learn to wrap the features around the head, even exaggerating the human profile and extending the eyes farther around the head, cutting them in more deeply. This is known as "letting light in" into the eyes, and it allows your head to be far more expressive. The puppet is, after all, a kind of kinetic sculpture, and you must learn to build for movement in light.

If you are satisfied with your work, it's time for you to unsettle yourself. Take the head to a mirror. Look at what you have created. It looks different in the reflected image, doesn't it? You will no doubt see that one eye is higher than the other, the mouth lopsided, perhaps several aspects of the features that weren't apparent to you without the mirror. Go back and correct them and recheck.

This is not to say that you must mourn a head that is not absolutely symmetrical. No face is exactly the same on both sides. Yours isn't, either. That's what makes it interesting. Just be sure that the asymmetry you mold into your puppet's head is the asymmetry you intend. And the mirror helps.

Now that you have accomplished a successful molding job, you are ready to turn to any of the mediums of casting for completion or to transfer what you have learned to constructing a felt or other cloth head.

You have already been given a body pattern suitable for a head of any type, but a few words need be said about building movement into the body. Yes, that is really what you do. You must first know what movements the puppet must accomplish and then construct the body so that the puppet will be able to do them. Remember, the puppet is not a human being, and he can't do everything a human can do. And it is quite possible that one specific movement, such as simply holding out his hand in a certain manner, is very important to a character. Then you must figure out how to tilt a hand or take a few stitches in an arm so that the specific movement can be accomplished. This may well mean that the puppet will not be able to make "normal" gestures with that hand, but try to work around the limitation. He is not a human being after all, and because he is not human, you can construct him to do many things people can't do. Bear in mind the comfort of the operator, and then make your first consideration building the puppet for the ability to move as you need him to.

Nor will your puppet always be a human being or an anthropomorphized animal. If your puppet is a teapot, how are you going to lift the lid? If you inserted plastic tubing with a syringe hidden in the "body," couldn't you puff talcum powder steam through your puppet's spout? Learn to think in terms of "what can my puppet *do*? What will he need to *do*?" And let your imagination and sense of fantasy run free.

Also learn, however, to make your puppet *not* do what you don't want. There are not as many pitfalls with hand puppets as with rod puppets and marionettes; even so, be sure that heads are securely sewn into bodies, hands well fastened, and wigs glued in place. Be sure to check your puppets during the run of the show; all manner of things can come loose. Something will, someday, in spite of your efforts, and the world will not end—but you will be embarrassed and vow to be more careful.

You can offset some of the difficulties of inexperienced operators who don't hold their arms straight and you can give character exaggeration to bosoms and bottoms and tummies by attaching a muslin "pillow" to the inner body under the costume.

Costume design, including the use of line and color and the adaptation of historical costumes to puppets, will be covered in Chapter 7, but you will need to know some basics about costume construction even for your first puppets. You have already learned, in remodeling a puppet, that the inner body is essential. When you construct the whole puppet you will make the inner body exactly the same way you did for your remodeled puppet. Remember the wire inserted in the hem at the bottom of the glove, and the metal ring attached at center back of hem for hanging the puppet when not in use.

Let's suppose that you have a completed head joined to an inner body with hands and you are ready to costume your puppet. Don't think in terms of dressing the puppet as you would a doll. If you sew a complete costume and put it on the puppet, you are extremely likely to create a constricting garment. Think instead of building the costume onto the inner body of the puppet. Unlike costumes for people, in a puppet costume you will leave some seams open for freedom of movement, and you will sew parts of the costume directly to the body. First, the sleeves. Cut two rectangles of lightweight fabric and gather them on both ends. It is very important that you develop a sense of what kinds of fabric will move well and what won't. Lots of time and care taken in choosing fabric will more than repay you later. You want to consider, too, what the fabric will look like after your show has been packed away—will it wrinkle? You should be able simply to shake a puppet out and have it appear fresh.

Attach the sleeves to the body by sewing them directly to the glove *before* attaching the bodice. Just how large to cut rectangles for the sleeves depends on how much you want the sleeve to blouse. You will gather them at the wrist, sew a seam down one side, and gather ever so slightly as you tack the sleeve to the inner glove. It's better to cut the sleeve a little larger than you expect to need; you can always trim it off. You won't want it to blouse so much that it covers or dwarfs the hand, but some fullness helps greatly in giving the illusion of longer arms than a hand puppet can really have.

The upper costume is also cut of two rectangles. You can gather it at the neck and waist for a lady's top or for a smocklike look. Or you can turn the side and fit the shoulders to taper a vest or jacket. Just be careful to leave it loose enough. Off the hand, costumed hand puppets usually look too wide, so put your puppet on your hand to fit it and see how it really will look. One important trick is not to sew the armhole seams to the sleeve; that is why the sleeve is sewn far in onto the inner body. You may want to tack it in a few strategic spots, so that no lining will show, but leaving it open as much as you can will help free the movement greatly.

The lower body will be either two rectangles for pants, sewn on to the inner body over the blouse, or it will be a gathered skirt. Either can be slip-stitched by hand at the puppet's waist. Blousing the top's front over a "pillow" will give a lady a bosom. If a gentleman is going to have a pot-belly, be sure that you fit the costume over the attached pillow; don't make the mistake of inserting the pillow into the finished costume and finding it is then too tight.

If you have a puppet with an animal body, the body may well be the inner glove, and you can give it some shape. If your fabric won't hold the shape well enough, build an inner body and attach pillows to tummy and rump. If the animal is to have a tail, put him on your hand. Make him bow. Attach the tail at the point where your wrist bends, and the effect will be quite lifelike. There are, of course, many variations on animal puppets, and you will think up some of your own. The animal that is all mouth requires a hinged stiffness piece, either of heavy cardboard or light wood, within the mouth. You then simply cover that inner mouth and join it to the outer head shape. Great success for fire-breathing dragons can be achieved with medical catheters joined in a T shape and proceeding down below the tubular glove. The end of the catheter is then connected to a rectal syringe partially filled with unscented talcum powder. It's a funny effect and has the advantage of being utterly safe.

Other animals can be created with or without moving mouths; when only their upper body is seen, they appear to be on all fours rather than standing in a human position. Often these are fun if they are large in proportion to the other puppets. As you work with them you can develop quite a skill in giving the illusion of realistic animal movement.

We've mentioned puppets that aren't animal or human—that are things.

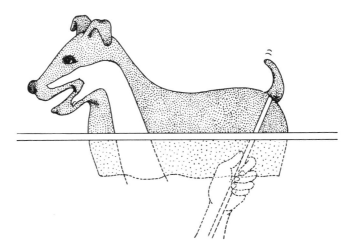

*A treatment of an animal on all fours when only the upper body is seen*

What about abstracts? You can, of course, build absolutely anything—shapes that move in fantastic ways. The difficulty with abstraction remains, as in painting and avant-garde theatre, that one must begin with the real and move toward the abstract in order to communicate. One must have a point of reference with which the audience can identify; if you are not in some way understood, your audience will not be entertained.

You now have ways to remodel existing puppets, and you have knowledge of the mediums you can use to build new puppets. You have, we hope, even developed some confidence in your ability to create your own "cast."

There exists the possibility that after trying construction you really hate it. Then, by all means, buy your puppets, or better, get someone else to build them. Many things must be done to create puppet theatre, as you are discovering, and it is certainly the better part of valor, when you come up against a necessary phase of the art that you hate or are really not good at, to find someone skilled to do the job for you. Just be sure to give anyone contributing to your work credit for what they have done. And choose an artist whose work harmonizes with your own concepts, so that the end result will be homogeneous.

Now, let's get on with the show! In order to perform with whatever puppets you have bought, built, remodeled, or found in the attic, you are going to need a script. Having come this far, you are ready to put a whole show together, starting with the backbone of a well-constructed, exciting script—for which our method follows.

# 4

## Building an Original
## Script for Puppets

You are ready now to take basic elements of story and literally "build" a show out of them, just as you would with so many wooden blocks. Perhaps your script will evolve from the puppets you have or, conversely, you may build your script and then create the puppets for which it calls. Either way you will need a working knowledge of what makes a good playable script.

"But," you say, "can't I just go to the library and find a book of puppet plays?" Of course you can, but most of them are awful. A few promising ones are noted in the Bibliography, but for the most part, available scripts are extremely wordy and lacking in action. Others, particularly of folk derivation, may actually play well, but because so much of their effectiveness comes from action often not described, it's difficult, from the written versions, to figure out what makes them work.

Guidance will be given here for determining the elements of a playable script, giving motivations and cues and critical movements—but no dialogue. You may eventually find or write out a delightful full script, but for the purposes of training and early work, you will accomplish much more for yourself and for your audiences by creating your own shows and by *not* writing them out in full. The advantage of this type of "script" is to free you not only from sounding "read" but from overwriting. Beautiful speeches that don't advance the action are thrown out with this method, and that's very healthy in puppet theatre.

Your first task in constructing a script is to choose your material. Will you expand one of your pantomimes or skits, make up a new story, or would you like to adapt a folk or fairy tale? Although it is certainly true that the bulk of puppet shows performed are for children, it is equally true that puppetry can be a highly exciting art form for adults. Determine, then, for whom you wish to perform. Some puppet theatre is so exquisitely executed and so tuned to the essential emotions of man that it plays equally well for children and adults. Arriving at such a theatre piece demands much work and a truly gifted puppeteer. In the beginning, do not discourage yourself by shooting immediately for the moon. Decide whether to develop a script for children or adults. This choice will determine your point of view, but your methods of script construction apply to puppet theater aimed at any age.

Let us suppose that you have chosen to expand your pantomime, to which you have added voice, and make a full story show of it. Is there really enough material there worth expanding? Can you take its beginning, middle, and end and elaborate on each, adding new complications and perhaps new characters, thereby enriching and expanding the story? It is a mistake to go on after the end with "and what happened then"; your story cannot go on after its conflict has been resolved. If it is to be expanded, it must be expanded from within. Each part—beginning, middle, and end—must be developed more fully, characters added, and complications introduced.

If your pantomime looks and feels capable of growth into a play and suits the age level for which you want to perform, find out where you can expand it in movement. Don't be afraid to try new actions or twists to the story; you can always cut them if they don't work, and they may lead you to fresh ideas that *do* work. Be strict with yourself when you are adding dialogue, remembering to pare away constantly any unnecessary talk. Probably your first small audiences have helped you find out what "plays." Don't lose those first tricks of the "take" and of building actions in series of three. Be especially careful to see that the actions build toward a climax, or your story will be level and the result boring.

If you are simply tired of your old pantomime, why not construct a whole new show from the characters you have now? Your play will be much more successful if it excites *you*. Writing an original script is more difficult and takes more work than adaptation, for which the groundwork is already laid out for you, but it also gives you the most room for expressing your unique ideas.

It is extremely helpful in puppet theatre if the script evolves around one central character, and, especially with hand puppets and children, it is a help if that character is onstage most of the time. When you set up the beginning of your script, you must be very clear about letting your audience know who your main character is and what he wants. It's important for this character to be someone you and your audience can like and with whom you both can identify. Then, you must think the story through, the beginning to the middle to the end, and, as Chekhov said, "put the gun on the wall in the first act." This does not mean that you will give your ending away. But if you will put some clues to what will happen later into the beginning, the end will seem an appropriate resolution, instead of appearing tacked on. Sometimes you can get away with the magic genie (or *deus ex machina*) that suddenly appears and solves everything, and this type of ending can even have a naïve charm. Whatever the type of ending, however, it must appear *deserved* by the hero and must satisfy the audience emotionally. For example, in the many variations of the Cinderella story, the heroine is not only put-upon but good and beautiful, and the Fairy Godmother figure appears early on to set up the idea that magical things can and will occur. Thus, we feel that what happens has a certain logic; it "fits." Do not be misled into thinking that because you are dealing with fantasy (and sometimes the unexpected), events do not have to have logic and order, progression, and a final resolution of the initial conflict you have established. Order, in fact, allows you to introduce *more* complications and characters without confusing your audience. You will develop a sense of just how many characters you can introduce. Never use a character just because you like him and want him in the show. He must provide an integral part of the story. Each supporting character introduced should enlarge on the complications presented to your main character, and must do so with action as well as words. Making the characters as different from each other as possible will help you "act" them and will help keep them straight for the audience.

Let the conflict build naturally, growing from the strong objective of the main character. The stronger you make the forces against him and the bigger the "fight" he must put up, the more exciting your story will be. This does not mean that there must be bloodshed or that your "villain" should be truly horrifying. In fact, in work for children, it is always best to keep your villains funny-horrible. Always ask yourself, "Is it too frightening to laugh at?" Sometimes it is very hard to strike the midpoint between too weak a villain and too scary a one, but if you remember the aspect of humor, you will be able to train yourself to achieve the right blend. You won't succeed with everybody all of the time. Some children have odd fears you couldn't know about; some parents are incapable of seeing with a child's eyes and will be horrified at what amuses their child. Just try to remember that your goal is to entertain, not to send your audience home to nightmares. It is definitely a question of taste and, as such, cannot be pinned down to a precise rule. Examples do help somewhat. Remember the wicked Queen in Disney's *Snow White*? Many children find her really terrifying. On the other hand, do you know Maurice Sendak's *Where the Wild Things Are*, which has become a classic among children's books? His monsters are ugly and awful, but they are also truly funny and they don't threaten the main character. Nor do they pop out suddenly. Children like to be scared—a little. Just remember some of your own fears as a child, and when you design your puppets and write your script keep in mind some universal horrors—things that pop out of the dark, for example, and certainly, mutilation. Severed limbs and heads are not the stuff that children's entertainment is made of, no matter what the Brothers Grimm wrote.

But, you say, what about *Punch and Judy*, in which Mr. Punch "does in" his wife, his baby, the policeman, the hangman, and the doctor, and finally is eaten by a crocodile? You're right, it's a grisly tale, but it works for very special reasons and has been passed down for several hundred years because of its essential psychological validity. (But you will find occasional parents and teachers who are appalled by *Punch and Judy* and its violence, so be prepared if you choose to perform it.) *Punch* works because it is the story of all of us. Mr. Punch rebels against every form of authority, just as each of us would love to, and each time he gets away with it; vicariously, we enjoy getting away with it along with him. But he must be punished (as are we, vicariously), and so the crocodile eats him. If he is not punished, the audience will go home feeling guilty. Some believe *Punch* is cathartic, expelling harmlessly emotions that would otherwise have to come out in some hurtful way. Others equate its violence with the death and gore of some realistic films and TV shows and find the tale ghastly. You will have to decide for yourself if the violence of Mr. Punch is cathartic or harmful.

You will be making many decisions as you build your own stories. After you have introduced characters who will aid or hinder your main character and been careful that each obstacle grow larger than the last, you must determine a point of central conflict—your big encounter between the hero and the villain. No, it does not work if a subsidiary character carries out the action for either one, though he may introduce interesting side issues or "help"; you really need the two main characters locked in conflict. Think what they can do *besides* beat each other up. Don't neglect trickery and the age-old "gimmick" that even Shakespeare loved so well: allowing the audience to know something that the character on stage doesn't know. The longer you can support this kind of situation, the more your audience is going to want to "tell" what they know, and they probably will.

Thus, you must now wrestle with the question of audience participation. You probably have experienced a little of it in your early pantomime and voice work; you now must learn to plan exactly where you would like an audience to respond vocally and what you would like them to say—*and what you will say and do if you get a reaction different from the one you wanted.* It is generally a good idea never to ask an audience any question that can't be answered by a simple yes or no. (Even then, you may get the opposite of what you expect.) If you ask a question that demands a sentence-long answer, you will get a horrendous jumble of babble from your audience, and how are you going to decipher it in order to answer? You want to lead the audience into the desired response by making obvious the answer that will advance the plot. One sure way *not* to accomplish this feat is all too often heard in live children's theatre and involves asking the audience any question beginning with "Don't you think I should . . ." or "You want me to change into a butterfly, *don't you?*" They know they have been told what to think and will invariably give you just the opposite response from what you sought. Learn to ignore the irrelevant response; it usually quiets down when no attention is paid to it. And getting the audience involved is really worth the price of putting up with occasional off-the-track or smart-aleck remarks. The audience will usually respond at the highest points of suspense in a children's show; you can learn to script for points where they can "help" the hero. It helps if you set up the fact that it is all right for the audience to talk to the puppets at the beginning of the show. In the United States, we train our children to "be quiet and watch the show," and they are used to being mesmerized by television. All the more reason to offer them an event in the theatre that requires their involvement and imaginative participation. You can have whoever announces the performance tell them to help the hero, or let your hero tell them himself at the beginning of the play. You can script an effective puppet play without audience participation, but if you do, you are overlooking part of the heritage of the art of the puppet. True, most adult audiences will be reluctant to answer the puppets, but they respond immediately with surprise and pleasure when the puppet addresses them directly. Depending upon the audience, you may be quite surprised at the amount of participation you do get, even from an adult house, if you have cleverly scripted your piece.

As do acting with puppets and constructing puppets, writing a script for puppets means learning some basic rules and then becoming confident enough to break them, for none are hard and fast. Interestingly enough, the rules that Aristotle set down so long ago for the construction of a Greek tragedy—including the importance of the three unities—apply equally well to the construction of a puppet play. For example, to hold an audience, a play must have a beginning, middle, and end. When enriching your primary plot with side issues that offer complications and variations within the story, never deviate too far from the central character's strongest objective. You will find that in your best scripts, after the conflict is resolved, something about each of the characters will be changed. After all, if things are exactly at the end of the play as they were at the beginning, that's not very interesting, is it? Clarifying the changes in the characters at the end of the play will help to unify the action and make the resolution more satisfying and complete.

Unity of place is extremely important in puppet theatre. Stories that have lots of scenes or are "travel stories" (like *The Wizard of Oz*) are extremely difficult to stage successfully. You want as few scene changes as possible; don't follow the lure that an exciting new set will be worth the break in the audience's attention. If you *must* change the scene, try to do so as quickly as possible. Sometimes it helps greatly to make sure that at all times *something* is happening, even during scene changes. For instance, let a character come out in front of the curtain while you change the scene behind. (Admittedly, this is almost impossible with a one-person show.) Music helps, but it won't really heal the break in attention caused by a scene change. You may find it useful to rely on film techniques with which every audience today is comfortable and familiar to the point of not noticing their use. Think how in film there is often an overlap of music as one scene fades into the next. You can utilize this technique by letting your puppets talk over the music as it fades out into the beginning of your scenes. Do keep your scene breaks as few and as short as possible. Yes, this is true in adult shows, too.

Can you have an intermission? Of course. It is advisable, though, if you want an intermission, to make it fall between two complete plays. It is too much to require of an audience to ask them to return their attention to a plot after an intermission. And keep your intermissions short. Do you want a rule? Figure five minutes is long enough for children and ten for adults. Be sure to blink the house lights or sound a buzzer to give them a warning to return to their seats. Remember: the attention span for puppet theatre in the United States seems to fall magically into twenty- to thirty-minute range, whether the performance is for adults or children. (It is doubtful that this is a conditioned response from television; we simply have not inculcated the tradition of two- to two-and-one-half-hour puppet performances.) Try to make your intermissions fall at about a twenty- to thirty-minute point, and while you can play an adult show for an hour and a half, an hour would be recommended as the outside limit for a children's show. Puppet theatre is small, the action is compressed and requires much concentration on the part of the audience. You will tire them out if you run your shows too long. Don't feel that by lengthening your show you are giving them "their money's worth." Far better to send them away happy with a short show than to tack on another act which will bore them because they have literally had enough. So, probably, have you. Sustaining a one-person show for an hour is all the discipline it is fair to ask of yourself, and even when you expand to working with a group, you will find an hour to an hour and a half about as long as you can all summon the necessary energy and concentration.

Time enters into consideration in other ways, too, and hearkens back again to Aristotle. While you certainly don't have to have all of the action of the story take place within a twenty-four-hour period as he recommended, it is difficult to dramatize for the puppet theatre plots that involve action over long periods of time. You will find yourself leaning on visual gimmicks of every sort to suggest time change: dimming the lights helps, but it won't do the whole job. One of your characters is going to have the hapless task of having to explain to the audience that x amount of time has passed, and this is always awkward. You will find that you can heighten suspense and increase the urgency of any action if you impose the condition that unless this action is completed by a certain time, your hero will suffer. The shorter the time your hero has to accomplish his goal, the tighter your script. For example, your audience will be far more concerned about a character who must recover a pot of gold by sundown or be killed than about the same character offered the same fate but with three years in which to accomplish the task.

Explaining *anything* to an audience without action is very difficult to do and should be avoided whenever possible. "But," you say, "how do I let my audience know where the characters are and what has happened before the beginning of the play?" What you have is the old playwriting problem of the opening scene (or passage-of-time scene) when the maid and the butler stand around dusting and informing the audience and each other what has been going on and what is likely to happen shortly. These scenes are incredibly awkward and equally hard to avoid. It takes real inventiveness, but you have got to think of a way to have something happen right away that is visual. Avoid like influenza having one character come out and remark where he is and, oh dear, what is going to happen. That kind of clumsy exposition will kill your show before it has begun. Let your first character (usually your hero) enter and *do* something. If he is clumsy, let him drop something; this shows something about his character and also gives him a chance to worry about what he has done and the effect it will have on information that has to be conveyed. As soon as you can, unless you are skillful at warming up your audience by involving them with the actions of a single character, introduce a second character who immediately causes interaction. If the main conflict is going to involve the tearing of a precious book, let a character enter in fear and trembling, looking for a place where he can *protect* his book, giving him a chance to explain, as briefly as possible, from what or from whom. In short, get your story moving as fast as you can—with action.

Please, please ban the use of a narrator. Yes, an offstage voice is one way of getting the exposition over to the audience, but it is a very dull way. You may think it will help to have action go on during a narration, but this usually leads to the main points of the exposition getting lost in general confuson. In rare instances, such as in *Peter and the Wolf, Our Town,* and *L'Histoire du Soldat,* the narrator is an integral part of the theatre piece. These are pieces by master dramatists. Narrated scripts represent an extremely difficult format—just the opposite of the usually assumed "easy way out."

Do not be afraid to let your mind run free, inventing all sorts of fantastic characters. Instead, remember that the realm of fantasy, of the magical, is the home of puppet theatre, and you want to present that which human actors cannot perform better. Be sure, however, that when you introduce fantastic characters you explain somehow who they are. A confused audience is a restless one.

Beware as you would the perils of the deep, the use of disguises. Somehow, they creep into the plans for many a show, and they confuse the audience *completely.* It sounds like a good idea to use them, but the only way you can bring it off is to be sure the audience knows who a character is before he *announces* he is going to go and don a disguise, and he is probably going to have to tell the audience who he is when he returns in disguise. For some reason, it is simply much more confusing to have a puppet in disguise than a human actor.

Never underestimate your audience. Especially if you are doing a "message" show (conserve energy, brush your teeth, take vitamins, whatever), you will want to respect what your audience, however young it may be, knows about your subject, how bored it may be with your message, and how much it will resent being told over and over again to do anything. The message may be worthy, and if you wish to win children or adults to a cause through puppets, you can; but be subtle. Have a good show with lots of action that would hold up as fine theatre whether or not it had a message to convey, and your audience will go home happy with your message and remember it. (They may not "buy" it, but they will consider it seriously). When trying to convey a message, humor is always your closest friend. If you have an impossible product to sell or a difficult message, let something funny happen to your hero. Let him be the victim of his circumstances, à la James Thurber. If your audience loves him, they will invariably champion the underdog, and they will buy whatever product or message he has to sell. Can you imagine refusing any request from Snoopy? Or, if you are old enough to remember his heyday, of Kukla? Characters must be loved to be believed, and they must get involved in interesting action to implant any message.

Make your hero beloved and he will be your trademark. Can Kermit or Kukla or Snoopy ever do real wrong? Of course not. They are for right and honor and valor, a little bit misunderstood, perhaps, as is my own champion, Edmund Mouse, but all of them are beloved wherever they travel. There is the universal predicament of mankind about these characters, and you will develop your own puppet "hero" around whom to weave shows. He (she) must be sympathetic, an underdog, and often the victim of circumstances, but brave and honest and true. Come on, now, work your imagination and evolve a "pet" character. Often, it will be the first puppet you create. He may even be a product of the first script you build.

Don't waste too much time worrying about the age level of your children's shows, that is, how old an audience they will appeal to. If it is an exciting, colorful show with well-designed puppets, you can count on its appealing to almost every age. If your sponsor insists on an age level for a successful children's show, tell him ages five to twelve. No child is ready to see a puppet show until he enjoys being told a story, and that varies with every child. Even if you give five to twelve years as the approximate age level for your show, expect that parents will inevitably bring some younger children who will enjoy the show and others who won't be able to sit still. You will probably even get babes in arms, though it is hard to understand why anyone thinks a child who can't yet talk will enjoy a whole puppet show. You will also have in your audience children older than twelve, some of whom will be fascinated by your technique and effects, others of whom will be bored. However, by stipulating an age range of between five and twelve years, you are capturing the optimum interest ages and protecting yourself from complaints from the parents of children whose interest is not as guaranteed. But, remember, you *must* have an exciting show or no child will give you his rapt attention!

We have spoken thus far mostly of children's shows and of principles that apply to scripting in general. Let us speak for a moment about the show aimed specifically at the adult audience, which is at once the same (because the principles of playwriting remain constant) and very different (because the age level demands a different subject matter, approach, and delivery). I have warned you not to underestimate your audience, but there is another side to this coin. You must not *over*estimate the background in theatre or appreciation of puppetry in your adult audience. If you are to perform puppetry for adults in the United States, where we lack the Europeans' long tradition of puppetry for grown-ups, you must also take on the job of educating your public. And the public is capricious in its tastes, ultimately influenced by reviews, though word of mouth will help you, too. Reasonably, you may expect that the easiest crowd to draw will be an elite and culturally sophisticated one, aware of the European tradition of puppet theatre. However, it is still very much your job to sell them on what you have to offer, to perfect a super product and prove to them that, yes, puppet theatre *can* perform for adults. And despite their seeming sophistication, you must still assume them to be very average citizens who are used to much film and television and are probably more than a little skeptical of what you have to offer. You will have to be just as clear and explicit in your scripting as in a children's show. They will be delighted if the production effects are smooth and exciting, but the backbone of your work is still going to be an arresting and well-thought-out script with a beginning that holds them spellbound.

Suppose you wish to do a "book" show or script that is a play for adults. From where will you draw your material? Though you may consider a serious play, bear in mind that that is the most difficult form with which to please your audience. Many people have the preconceived notion that puppets *must* be funny, and if they have come to see an adult puppet show those people want to be "entertained." It might be a good idea, then, and the easiest way to reach your public, to consider comedy. The bonus here is that you have free reign of satire, which is certainly the puppet's rightful domain. Frequently the puppet can get away with what the human or the live actor could not attempt, simply because he is *not* alive. Puppets have been used throughout all time for propaganda in countless wars and political causes. The puppet is, in a mystical way, inviolate.

For sources of skit and play material, look to your local news. Let your puppets weave their material around what is going on in the world *now*. Around 1800, Guignol, puppet hero of Lyons, fought for the silk workers in his city, and he won his audience to his cause through his comedy, his inventiveness, and he did so because the people loved his invincible spirit. During the Second World War, the information from the Resistance in France was conveyed to fellow members through puppet shows in public gardens; the Nazis in the audience had no idea what was going on. You are blessed. You do not need to be guarded and mask your ideas. If you are successful in your puppet theatre attempts, you may change a mind, alter a viewpoint, give the memory of love to a bitter soul, or make the gray, pallid person laugh. If you are true to your art, your work will never be without initial purpose, whether you wish to convey deep themes or simply to entertain.

One cardinal rule in working with serious drama is to set the tone of the play *immediately* in your first scene. Let your audience know that you expect to be taken seriously and establish this with the entrance of the first character. You may well have comic interludes to provide relief, and you still can utilize "the take," and the exaggeration and simplicity of puppet theatre, but don't "pull the rug out from under your audience" by letting them anticipate one outcome and giving them (unprepared) another.

Experiment. You will not and cannot reach everyone, particularly if you deal with controversial material, and some people simply will not understand what you have to say. However, if *you* are satisfied, then a large portion of your audience will be reached by your sincerity and will come to realize that puppetry isn't all comic or limited to children's shows and stock revues.

Puppet theatre offers a new mode and dimension for adult works. Start thinking about how you can combine types of puppets, masks, abstractions, how you can take advantage of the puppet's fantastic nature. Be careful that in dealing with abstraction you are able to define and state your theme and plot in clear and simple terms; remember, "abstraction" can become an excuse for fuzzy thinking. Your goal is to communicate, remember?

There is a wealth of material from live theatre that can be played beautifully by puppets. Noteworthy triumphs were Ralph Chessé's mounting of *The Emperor Jones* and Remo Bufano's production of *Oedipus Rex* with its towering ten-foot (or taller) figures.

Adaptations of scenes will require skillful editing of long speeches and sometimes combining scenes, skills we will examine in the next chapter. If you perform excerpts, *never* assume that your audience has any knowledge of the original play. You will have to figure out a way to prepare them, or they will be lost. There are some whole one-act plays that were originally written for puppets that you may want to consider, but it is difficult to find one that will play for a contemporary audience, except perhaps as a college exercise. Be sure to take a look at the one-acts by Federico García Lorca and also those by Maurice Maeterlinck and Anton Chekhov. A surprising number of playwrights produced works for puppets, and it is well worth getting acquainted with them; however, many of these plays now seem wordy and ponderous and it is likely that after reading them you will be spurred on to writing your own scripts.

The final performance format to be considered is that of the revue, which, of course, can be used for adult or child performances. It is the format most frequently favored for adult shows and is thought by most people to be the easiest one. However, unless you are content with a very run-of-the-mill show, the revue is not as easy as you may think, and you will need more of a "script" than you may suspect. Though there is no real plot to a revue, you must arrange your acts with utmost care in order to sustain audience attention. You will need a "snapper"—a very interesting and preferably original number—with which to open your show. If this initial number captures your audience, you can follow it with almost anything for the next two or three numbers, and as long as you perform with reasonable skill, you will be well received. You will want to vary numbers in length, but make none so long that they seem to dominate the show. Music will help you to keep the show moving. There must be a sense of flow throughout. Remember the importance of keeping the action going and of avoiding scene breaks; try never to leave the stage completely bare. When a revue is played entirely by one person, keeping something interesting in front of the audience is an extremely difficult task, but it can be accomplished.

Often a "running gag," or character who reappears at intervals throughout your show, can help the pause between acts as well as the sense of unity your production will need. There is no reason why a revue has to be all comic, but you may have trouble inserting a truly tragic piece. Audiences have a tough time adjusting to abrupt changes in style or subject matter. It is even tricky to offer a total change of content in sections of a show spaced by the divisions of intermissions. Generally, just don't demand too much of your audience; and if you want a standing ovation, do save your most effective piece for last!

In order to construct a successful revue, especially with hand puppets, you need to train yourself to think in terms of what ideas can be developed in a short time (possibly only five to seven minutes). Even without plot you will need to determine a beginning, a middle, and an end. Each little scene must have its own such structure, and the end must be definite enough so that you can "black out" your lights and cause your audience to applaud immediately. They must never wonder if a sketch is over. Try to develop a sense of progression, so that your audience can actually feel a build toward your final number. Often it helps to have a theme for the entire show, but this is not absolutely necessary, provided there is a stylistic unity to the whole production. You may find the "A-B-A" idea useful, that is, returning at the end of your show to characters introduced at the beginning. In both musical and dance composition you will find inspiration for "variations upon a theme" and satisfying ways to unify a program.

Now that we have covered most aspects of building an original script, you should get busy and try out some scenes. Some of your ideas will work. Others you will throw away, but they may give you fresh solutions and more ideas. Once in a while a script simply refuses to "take off." If you have gone back over all basic script needs and it still isn't satisfactory, don't worry it like a dog with a bone; give it up and start over. Save the idea, put it on the shelf, and maybe at a later time you will think of exactly what the show needs to succeed. Above all, do not be discouraged.

Even though I've advised you not to write out all your dialogue, this is the time to get out pencil and paper, because you will need to clarify actions and motivations. You will also have to determine which puppet will go on which hand (and to be sure that you have hands enough to accomplish your ideas!). A detailed outline of your show will not only clarify motivations and the progression of action, it will force you to define character relationships, making sure that each character you introduce is really contributing to the advancement of the plot.

After you have determined the beginning, middle, and end of the whole show in the most simple terms, start working on the show scene by scene. Yes, get up on your feet and act it out! If it is a show for which you do not yet have the puppets made, use glove-and-ball puppets, or any puppets handy, as long as their looks do not distract you from the characters you are making them play. After each scene, sit down and evaluate it. Is it really contributing to the action? How much have you caused your characters to say that was unnecessary? It will help greatly if you will write down *one line* that your character says on each of his entrances. These few written lines of dialogue will act as cue lines later when you have pared down your outline to the simple cue sheet of entrances and exits that I've suggested you post backstage during a performance.

Take a look at the first line you have written for your entering hero. If you have written, "Like the dawn of a new moon with a shimmer of stars, I have come to rescue the fair Princess, fairest of the fair and delicate as the minaret towers of my Father's land," you are getting carried away with the sound of your voice. Give him instead a simple cue line like, "I must think of a way to rescue Princess Whatever-her-name-is."

Include in the cue line what the character *wants* at the outset of the scene. This line may not turn out to be the first line that your character speaks in the final version of your show. It is written in your outline for the sake of your memory and the development of your plot.

Though you may be working with a partner, for the purposes of illustration we will assume that you are scripting an original one-person show and will furnish you with the bare-bones sample working outline. Following the next chapter on adapting a script from existing story material, there is a sample outline for "Beauty and the Beast" which involves five operators, and you will find in the chapter on directing the play many suggestions for working with groups. It would be a mistake, however, for you to tackle a group effort for your very first show. Learn to develop your own capabilities first.

Note that in the working outline script, music and props (unless they are important to the development of the action) are left out. However, your final "script" to be posted backstage during a performance should include cues for anything that must happen, not just entrances and exits, but lights, curtains, props, and special effects. If you are doing the show yourself, you won't have to note who is responsible for these cues, but it will help greatly to remind yourself when they have to happen. Compare the differences in the two outlines following. The script is for one scene in which your central character stays on your left hand throughout the play, even if he exits. (You will involve yourself in all kinds of unnecessary agony if you transfer characters from hand to hand. Even if you have a progression of characters on the right hand, it will help you immeasurably to keep the action going clearly if the hero is always on your left. You can, of course, reverse the process and put your hero on the right and your chain of other characters on the left. You should be working equally well with both hands by now, and it is even possible to program two short shows, one scripted for the hero on the left, the other the reverse. This way you will be able to hang all of the characters for both shows at the beginning of your program.)

## SHOW TITLE

| *Left Hand* | *Right Hand* |
|---|---|
| Name of first character to enter.<br>Cue line of dialogue.<br>(What does he want?)<br>Be able to answer: where did he come from? where is he going?<br>Jot down details about him: age, health, physical characteristics.<br>First action briefly described.<br>What are the consequences? | |

*Left Hand* (cont'd)                    *Right Hand* (cont'd)

Second character to enter:
name
Cue line of dialogue.
Repeat for each character
the questions and answers
you applied to the first
puppet.

(Do the characters meet? What is the consequence of their meeting?
How does it advance the plot? Write the important interactions in this
middle space.)

If the first character exits,
note when and why in
this column, along with
any action he performs
alone.

Second character exits.
(Remember this is an
hypothetical example,
not a formula for a
play! You may have
many characters or few,
and their entrances and
exits will be determined
by the action of the
plot.)
Third character enters.
Answer questions as be-
fore. Cue line of dia-
logue.

Note if hero returns.
Why? What does he
*do*? Cue line of dia-
logue.

(Define your central conflict, noting which characters are involved in
it. By outlining this way you can *see* whether you have sufficiently developed your plot by the time you have reached the central conflict or
climax.)

If hero is onstage for *falling action,* or that which occurs after the central conflict, note what he does to tidy up any loose ends of action.

(Define the final action of the play. For a "security blanket" write down the final or "tag" line of the show.)

As you can readily see, this is basically an outline of who does what to whom and why, but it puts it in a written form that makes the structure of your play immediately evident and starts training your memory for rehearsal and performance. One curious thing that you may discover while creating your first script in this fashion is that if the reasons for a character's entering or exiting are clear to you, he will probably have to say very little to explain himself or his actions to the audience. Usually, if *you* know why he is there, the reason will be obvious to the audience. And if you answer all the character questions for yourself in making a working outline, not only will they affect how a character carries out action, but your very answers may suggest new action and plot twists. If your play is in more than one scene, you will be able to see what characters are onstage and what they are doing at the beginning and end of each scene.

Compare the above working outline with the following performance "script" for posting backstage.

## SHOW TITLE

| *Left Hand* | *Props* | *Right Hand* | _____Music |
| --- | --- | --- | --- |
| | | | _____Curtain |
| First character | Prop he handles | | |
| | | Second character | |
| First character out | | | |
| | | | _____Light dims |
| First character in | Prop he carries with him | | _____Sound |
| | | | _____Light up |
| | | Third character | |
| | | | _____Music |
| | | | _____Curtain |

This outline can, of course, be quite long, depending upon the number of characters and the complexity of the script. It will help you to use different colored pens for music, sound, and light cues, and if the cue for them is something a character says, that line *cannot* be improvised. It must be kept consistent and be written on the cue line. This is especially important if you are having someone assist you by gloving you (getting you into the puppets) and working the curtain, lights, and music. If you have a second operator, make sure that entrance and exit cues are set. They need not be worked *exactly* the same way each time, but if you change them completely, you are likely to cause a missed cue. Absolutely nothing sounds worse than hearing one operator whisper to the other that they are supposed to be on or off stage, or indeed, any out-of-character comment by the puppeteer at all. For some reason, whatever is said accidentally behind a puppet stage is *very* audible out front—and be doubly wary if you have microphones turned on!

As soon as you have your first play outlined and rehearsed until you remember the progression of action, assemble a small audience and try it out. No one can teach you more about playwriting than an audience. From them you will learn what to drop, what to expand, what dialogue works, and when you hear a murmur of inattention, you'll know you are talking too much instead of *doing*. Most of all, however, you will be gaining not only skill but the incredible satisfaction of knowing that you are increasingly successful with your audiences. Your acting skills will strengthen as you continue to perform, and you will have ideas for new programs. As soon as you feel ready, tackle a larger audience.

You will, we hope, do original work, for new work is what keeps the puppet theatre from stagnating. As you interpret the world through your puppets, you contribute to your art.

# 5
## Adapting Material for a Puppet Script

It is not always necessary that every germ of your script be new with you. You can be creative and original by adapting and giving your own interpretation to existing material. Many types of stories, myths, and poetry lend themselves to adaptation and can provide you with a rich and varied source for inspiration. Adaptation does, however, require a slightly different approach than creating original material and in this chapter we will explore the special skills that are necessary to achieve successful adaptations.

There are both advantages and disadvantages inherent in adapting stories or other existing material to fit the puppet stage. One obvious advantage is that some of the groundwork will have been done for you: the characters basically set forth, the locale defined, and the framework of the story line already established. The audience's familiarity with the story you are about to present may also work in your favor, though, as you will see, this familiarity is a double-edged sword. It sounds like much the easier path to adapt than to create an original play, especially if you do not feel "creative" when it comes to story. Adaptations may provide you with many answers to "What play shall I present?" Be aware, however, that in tailoring other people's material to your own dramatic needs and that of your puppets, you are going to require as much playwriting skill as if you started "from scratch"—and extreme discipline in the area of selectivity as well. This is not to deter you from adaptation; rather, it is to prevent you from choosing to adapt as an "easy way out." Adaptation is difficult, but often worth it. Adaptation has given us some of the most beautiful and exciting work that has been done in puppet theatre, and if you wish to take puppetry seriously, you will surely at some time be faced with the challenge of adapting material.

After you have decided whether you wish to do an adult or children's play (the same phenomenon applies here as to original work: some rare and beautiful works are universal in appeal, but they are few and hard to find), start looking for a story that suits your present capabilities. If you are going to do a one-person show, you will presumably not start off with trying to adapt "The Twelve Dancing Princesses." Frequently, less important characters can be combined, sometimes several compressed into one new character, but there is a limit to how much tinkering you can do and still preserve the original story. Just try to pick a story that excites you, that you think will appeal to your audience, and that you can perform without too many changes in characters or plot.

Before you put pen to paper at all, and as soon as you have chosen your story (or poem or musical piece or whatever), do check to see if it is in the public domain. In other words, is it by a living author, or by one whose estate may have rights to the work? If so, you must ask the publisher for permission to perform the work, and you may be asked to pay a royalty if permission is secured. If you have chosen a work by a living author, he or she may not want the work adapted or may ask to approve your adaptation before it is performed. All of this may sound unusually picky if you are planning to perform the work where admission is not charged and you do not receive a fee for your performance; but better to obtain permission than go to all the work of building a show and then be prevented from performing it or embarrassed because you did. You are, after all, using someone else's property. If you will be charging admission, you *must* clear the work. And you may be quite surprised: the author might be pleased to have his work adapted.

If you are planning to tour a show, perform it on television, or in any way subject it to broad viewing, it would be worth your while to check to see if Disney or any other large house holds an option on the work. If you find that is the case, you are better off choosing other material, because the intricacies and legalities of such rights are legion. A French candy company was once reported to have been sued (and it was reported that they lost) because they named a candy bar "Blanche Neige" or "Snow White." While the foregoing seems preposterous, the fact remains that a large studio can tie up a work by putting it under option until their version is released. How far this process can be carried in the case of works in the public domain is probably a question only an attorney can answer in each specific case. Usually any material in the fairy tale or myth categories, especially that of unknown authorship that has been handed down through generations, is free for anyone to use in any way they please. Certainly in your early work, a large company holding an option on a story is not going to bother you. Just be aware that the complication exists, respect authors' rights, and be careful to clear that which you *know* isn't in the public domain.

Now that you have cleared your material, you can get to work on it.

You will probably have to do considerable "pruning" in order to isolate the beginning, middle, and end, but isolate them you must. It is possible that you may have chosen a story that really doesn't have much of an ending, but just sort of fades off. You will then have to invent an end that grows as organically out of the beginning and middle as the one you worked out for your original script. Many fairy tales that are fine for storytelling are very difficult or even impossible to adapt. Even if you can work out a satisfactory ending, you are going to have an uphill task with a story that has little or no dramatic action. "The Little Match Girl" by Hans Christian Andersen, for example, just does not make good puppet theatre material because it has almost no dramatic action. It ends as the child dies and is welcomed by her beloved grandmother into heaven, and how are you going to make dramatic theatre out of that?

So, you will want to look for a story that has lots of conflict and visual action, even if you have to evolve a new ending yourself. Try to find a story with interesting characters that can't be played better (or at least as well) by live actors. Consider "The Musicians of Bremen" before "Sleeping Beauty," despite the latter's spectacular appeal. How much more fun to craft and perform the animal musicians than a group of courtiers and a handsome prince and beautiful princess. There is also in "Sleeping Beauty" (used here as an example because of its familiarity to most of you) the disadvantage of many scenes and a long passage of time to be established. It can be managed, but not without technical problems of grand proportion. Someday, you may think it worth it all for the bad fairy, but can you imagine staging the banquet scene with hand puppets . . . thirteen fairies, a king and queen, and several courtiers? Do stick to stories with small casts. Sometimes you can put several puppets on a multiple control, but they usually look just out of the grave (which is *always* the case if you prop them up somehow and leave them visible but motionless). No, hand puppets, especially, do best with an intimate cast of characters, at least the ones that have to be on the stage at the same time. Sometimes you will find yourself, even with a small cast, searching for a reason for a character to exit because another must take part in the story and you have to have a hand free!

For many years fairy tales have been the staple of most puppeteers' repertoires. Children liked to see the familiar tales, and you could usually count on a full house for the best-beloved stories. Today, sadly, not that many children know the stories, for whatever reason. Their mothers still bring them to fairy tale puppet plays because *they* know and remember the tales, but usually have not read them to their children. The children do still love the old tales when they are beautifully presented by puppets, and puppeteers have at least a few years' grace in selling them at the box office, since parents buy the tickets. What will be the state of the fairy tale in another twenty years? When today's children are parents will they remember the tales at least enough to bring their children to see the puppets play them? The loss of fairy tales in a child's early experience would be tragic. Listen to Bruno Bettelheim's eloquent plea for the preservation of these tales, of their importance to the child, and hear how exactly they fit the requirements and possibilities of the puppet theatre as you have come to understand them. Of all the material available to us for adaptation, the fairy tale is perhaps best suited, and, indeed, needs us most.

It is characteristic of fairy tales to state an existential dilemma briefly and pointedly. This permits the child to come to grips with the problem in its most essential form, where a more complex plot would confuse matters for him. The fairy tale simplifies all situations. Its figures are clearly drawn; and details, unless very important, are eliminated. All characters are typical rather than unique.

Contrary to what takes place in many modern children's stories, in fairy tales evil is as omnipresent as virtue. In practically every fairy tale good and evil are given body in the form of some figures and their actions, as good and evil are omnipresent in life and the propensities for both are present in every man. It is this duality which poses the moral problem, and requires the struggle to solve it.

. . . Only by going out into the world can the fairy-tale hero (child) find himself there; and as he does, he will also find the other with whom he will be able to live happily ever after; that is, without ever again having to experience separation anxiety. The fairy tale is future-oriented and guides the child—in terms he can understand in both his conscious and his unconscious mind—to relinquish his infantile dependency wishes and achieve a more satisfying independent existence.

Today children no longer grow up within the security of an extended family, or of a well-integrated community. Therefore, even more than at the times fairy tales were invented, it is important to provide the modern child with images of heroes who have to go out into the world all by themselves and who, although originally ignorant of the ultimate things, find secure places in the world by following their right way with deep inner confidence.

The fairy-tale hero proceeds for a time in isolation, as the modern child often feels isolated. The hero is helped by being in touch with primitive things—a tree, an animal, nature—as the child feels more in touch with those things than most adults do. The fate of these heroes convinces the child that, like them, he may feel outcast and abandoned in the world, groping in the dark, but, like them, in the course of his life he will be guided step by step, and given help when it is needed. Today, even more than in past times, the child needs the reassurance offered by the image of the isolated man who nevertheless is capable of achieving meaningful and rewarding relations with the world around him.[1]

Precisely because fairy tales are so replete with psychological truths, one must be very careful in adapting them. First, because those in your audience who are familiar with a story and love it are not going to want to see it changed drastically. And, second—and most importantly—you want to be careful that in working for dramatic intensity, unity of action, place, and time, and especially in altering the characters or their relationship to each other, you do not alter the intrinsic values of the story. Prettifying fairy tales and changing (or losing) their potent messages constitutes a real wrong against the cultural and psychological heritage of healthy children. Cinderella, poor dear, has been a real victim, most adapters, including Disney, choosing Perrault's sugar-sweet and insipid heroine over more believable heroines of earlier versions. It is always best to go back to the earliest sources you can find and then to read all the versions of a given story that you can get your hands on. The more you read, the more you will be struck by the similarities of stories in different countries, and by comparing them, you will be able to sift out and save the important elements.

"But," you say, "some of the stories have really horrible elements. Must I keep them?" No, you should keep the essence of the relationships and try to determine why the horrible elements were there in the first place and what value they have psychologically and dramatically. It is not necessary, for instance, that the wicked stepsisters of Cinderella cut off their toes in order to fit into the slipper, but the necessity for them to feel pain in the fitting of the slipper while Cinderella is perfectly comfortable is quite obvious. And before you start inventing fairy godmothers who look like retired tooth fairies, go back and find out what the original one in the story was like and analyze for yourself why she is there. If this all seems like too much trouble to you and you don't want to search out sources or use (or acquire and use) some knowledge of the psychological truths behind these tales, then you really have no business tampering with them. They have too much to say to be spoiled. Either go to the trouble, or leave them alone.

Because of the importance of fairy tales and the difficulty inherent in their adaptation, "Beauty and the Beast" has been chosen as the sample script that appears at the end of this chapter. It is hoped that it will help you in adapting, not only fairy tales, but other forms of literature and music

[1] Bettelheim, Bruno, *The Uses of Enchantment* (New York: Alfred A. Knopf, 1976), pp. 8–11. Copyright © 1976 by Bruno Bettelheim.

to the puppet stage as well. Before we detail this example, though, let us examine some of the other material available to you for adaptation.

Closely allied to the fairy tale are myths, which usually deal with gods and heroes and seek to explain some mystery of the universe or impart some great moral truths. Probably, they are not as powerful as fairy tales for us today, but some of them are inherently dramatic and are eminently adaptable. Admittedly, nobody has ever been able to do anything with Prometheus chained to a rock, but consider his earlier search for fire. Consider Pandora's box, which has all sorts of possibilities. It has suspense, a secret the audience knows that the main character does not, and Pandora is basically sympathetic. Many myths have been transferred into modern dress or some other period, but why? How much more interesting to teach a child something of Greek or Roman culture painlessly while enacting a good, exciting story.

Some American Indian tales, if you can give them dramatic structure, are fun for the audience and evoke a culture and its traditions. When you adapt, try to keep as much as you can of the flavor of the source, the time in history, and the people who told the tale. Then you will be following the great tradition of folk puppetry and transmitting history through story.

In the common domain along with myth and fairy tale—available to you with very little difficulty or expense—are a number of musical works. *Peter and the Wolf* has often been done with puppets, Bil Baird's production being one of the most inventive. Bil was one of the few puppeteers to deal successfully with the long passages of music when little or nothing dramatic happens. Peter dances in the meadow. Peter dances for a long time. The music is charming, but if you are stuck out there with a puppet you are going to have to *work* to think of enough variations to fill the time. And you must not start inventing action that is superimposed on the original plot and introduces irrelevant story material or suppresses the audience's attention to the music. Any action by the puppets must enhance and delineate the music, never defeat it.

Frequently presented by puppets, Manuel de Falla's *Master Peter's Puppet Show* presents similar problems. There are long solos by the boy narrator, who is explaining the actions to take place among hand puppets. These passages are difficult, and unless the singer is extremely skilled, they are often unintelligible, so that when the action of the hand puppets does take place, it is very hard to make clear just what is happening. It can be done successfully, but it takes fine musicianship and some very skillful puppeteering. In "adapting" the work, one cannot easily alter the score, but there are numerous ways to be inventive with movements and combinations of various types of puppets and manners of staging. If you cut these works, you must do so very carefully, so that you do not do them musical damage; sometimes cutting is necessary, however, since it is very hard to fill some of the long musical passages meaningfully.

Opera can be successfully brought to the puppet stage, though it definitely must be cut in order to work properly. The Kungsholm theatre-restaurant in Chicago performed entire operas with a unique kind of rod puppet for years to full adult houses. And the Salzburg Marionette Theatre has been enthralling audiences for many decades and continues to do so with full renditions of recorded operas, faithful in every detail to the music and to the composer's style. Their *Magic Flute*, though long, is sheer delight. In some puppet operas the puppets have been allowed to make contemporary slang remarks, totally out of keeping with the period of the work or its style. It is a temptation to throw cute little remarks in, but watch yourself. It never works. Be consistent. Stick to the style of the work. Appreciate your source.

It is necessary to give this same appreciation, but not to grovel in a frenzy of self-abasement, if you wish to present Shakespeare to your public. Be true to his intent, but do be careful to choose those passages that befit the puppet theatre. It is embarrassing to see the "closet actor" who brings out a complete puppet cast of *Hamlet* and acts all of the parts himself, because he is a frustrated Thespian. On the other hand, why not try some of the scenes from *The Taming of the Shrew* (which has a lovely comical exaggeration that puppets can handle) or the final play within the play from *A Midsummer Night's Dream*. Both plays would require a number of puppets, but if you have the hands to work them, these are plays that would do very nicely in puppet theatre. You will need to cut carefully, or to find someone who really knows Shakespeare if you don't, to use the scissors. There is no mystery about it; just delete what a puppet can't convey or material that involves a scene that you are not presenting. The catch is that you must not disturb the poetry, and that does require skill. But it is worth it. Playing Shakespeare when you know you are good is like riding the crest of a wave on the most marvelous surfboard ever invented.

If you choose to use a recorded tape—and you may have to with Shakespeare, since puppeteers or those whom you have trained to manipulate your puppets may not know how to read him—you will need the help of a very good sound studio. It is not that expensive, and you *can't* do it at home. The noise of a truck going by or a child howling in front of your house is not going to add to the total effect of your performance. I have argued against tape, but with Shakespeare you may have to resort to it. Find actors who know how to read the iambic pentameter. And if you are going to participate in the tape, you need a director. It is impossible to read in a scene and listen to the overall effect as well. You will need to direct (or have directed) your scene(s) for the most dramatic impact. You are out there to prove that puppets can present Shakespeare in an intelligent and entertaining fashion. It is not going to help your cause if your tape is dull and your audience falls asleep, no matter how beautiful your puppets may be. Go over the scene for beginning, middle, and end. Plot its rise and fall. It is a challenge, it is fun, and it will be a new experience for your audience.

Cutting any existing plays written for the live theatre in order to adapt them for the puppet theatre is not really very different from adapting stories, except that the amount of original addition you can make is limited. You may occasionally need to insert a transition line between two scenes that you have combined into one. In this case, you must try to write your line or lines in the style of the author whose work you are playing, conveying the original sense he intended. You will want to cut long speeches drastically, remembering that long speeches just aren't handled very well by puppets. Again, you will have to cut and splice in such a way as to preserve the original meaning. Adaptation of any kind always involves the delicate balance between bringing the work alive in a form that fits the puppet stage and retaining the style and essence of the source work. It is never easy, but if you make your first order of business defining the style and intent of the material you are adapting, you will find the job much easier.

Once you have defined what you want to keep, then think, "How can I best make this dramatic with actions that suit the puppet?" A book of source material long neglected by puppeteers, unless they were making puppets with a Sunday school class, is the Bible. If you think it isn't dramatic in contemporary terms, go and see *Godspell*, the musical of parables that has swept the country with its fun, fantasy, and vigorous dramatic flair while remaining faithful in both content and spirit to its source. One effervescent production witnessed recently (directed by Robert Kelly of Theatreworks) used rag-bag puppets to portray the story of the Good Samaritan, and it was the hit of the show. And do not say, "Yes, but *Godspell* was a Broadway show; they're professional, and I can't do that." *Godspell* began as a master's degree production when the authors were graduate students at Carnegie-Mellon University. No matter what your training or experience, if you find material you like and approach it with solid playwriting discipline, you can bring it alive and still keep its original meaning. After all, that meaning is probably what attracted you to the material in the first place!

Some puppeteers work very well using folk songs or other short musical pieces as springboards for their ideas. Having puppets simply dance to the music can sometimes be fun in a revue or form the backbone of a company's style, as in the case of André Tahon. It is also possible to take a song, especially a ballad, and invent a solid dramatic story around it. A good example of a highly successful "adaptation" of this sort for live theatre would be Howard Richardson and William Berney's *Dark of the Moon*, which is based on the haunting folk song "Barbara Allen." Though this play was not written for puppets, it has many of the qualities of a fine puppet play; it has the fantastic aura puppets portray so well, the simplicity, and the ability to convey so much with so little.

When you are searching for material to adapt, you must be prepared to read through a great quantity of stories, plays, et cetera, that just won't prove suitable, for one reason or three. Don't be discouraged. Sometimes you can combine two or more stories that involve an interesting main character. And there will be times when, try as you will, you cannot come up with anything on a given theme . . . possibly just because it is given. It is very hard and probably not fruitful to force inspiration. Give yourself a chance to get away from the *necessity* of producing a given type of play, and an idea will come.

If poetry excites you, you may want to dramatize a poem. Sometimes, as in the work of Walter de la Mare, a narrator can be effectively used. Yes, you have been told to ban the use of a narrator, but that was when the role was used to convey information to the audience that is better told by action. In the case of poetry, especially if the puppets are just to move and not to speak, you will be able to keep the poem intact, preserve its rhythms, and convey a unity to the whole by having an offstage voice recite the work. You will have to allow plenty of time for action, and if you *must* tape the narration, do rehearse the piece well in advance of taping to be sure that enough blank spaces are left to provide time for all of the action you need.

Let us now move to a discussion of an adaptation of "Beauty and the Beast." First, we will turn to the original story and examine its elements, explaining why certain characters and scenes were cut and why others were added. The script that follows at the end of the chapter represents *one way* to solve the problem of presenting this story dramatically with puppets. Other successful puppet productions have been quite different. Yours, too, may be different yet equally effective. The example is given in order to illustrate the processes of selectivity and invention that are necessary in adapting any material for the puppet theatre.

"Beauty and the Beast" exists in many versions, but the best known is probably that of Madame Leprince de Beaumont, which made its first appearance in print in English in *The Young Misses Magazine* in 1761.[1] It is part of a whole group of stories in which the hero, who has been transformed into some sort of animal (see *The Frog Prince*), via a magical spell, falls in love with a young girl and is redeemed by her love. It is revealing of the universality of the symbolism in the story that our script was worked through by the company as a group and when it was compared with Dr. Bettelheim's analysis of the story,[2] we had wrestled with nearly every point he covers and arrived at almost identical conclusions.

Let us start with the concept of the Beast. The presence of sexual symbolism is immediately evident, but most adults think first of his "beastliness" and wonder about the undercurrent of bestiality lingering over the story. Such is not the case at all, and the child sees this immediately. The Beast, though ugly, has a beautiful inner self, and it is our duty to present in action enough aspects of his character so that the audience can appreciate why Beauty would see him as kind and "good" enough that she will eventually break his enchantment with her love. Dr. Bettelheim advances the theory that the Beast represents the child's repression of sexuality in preconscious years and that repression retained throughout the Oedipal phase. Thus, at first, Beauty's love is given only to her father and she sees the Beast as "beastly"; when she matures in years and in appreciation of the Beast, she is able to transfer her love from her father to the Beast, and her "dear, kind, good beast" can be seen by Beauty safely as good and the object of her adult love.

By digging this deeply into the psychological symbolism of the story, we have solved several questions about dramatizing it. We will have to make the Beast ugly, and he can't be ugly-funny, or we cannot expect the audience to take him seriously. How, then, can we avoid frightening the small child in the audience, especially since we know that what the Beast represents and what the child unconsciously understands *is* frightening to the child? Our solution was to make him not horrifying but ugly-sad. He deeply regrets the effect he has on others, and by his *actions* shows the audience that he is really not to be feared. It seemed totally unnecessary to us to explain why or when the Beast had been enchanted, which goes along with the theory that the child's "beast" was enchanted or tabooed in times before it can remember. *Audiences* simply accept that he was and is enchanted, and by whom or when is just not important. So much for

---

[1] Bettelheim, p. 322, N. 105. The tale can be found in Opia, Iona and Peter, *The Classic Fairy Tales* (London: Oxford University Press, 1972).
[2] Bettelheim, pp. 303–10.

*that* exposition; it doesn't have to go into our script. We have never been questioned on this point after a performance.

It is apparent from the nutshell analysis that this is a love story on several levels. It concerns Beauty's love for her father and his for her; and it concerns the love between the Beast and Beauty. These, then, are our central characters. We will use the two sisters antiphonally and as comic relief; by exaggerating their greed, we will point up Beauty's goodness, which will save her from appearing an obnoxious goody-goody.

When shall our story begin? At first one would think that Beauty must be introduced at once, but why? Think where the highest point of early action occurs. Isn't it when the Father picks the rose for his daughter; after all, that is the *action* that really sets the story in motion. Again our analysis aids us, for the Father picks the rose out of love for his daughter, who is his best beloved. We determined to open our play with the Father and his horse, laden with many gifts for the two sisters, lost in a forest. The Father confides to the audience that he is lost and begs their help in determining which way to go. At this point we needed a character or characters to set up the magical nature of the forest without frightening the audience. The "woodsie-mossies" were created: odd blue-headed creatures with branches and leaves in their hair and simple muted-print glove bodies. They were distinctly nonhuman, but they were also graceful, with gentle strands of silk falling from their arms, and definitely not menacing. We decided to have them open the curtain. Then the audience would be immediately aware that something magical was about to happen. The effect was heightened when the prosaic problem of the Father's plight was revealed. Poor Father would have had a lot of heavy exposition to hand the audience alone if he had not been interrupted by the woodsie-mossies (how they ever got named that, I don't know, since no one called them anything but the "Beast's servants" or "creatures" in the actual play). They became mimes, and as you will see, provided very useful connections between scenes. The woodsie-mossies are a good example of added characters who facilitate the dramatic action while in no way tampering with the original material. We had them lure the horse offstage, for example, to show that they could be naughty—and to help us get rid of the horse in order to get on with the action (the horse would have distracted from and provided no contribution to the action if we had kept him on stage. So off he went.)

We didn't give the Father much time to moan about his lost horse. Thunder and lightning and some marvelous music began. A bush, which was two green-gloved hands painstakingly covered with plastic leaves, appeared as if growing out of the playboard (Appearance: 1). The bush grew, and a bright red rose appeared above it, which the Father marveled at and picked (Rose: 2). The bush trembled, the music swelled, and the Beast appeared (Beast appears: 3). Then, after the familiar device of building up action in a series of three, the Beast menaces the Father, telling him he must pay for the rose with his life. We allowed the Father to protest that he had only picked the rose for his daughter Beauty, because it seemed illogical that the Beast would have foreknowledge of her existence. The Beast immediately seizes his opportunity and demands that Beauty come to live with him at the Castle within three days (notice the imposition of a time limit) or else the Father's life will be forfeit. The Father sadly exits for home, led by the good old woodsie-mossies, who, summoned by the Beast, will show Father the path.

Lest we get bogged down in dreariness, we moved quickly to bright music and a light scene between Beauty and her cat. The cat was very naughty and funny and was supposed to fold some laundry. Beauty tells him her sisters have threatened to get rid of him, if he doesn't do a good job. He again uses the triad of action and scrambles three cloths and gets paw prints on the last one. As he is sent into the house, never to be heard from again, he spits at Isabella, the first sister to enter. His purpose has been accomplished. He has allowed Beauty to meet the audience and show them that she is kind and intelligent. He also sets up the relationship of Beauty to her sisters. Again an interpolated character has contributed to the weaving of the plot without changing its intrinsic focus.

Our use of the sisters deviates somewhat from the original story, but preserves their psychological function. They appear older than Beauty and are, later in the story, not afraid of the Beast, nor are they particularly attached to their father. In fact they are only concerned for the multitude of gifts for which they have asked. In the original story there are also brothers to Beauty, but since they provide no real dramatic purpose, we chose to cut them. In some versions, the Father is given a choice of which daughter to send to the Beast, and only Beauty will go. We chose to make the Beast demand Beauty; in any case, her resolution to go (1) spares her father's life and (2) allows her to accept the responsibility for the situation, since it was she who had asked for the rose. Whether we accept the theory that the rose is a symbol of Beauty's virginity is beside the point, which is that the problem of what to do about the rose, Father, and the Beast is ultimately hers.

We made the sisters horribly greedy, and they were wonderfully funny. Just before the Father's entrance they got into a dreadful fight over who was to get which present. They ended the scene in a huff at opposite ends of the proscenium, vowing over and over never to speak to each other again. Their fight provided a chance for Father's entrance. Their greed counterpointed Beauty's worry over their Father's lateness (we couldn't decide *how* late and finally settled on two weeks). As you will see shortly, the play is fraught with time problems that must be solved, as well as travel scenes that must be worked out. Somehow, after farewells, Beauty had to be gotten to the Beast's castle and, because it seemed too abrupt to have her simply appear there, we included a short scene in "another part of the forest," which, as a result of its gentle character and the puppets we introduced, acted as a contrast to the Father's first scene there. Beauty, in trying to find the way to the Beast's castle, meets a little faun and a butterfly, both of whom flee upon mention of the Beast. Finally we introduced one of the woodsie-mossies, who bows, and who conveys to Beauty via dumb show that he will take her to the Castle.

In many of the versions of the story, including the lovely film by Jean Cocteau, the Father is wined and dined in the Castle by an unseen host before he meets the Beast. We considered including this scene, but there were good reasons for eliminating it. First, we very much wanted to cut down the number of scenes, of which there would be six as it was. Then, too, we wanted the Castle to be a surprise to the audience when Beauty entered it, so we saved the wining and dining scene and gave it to her. The way it was handled proved particularly effective and involved many abstractions and scenic devices that only a puppet could employ believably.

We dimmed our lights as Beauty entered the Castle and she was escorted in by a gloved hand holding a candelabrum. When it disappeared, she found herself alone and called out, "Is anyone home?" (Many little children in the audience remembered this scene to tell us they knew just how she felt, or that they had felt just like that once.) We used differently colored gloved hands to bring a table, pour her wine, and bring her food. No one got scared in this scene because we brought up our lights, because Beauty wasn't scared, and because the food was funny: a drumstick brought to her by a glove and immediately followed by another glove that offered her a napkin to wipe her hands and face. The "servants" cleared, Beauty fell asleep in the chair, and we were ready for the Beast.

His entrance was a good chance for the audience to get involved. Of course they saw him upstage behind the curtain and tried to wake Beauty as he came near her chair. His first remark was about her beauty, which eliminated any fears of violence on the part of the audience. We allowed her to be terrified, but to come out of hiding because she feared she had hurt his feelings when he said that he knew he was ugly and she didn't have to look at him. We were now entering the really difficult parts of the adaptation. The Beast's actions must somehow convince Beauty that he is lovable. We had him give her a cape and jewels (brought by the hands), but we were very bothered that he should win her over simply by giving her things. After all, she shouldn't be "bought." The very last thing we wished to inculcate in our audience was the idea that "people who love you are people who give you things." How could we show other aspects of the Beast's character and of his relationship with Beauty?

We decided on games and had the two enter laughing from playing tag in the garden and deciding to play a game of hide-and-seek. This device worked very well, and it also gave the audience a chance to participate in their relationship as they helped Beauty find the Beast. It also gave us a chance to have the Beast and Beauty touch, showing that there was no fear anymore. What did give us a problem was the passage of time. We dimmed the lights and played some music, but our prayers for a better way to establish the fact that Beauty and the Beast come to love each other over a year's time just weren't answered. We kept feeling the need for another scene, and I think the lack of it does let the original story down, because if the time spent in the castle is experienced as too brief, we don't see Beauty grow to the point where she can transfer her love from her father to the Beast. But we were unable to evolve a dramatic moment that would show both time and character change without being repetitive and simply lengthening the play. Perhaps one of you will come up with the answer.

We did make one fairly drastic change in the story. After Beauty refused the Beast's proposal of marriage, we had her beg the Beast to let her visit her family because she missed them. In the original story, she sees in a mirror that her father is ill, and she thus wants to return to him. In the narrative it works very well that both the Father and later the Beast fall ill for lack of Beauty's loving presence. But on stage the two incidents would have followed too quickly upon each other. We were afraid the sight of the loved father sick followed so soon by the near-death of Beast would seem comic. Our treatment worked, and I don't believe it weakened the audience's recognition that Beauty needed to return to her father (she must have his blessing in order to return to the Beast, be free to transfer her love to him). The Beast allows her to go but she must return in ten days (time pressure) or he will die. The rest followed quite closely to the story and worked well for the audience.

This discussion of our development of the "Beauty and the Beast" script will, we hope, aid you in your own efforts to script both original and adapted pieces for puppet theatre. At least you are now aware of all the necessary elements, the needed structure, and most of the pitfalls as well as the rewards of creating a script. Our bare-bones working script for "B & B" that we post backstage follows.

## BEAUTY AND THE BEAST

|                    |                      |
|--------------------|----------------------|
|                    | _____ music      |
| Woodsie-mossies    | Curtain              |

*Scene I*

Father leads horse.
   "I want to find my way"

                                          _____ thunder and lightning

Horse wanders off,
   lured by woodsie-mossie

                                          _____ lights dim

Bush up                         _____ music

                                          _____ lights up on bush

                                          _____ music

Rose                            _____ music

Beast enters. "I want your life" to
            "I want your daughter"

Beast out.

Woodsie-mossie in with horse.

All exit, Father last.

                                          _____ music

                                          _____ close Act Curtain

*Scene II*

Beauty and cat. "I want you to do a good
   job so that I can keep you, cat"

Cat out.

Isabella (sister) in. "I want you to get rid
   of that cat" to "I want my presents"

Evelyn (sister) in. "I want Father to come home,
   so that I can have my presents"

Beauty out to prepare to search for Father.

Father in. "I want to tell Beauty the awful news"
   Father-sisters scene. Presents not enough.
   Sisters out to get Beauty and their presents.

Beauty in. "I want to welcome Father"
   Awful bargain. Beauty resolves to go.

Beauty exits to pack.
Sisters in to gloat. Father laments.

_____ music
_____ pull forest
scrim

*Scene III*
Beauty in. "I want to find the Beast's servants"
Faun in.
Butterfly in.
Woodsie-mossies in to lead Beauty out to castle.

_____ Act Curtain
_____ music
_____ gloved hands
set chair
_____ get rid of forest
scrim
_____ dim lights

*Scene IV*
Beauty in, led by glove with candelabrum.
    "I want to find the owner"
Gloves bring table, wine bottle, chicken leg, napkin.
Gloves remove table.
Beauty sleeps in chair.
Beast in upstage behind purple drape.
    "I want to see how lovely she is"
Beauty frightened, runs behind chair.
Beast gives gifts.
    Hands bring cape and jewels.

_____ music
_____ dim lights

Hide-and-seek. "We want to play"
Proposal.
Permission to leave.
Woodsie-mossies bring mirror.
Exit Beauty.
Beast wonders if she will return.

_____ music
_____ Act Curtain

——————————— gloves strike
chair

*Scene V*

Father in. "I want to know if you are happy"
Beauty in. "I want your permission
  to be happy with the Beast"
Both out.
Sisters in. "We want to make her stay longer,
  to trick her and take her place"
Beauty in. "I want to say good-bye"
  Sisters convince Beauty
  to stay a little longer.
Sisters out.
Woodsie-mossies and mirror in.
Beast in mirror. "I am dying without you" Then out.
Beauty out quickly.
Sisters run in and follow in chase.

——————————— music
——————————— open Act Curtain

*Scene VI*

Beast dying.
Beauty in. "I want to save you"
  "I love you"
Transformation.
Explanation and proposal.
Sisters in. "We want a chance at the Prince"
Transformation of sisters into trees.
Tag lines.
Woodsie-mossies with bower of flowers.
"Dear Beast"

——————————— music
——————————— Curtain

*Curtain Call.*

# 6
## *Directing the Puppet Play*

In any theatrical endeavor, the director is probably the most important person. He or she determines the style of the production, unifies all the elements of design and performance, and draws from the actors an interpretation faithful to the playwright's work. Responsibility for what the audience finally sees and hears ultimately rests with the director. Assuredly, there will be differences in the director's job if he is working in puppet theatre rather than live theatre, but you will find that many directorial skills can be borrowed from live theatre and applied to the puppet stage. Although there will be differences in directorial craftsmanship when you are working with a group of puppeteers and when you are working alone, these will merely be differences of degree and selection; the need for directorial skills remains constant. A sound basic vocabulary of stage direction techniques will help you mount your production, however small, for its greatest effectiveness; it will also help you strengthen your shows, enabling you to spot weaknesses and supplying you with solid "first aid" when a production just doesn't seem to be going well.

Directing the play is far more than "directing traffic," though that is often what it feels like. Basically, there are two elements: uniting the visual and audio aspects of the production to achieve a particular effect (corresponding to technique in acting), and extracting the best possible performance from the puppeteers (corresponding to inner life). The more tangible aspects of visual techniques are usually more easily approached first.

Just as in the live theatre, the puppet stage can be divided into acting areas, though if you are using traditional puppet staging (either the scrim or overhead stage) you will have much less depth to work with. The stage floor of live theatre is usually divided into areas of equal depth. The puppet stage areas correspond, except that all three upstage areas are quite shallow.

Down center (DC) is always considered the strongest area, or that which commands the greatest attention, and the character who is most important

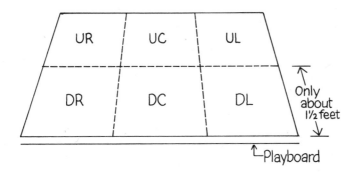

*Stage "floor" areas of puppet theatre, overhead stage for hand or rod-puppets*

at a given moment often occupies it. Up center (UC) is the next strongest area, followed by downstage right and left (DR and DL). (There is some disagreement as to whether DR is *really* stronger than DL.) Two upstage areas (UR and UL) are just too weak for the audience to sustain attention to any important scene taking place there.

Though the upstage areas are very weak in most puppet stages, using *all* the areas will prevent you from always keeping your puppets down next to the playboard in a boring line. Contrary to what is so often seen in the puppet theatre, puppets do *not* have to stand in a line, and the use of the upstage areas for entrances, exits, and for puppets not dominant at a given moment lends depth and interest to any production. Less depth to work with than in the live theatre does not mean total lack of depth. You will need to train yourself to arrange action to occur in a variety of areas and to assign areas for whatever emphasis you may need in a given scene.

Ordinarily, as an actor retreats upstage, his position loses strength; this fact is also true for the puppet, except that the degree of loss is much greater. Consider, too, the height of the puppet. As you move him upstage, he will appear to grow smaller, unless you compensate by raising him up higher as he progresses upstage. How far upstage he can go will be determined both by the depth of your stage and by how far you can raise him up and still have him seen. Here you will have to bear in mind the audience's sight lines. They will see a different picture if your stage is on a floor level with them than if you are on a raised stage or platform, and their view will be different if your seating area is flat or raked (slanted), the latter being, of course, much more desirable. Because of their size, puppets are hard enough to see without obscuring them behind myriad heads. A flat audience floor is especially undesirable for a children's production, since a small viewer may well be seated behind a very large one. In Europe, one often sees parents seat their children in front at a puppet performance and themselves retire to the back or side of the hall. If you can get parents to comply with this practice, it enhances the performance for their children, but often, though a child may be quite comfortable, a parent will be reluctant to let him sit alone. It is therefore difficult to make such desirable seating a rule, especially if you want to remain popular with the parents who are buying the tickets.

One director's "rule" that you can borrow from the live theatre and, indeed, exploit, is that the actor of greatest height dominates the scene. This may be tallest, but also applies if one actor is seated and another standing, or if someone is raised on a platform. Usually, the largest puppet (and tallest) will dominate the scene. You will be able to build your "actors" for his dominance. Think of the Greek tragic actors who wore high shoes and giant headdresses in order to appear larger than the chorus. You can actually build into your "actors" the *emphasis* size creates. But what happens when you wish to weaken the position of a large puppet playing a scene with a small one? Put the small one DC and move the large puppet to a weaker area. Sitting and standing can be used to some degree, as well as kneeling, which hand puppets do rather well. Care must be taken to concentrate on the transference of bodily weight as the puppet gets into the kneeling position and rises from it. Kneel yourself and rise. Now try to copy the motion with your puppet, concentrating on what the action felt like when you did it yourself. Puppets appear to sit down believably if you raise them up slightly and then lower them onto a rock or chair. The lower part of the puppet will disappear below the playboard when he is sitting, but rather than looking "half there," he will simply appear seated.

Care must be taken even in a one-person show that one character never "upstage" another, that is, force a puppet to look upstage to talk to him. If this happens, the audience will see only the back of one of the puppet's heads. Puppeteers sometimes do not realize that their puppet is facing upstage because to *them* the face is evident. It is necessary to get into the habit of bearing in mind the audience's view of the puppet. Conversely, if you wish to de-emphasize a puppet, having him turn upstage will do the trick. The old rule of "never turn your back to the audience" is one that can sometimes be very effectively broken. A puppet dead center that suddenly turns and delivers a line upstage can have real impact. Generally, however, when puppets are conversing, it is best to have them in profile to each other, though if you retain eye contact you can "cheat" and have them in almost a three-quarter turn toward the audience.

Though it might be difficult to put a hand puppet on a "platform" in order to command emphasis, there is a very practical way of using different levels as well as areas that adds considerable interest to a puppet production. You can suspend from above or support from below a groundrow or masking piece of almost any height and thus have another whole plane on which your puppets can play. If this area is well lit and not too far upstage, fairly important action can take place there, and it is absolutely great for processions and traveling sequences. You can, of course, use three or more of these masking pieces, but bear in mind that the farther back you go, the less the emphasis. A delightful trick to pull on your audience is to have a puppet exit downstage and have another puppet who looks like him but is smaller enter on a higher plane behind a masking, thereby giving the illusion of great distance.

Though it is difficult to obtain great variety in the use of areas because of the limited depth of the puppet stage, be careful that you don't allow one area to be overused. Try not, for instance, to play three scenes in a

*Tiered masking with smaller puppets entering on*
*succeeding levels to give appearance of distance*

row DC; rather, vary the action so that you utilize the whole stage, and do not use the areas always in the same sequence. Don't be afraid of having one character cross behind another (unless you are using a scrim stage!); crosses lend variety. Though you will not want to overuse either right or left for exits, you do need to watch that you are consistent. If one character exits "to the house" DR, then DR is established for anyone else going "to the house." Audiences have a remarkable memory for what you establish as being directly offstage.

One way to attain variety in the use of area is to make sure that any dominant piece of furniture, like a throne, is not placed in the same area that was occupied by an equally dominant piece in the immediately preceding scene. Usually with hand puppets you will want as little furniture as possible, because it uses up what little valuable playing space you have, but when a furniture piece has a purpose in the action, it can be used as a pivotal point around which the puppets play and greatly helps to define an area.

You have previously learned how to focus the audience's attention on the speaking puppet by having any puppets on stage look at him. This same use of focus can be used for emphasis to point up a puppet's entrance or exit. Simply have the eyes of any puppet or puppets onstage follow him offstage. You will double the effect if this is done in silence. A totally different and suspenseful emphasis is created if a puppet or puppets look *away* from the direction of an entrance (usually most effective if the entrance occurs upstage, especially if it is to be ghostly); this allows the audience good time to see the new character, perhaps even allowing him to speak, before the other puppets turn and notice him.

Substantial variety can be given the stage picture by the use of circular crosses, which again utilize the upstage areas and help break up the linear plane. Such crosses are very effective on entrances and help a character to "command" the scene. You won't want every character using the circular cross, but it is a happy addition to your bag of directing. Simply let the characters enter downstage and make a circular cross upstage and back down again to whatever frontal point on the playboard you desire.

In a one-person show, you will have few problems creating the stage picture and establishing emphasis, since you will at most be concerned with two puppets and perhaps a piece of furniture, but when you increase the number of puppets and operators, you measurably increase the problems of creating a pleasing stage picture. Take the trouble to study some paintings by the old masters that concern themselves with groups of people and you will learn about the placement of figures in a group. Notice how everything in these paintings builds toward a central point of emphasis. For example, look at Da Vinci's "Last Supper" and follow the line of the hands around the table; they make a fluid and unbroken line toward the central figure of Christ, who is also set off by space for emphasis. Take a look at Rembrandt's "Descent from the Cross," and you will notice that the action forms a perfect triangle, really one triangle superimposed over another. Sometimes you will want to form stage pictures of shapes in this way to provide emphasis, or you will use a series of geometric formations in different scenes to provide variety.

You will need to develop a sensitivity to line and balance within the stage picture. Any collection of classical masterpieces in painting will afford you many examples. Look at some of the Flemish and Dutch paintings and notice the arrangement of detail to point up a certain figure. "The Idle Servant" by Maes shows one kitchen maid begging us to regard the slovenliness of another; no better study in line and leading the eye could be found. The composition is triangular, the seeming emphasis on the standing figure, and only because she is pointing to the seated figure do we look to the real subject of the painting. Look for paintings of groups of people and note how the artist arranges details in order to call your attention to the central figure. Almost anything by Watteau in which numbers of people are enjoying a garden will give you an insight into arranging groups of puppets for the greatest seemingly natural effect.

Notice how the artists balance the weight of the various parts of the canvas, so that it is aesthetically pleasing. Mass is balanced against mass; if it were not so balanced, the painting would appear to "tip" in one direction or another. If your stage picture is off-balance for any long period of time, your audience will become nervous, though they may not be able to tell you why. Notice in the paintings you study how the artists will use the figures at the sides of the canvas as "bookends," that is, they are often turned to face the central figure, thus leading the eye back into the canvas. Sketch even a stick-person picture yourself and reverse the procedure, having the figures at the outer edges of the drawing looking out of the picture; they will appear to be almost falling out of the frame and will distract from the central point of focus. You can use figures at the DR and DL (and even UR and UL) positions on the puppet stage to help "bracket" the action and focus the audience attention where you want it.

Though color is often breathtaking in paintings by the old masters, try to abstract yourself from it while you simply get a feeling for line. Notice that a rhythm is created by the seeming movement of the figures, or simply by the basic line of composition. Observe rhythm in a painting of only one or two persons, such as Velazquez' "Venus and Cupid." Here the line of the woman's body and the drapery upon which she lies create the lower half of an oval. Our eye is then returned to completion of the upper half of the oval by the crook of Venus's arm and led through her portrait to the arm of the kneeling Cupid and through his form back to the left side of the lower half of the oval. Notice how the use of the oval gives the feeling of restfulness and contemplation, whereas the use you have seen of the triangle in former examples or ones you have found, creates the illusion of action. Can you feel that though nothing is actually "happening" in this painting, no action except contemplation, there is a rhythm intrinsic to the quality of line?

You will need to train yourself in seeing and using rhythm in your stage pictures. Do not be discouraged if you do not sense it right away. The moment of "Aha! I know what it means!" may even have to wait until you see a particularly bad example in (we hope) someone else's show. An irritating break in the rhythm of a production can occur when a puppeteer whose puppet is not speaking appears to "go dead," almost invariably because the operator's concentration is just not there. Though you have been told in your early work to freeze any puppets not speaking, now that you are developing a sense of the use of focus, you will discover small motions that the nonspeaking character can make, which retain a bodily animation and help him continue to appear alive and part of the scene. The puppet may simply fold his hands or touch his face, nod slightly; any smooth, small, and not too quick gesture that feels appropriate.

After you have isolated line and balance and their uses in rhythm and motion, it is time to consider color. Though we will detail the use and effect of color in discussion of scene design, costume, and makeup, be aware that it is the director's job, even if he is lucky enough to have someone else executing design, to utilize color most effectively in the creation of the stage picture. He must learn how to give enough emphasis to an important character dressed in a dull hue (Cinderella?) through line and movement and area so that the audience will take its eyes off other brilliantly dressed characters and focus their attention where he wants it. It is the director's job to give unity to the entire production, tying all its many elements into a whole in which each of the parts is complementary. Since the puppeteer is often responsible for design, acting, writing, and direction, he has a unique opportunity for providing stylistic unity in his productions, a fact that is both challenge and reward.

Again, you must have patience with yourself. The ability to bring unity to a production and to provide that special manner of expression through your work that is your "style" does not develop overnight. Some people have more of an innate sense of style than others. Probably it cannot be taught, but it can certainly be brought out and developed. Webster defines style as "distinctive, characteristic mode of presentation, construction, or execution in any art . . ." and also as "the quality which gives distinctive character and excellence to artistic expression." As with many "qualities," style almost defies definition, and it is frequently more remarkable in its absence than in its presence. In direction it is perhaps best defined as the ability to unify the entire production into an expression that is uniquely your own. The most difficult element to conquer in any art, but the most necessary if that which we convey is truly to be art, style develops with time, practice, experimenting, and most of all, perseverance.

In pursuit of style think first of the overall feeling you get from the script you are about to produce. Is it light and airy and full of fantasy? Is it tragic or somber? Is it funny and brisk? Try to determine a general mood and then think what colors it brings to your mind. Does your story take place in a given time and place in history? Does the period seem to fit the mood of the script? If not, you may want to set the story in another period that better harmonizes with its mood. With fairy tales you have wide range of choice from Gothic right up through the Renaissance and later. Or you might want, for instance, to set a Greek or Roman myth in the present day. Answering as many questions as you can about the inherent qualities of the script and how they make you feel will help you to determine your approach and to define the style of your production. Once you know the direction you wish to pursue in interpretation and design, your byword must be "consistency." You will be checking and rechecking to be sure that every element of your production "adds up" to a harmony in the total stage picture, every element complementing the other.

Though it is perhaps easier to develop stylistic unity in a solo production in which all of its elements are created by you, the one-person show has its own pitfalls. You are your own director. Somehow you must turn your critical eye upon your own work, just as you did in your early acting exercises, and eliminate anything that does not contribute to the overall effect. Nor is it easy to develop a discipline of rehearsal when you are working alone. It is so comfortable to let things go until the last minute, because there is no one there to push you onward or to catch your mistakes and correct them.

To aid your self-discipline, make out a rehearsal chart, plotting rehearsal times until the day of performance. A worklist helps tremendously while you are constructing puppets and settings, and it is so gratifying to be able to burn it or tear it up when everything is finally done! Organize your work so that you are confident you have allotted enough time to be ready by your performance deadline. It is no fun to panic at the last minute. Plan on having a "dress rehearsal" for some friends, scheduling it close enough to production for all the construction and basic plot work to be done, but early enough to make corrections. Plan another "dress rehearsal" just before the show. Then you will *know* that everything is ready and that you are too. If you find that you have to skip a rehearsal (or the weather is lovely and you just want to), write in an alternate time, and make yourself stick to it. Remember, if the show is not a finished product by performance, you have no one to blame but yourself. Give yourself deadlines (completion of puppets, finished script, et cetera), which will break up the work into smaller blocks and let you feel some encouragement as you progress. After all, if you are going to be your own taskmaster, you have to learn to give yourself some rewards, too!

Having someone you trust sit in on rehearsals can help you mold your performance, and you may also find the use of a mirror helpful. You can simply take a puppet or puppets to a mirror and try out certain effects and movements. Or you can hang an inexpensive mirror facing your rehearsal stage, wide enough to show the whole stage and at a convenient height for you to see yourself working. While mirrors are dangerous for the live actor, lest he become preoccupied with the way he looks and his technique, blocking his concentration on inner life and objectives, mirrors can sometimes provide much needed help for the puppeteer. The same dangers, of course, lurk in their use for the puppeteer as for the actor; he, too, can become preoccupied with the way he looks and neglect to concentrate on inner life, but if the puppeteer can train himself to use the mirror as a way of checking on himself, when he believes things are set he can correct faults not obvious to him from backstage. He should never use the mirror all the time or become dependent upon it, but it can supply his "third eye" when needed. Even better, of course, is the use of video tape, if you have access to it. With tape you can concentrate completely on your performance and then devote your full attention to the playback, actually becoming your own audience. Few puppeteers can afford the equipment themselves, but more and more schools and colleges have excellent systems. Check out what is available to you. You may find that a class would be as interested in learning from the creation of your production as you would be in using the school's equipment.

As we have moved from a discussion of some of the techniques available to you as director to the problems of being your own director, we begin to see the bipartite nature of directing the solo play; the visual aspects and what you want to achieve synthesized because and in spite of the aspects of temperament, which often determine how or even if you achieve your technical goals.

You now have some guidelines for directing yourself, but what if you find yourself directing a group? Though the Übermarionette, that perfect abstraction of life longed for by Gordon Craig, was supposed to have the advantage of absence of temperament, this wonderful creature has never appeared. Could Craig have forgotten that behind every puppet (or at least every two puppets) there is a puppeteer? Whatever Craig envisioned from his pinnacle of abstraction, puppeteers are people, and people possess not only varying skills, but emotions, opinions, health problems, and part-time jobs around which you have to schedule your rehearsals. No, Mr. Craig, melding a group of personalities into an ensemble that works well together to produce a puppet production is not an easy task. Every director will handle his problems differently, and there are no hard and fast rules. (What follows is a system for the beginning director; we hope his problems may be reduced because he knows how to plan and what he may expect.)

The first thing you must do after you have chosen your material is determine how many people it will take to perform it. If you are going to improvise with a group from a working outline, you can still quite closely figure out how many hands you need to present your show. Don't forget that you will need hands to work curtains, lights, music, and to set props. Consider the leading puppet's operator occupied; unless he is very versatile he will have enough on which to concentrate without being given another puppet or effects to accomplish with his free hand. If you have a group assembled, think what they each like to do. Once in a while, you will have to assign a duty, say dimming lights, arbitrarily, because only one person has the hands free to do it, but when it comes to putting people *in charge* of lights, or sound, or even particular puppets, consider both their capabilities and their likes and dislikes. They will do a much better job for you if they are happy.

Do try to keep your cast as small as possible. In any kind of traditional staging, the playing area is strictly limited, and bodies take up much more room than puppets. Remember that before you can do anything artistic, you have to direct traffic. Even with a group of adults (we will discuss children's work in Appendix A), you will have fewer lost tempers if people are not cramped and aren't falling all over one another. Let us suppose you are working in an overhead stage with four or five operators. Unless your stage is very large, you are going to have to teach them to step back away from the playboard when they are not involved in the action. When a puppeteer is rightfully concentrating on a puppet, he is looking at his puppet or the one with whom his puppet is playing a scene. He cannot be held responsible for stepping on or bumping into anyone standing in his way.

As you work, always try to bear in mind the comfort of the operators. Remove any drapery or masking from the lower part of your stage, so that you can see your people as they work. Be aware when their arms start to sag because they are tired, and give them a break. One of the difficulties in working for television is that the director usually has little or no knowledge of what physical contortions a puppeteer may be going through behind the masking that conceals him. Many a puppeteer has been nearly finished off by "take number 92" in a television commercial. The cardinal rule: have mercy, and whenever possible, find a more comfortable way for the operator to work.

You will not always be able to relieve the puppeteers' physical torture, since few companies have persons all of the same height, and the playboard cannot be raised and lowered to suit each puppeteer. Tall puppeteers may have to crouch (most uncomfortable) or even kneel (not fine for everyone); short puppeteers may have to take an old pair of shoes and build them up with cork until they are tall enough to have their puppets appear at the desired height. Whatever the case, do as much as you can to alleviate discomfort, so that your company can concentrate on their puppeteering instead of on the pain in their backs or legs or necks.

Assembling a company and casting a play is not always an easy job. You will want to consider not only a person's talent, but his schedule and reliability as well. It won't benefit you at all to have a talented lead who doesn't show up for performance, or a puppeteer who has several responsibilities of a technical nature and upon whom the rest of the cast is dependent, who is frequently sick or seems to be prone to accidents or crises that prevent attendance at much except dress rehearsal and performance (the most interesting times). Sometimes you will want to cast such an unreliable person because of talent, but do back yourself up with an understudy or nerves of steel. Usually it is better to double cast, that is, arrange for both people to be able to play the part in a performance than to have an understudy simply learn the part and never play. The understudy will like it better, even if he or she only plays once in a run, and you will have the assurance that the part will be learned.

If you have open tryouts and do not know the people you are casting, you will have to become very good at divining not only the potential puppeteer's personality but also his "trainability." Two things will help you greatly: a questionnaire prepared by you to be filled out at tryouts, and a chance to see your candidates improvising. A questionnaire should tell you vital statistics, including amount of experience and indicating any physical disabilities, and give details of when the individual is available for rehearsal and performance. Obviously, you can't use someone if he is not available when you need him, but you may be able to work around people's schedules by working different scenes on different days. You need to know physical disabilities so that someone with a bad back or chronic arthritis isn't cast in a role that later proves painful or impossible (this same person may become your best electrician or seamstress or publicist, so by all means let everyone try out). It is vital to know the amount of experience, but you may often want to choose the person with less experience rather than someone with a little (who thinks he knows a lot) or a lot of experience (who thinks he knows everything). Remember, this is your production, and you are going to need people who are willing to work your way. Often, this end is best achieved with the inexperienced but trainable person.

How do you know if a person is "trainable"? Letting them improvise usually tells you the most, for then they are relaxed and show themselves off to best advantage. You may want to use situations and characters from the play you are going to do. While you won't expect a finished piece of work, you can easily give suggestions, like, "Would you try it this way . . ." You will quickly find out whether or not a person is willing and able to take direction. Note, too, how each person interacts with the others. You are going to make an ensemble out of those you choose, and someone, however talented, who appears hostile or antagonistic to other people—or is simply unable to accept being part of a group instead of being in the spotlight by himself—is better off working alone. You will have to do some guessing, but facility in casting, like many other directorial skills, comes with experience and not without some mistakes. Do try to disregard what the people trying out look like; you are casting puppeteers, not actors. Your most important consideration is whether they can project through the puppet. Sometimes you will have to make difficult compromises, like deciding whether an actor who moves a puppet well but does not have quite the right voice for a part should be used instead of one unsure of movement (can you train him?) but with control of a good voice. Notify your cast within a day or two (they may want to make other plans, and you don't want to lose them); and let those know who were not cast, perhaps offering them jobs in production and letting them know that you may call upon them in the future (you may need them).

Next, you must set up a rehearsal schedule, if you have not already done so. You may have had to wait in order to coordinate your cast's schedules, but you must get it down on paper and copies into each person's hands at the very beginning of rehearsals, so that they know exactly how much time is involved and when. If someone is going to back out because of time commitment, you want to know now, at the beginning. *Always* make lots of extra copies of both your rehearsal schedule and your working script; no matter what you say or do, many will get lost, and replacements will be requested.

There is no absolute way of determining the number of rehearsals you will need, for the complexity of productions and the skill of the performers varies so greatly. Better to consider rehearsals in terms of blocks of time needed for each phase of preparing a production; then you can plan according to your individual needs, bearing in mind a few universal constants. First, you will need an initial rehearsal which is designed simply to acquaint your cast with your working script and, vaguely, with what each operator's character wants and does and what his relationship is to the other characters. You will want to tell your cast whatever you feel necessary to their interpretations of your overall concept of the show, without burdening them with unnecessary lectures on your philosophy or why you are approaching the material in a given manner. Accept their suggestions, by all means, but start from the outset by regarding this as *your* production. The next rehearsal or two will be devoted to blocking, that is, simply telling everyone who moves where and when, walking them through it, and then letting them repeat the movements to "set" them in their heads and bodies. Disregard interpretation now, unless you feel really bad habits are being formed. Some directors write out all of their blocking in diagrams; other like to carry it in their heads. It really doesn't matter which way you work, as long as you are clear in what you want your characters to do. Either way, you will probably find that some movements you have thought out do not work when actually tried; be flexible and change them as you go along in rehearsal. Always be looking for what might work better, and while you are making the final decisions, your production will much benefit if you will be free enough to draw on the inspiration, sometimes sudden, of your puppeteers.

After you have blocked the show and everyone is familiar with the bare bones of the working script, take time to talk out character relationships and motivation. Question your puppeteers on *why* they are doing this or that; let them argue, and encourage them to think. If they seem unsure of motivation, go back and discuss it. It often helps to declare one rehearsal to be completely technical and another to be completely concerned with inner life. Your cast will perform better if they know what you expect of them. Do get them into the habit of waiting till the end of each rehearsal to tell them what went well, what didn't work, and what you want changed. During some rehearsals you will stop and start and make changes. Then, as soon as you feel your cast needs to get an idea of the continuity of the script, you will call a "run-through" rehearsal, in which you will not stop except in case of disaster and give notes at the end.

You need to allow your cast enough rehearsals so that they feel sure of the show, including its technical aspects, and ready to meet an audience, but you must not over-rehearse, or your cast will lose interest and the production will go stale. Even in an ideally planned rehearsal period you will have to think up ways to revive flagging imaginations and keep the material fresh for your cast. There just is no absolute rule, but for a very general guide, a group show might take four weeks to prepare, if all puppets are complete when rehearsals begin. Whatever the time period for rehearsals, however, by all means allow for a technical rehearsal and preferably two dress rehearsals at which *you know everyone concerned can be present.* At your technical rehearsal, run only cues, no dialogue, unless it is needed to warn that a cue is coming. Run all curtain cues, lighting cues, music cues, sound cues. Make sure that everything is working. If you have complicated lighting, have a "dress parade," as is done in live theatre, and take a look at every puppet under the stage lighting conditions in which they will be seen. Note and make correction of any costume changes *now.* This is the time to be sure that there is enough room for entrances, that the chariot can really be gotten out of the way in time, and that that beautiful backdrop can be changed in the time you have allotted. All technical changes must be made directly after this rehearsal, so that your dress rehearsal can be a complete run-through of the whole show with everything just as it will be in performance. Don't stop for *anything,* no matter how ragged things may look. Your cast needs to know what it feels like to *have* to go on, as they will in performance. After you have given notes and allowed them another dress rehearsal, preferably the next day or evening, you will find your cast ready to do you credit in performance.

While some of the foregoing may sound as though you will constantly be delivering rules and regulations, there is no need for you to become a little dictator or even feel that you are. On the other hand, you cannot afford to sacrifice discipline, and you must be firm about it from the beginning. Without discipline, any theatrical endeavor falls apart. Failure to learn a part, habitual lateness at rehearsal, missed rehearsals without excuse, et cetera, simply can't be tolerated. Make clear what you expect at the beginning and stick to it. Since, if push comes to shove, "sticking to it" may mean dispensing with a puppeteer's services, it is an excellent idea to have a list of possible replacements. It is awful *having* to back down on stage discipline and work with an uncooperative puppeteer simply because you have no one else.

One special complication that may arise for the director of puppet theatre is that he may be playing in the production himself. If this is the case, you will find yourself with a difficult, though not impossible, double task. You will be constantly jumping in and out of the production, and it will be very hard to get a close idea of what the show really looks like. It helps to have one of the cast members who isn't busy in a scene play your part. Then you can concentrate on how the other puppeteers come across and probably even get some insight into how your own work is projecting. You can also ask one of the cast members whose judgment you trust to watch your scenes and take notes. Try not to ask the whole cast in a body how you are doing; this practice invites mass confusion and a large question about who is directing the play. The role of director is complex enough without complicating the issue. You will find yourself playing the roles of coach, teacher, traffic cop, occasional nursemaid, and always of diplomat. You will have to retain a constant balance between remaining flexible and retaining your authority. In many ways your role resembles that of the parent, and do not be surprised if you find yourself so regarded by your cast, whatever your relative ages.

If you treat your "children" well, respecting their intelligence and inventiveness, they will reward you by working together and forming that ideal performing unit in the theatre, the ensemble. Your goal is to draw from each puppeteer his best possible work. Whenever you can, except in matters of pure technique, try to let the puppeteer discover "how to do it" by himself. Give line readings only as a last resort, and keep demonstrations of movement to a minimum if you want the most creativity from your players. Above all, refrain from sarcasm, and never humiliate; you may get a performance from a puppeteer by bullying—once—and you will also gain an enemy who is not going to want to work for you again. Try to keep harmony among your players by not listening privately to their gripes about each other; if something serious comes up, let the offended puppeteer bring his grievance out into the open. Your reward for keeping harmony in the group and encouraging creativity is not only a better production but the excitement of seeing individual puppeteers surprise you with a quality of work and occasional brilliance of which they had not known themselves capable.

One directorial relationship we have not touched on is that of a pair of puppeteers working together, when the division of labor and responsibility is just about equal. Such a relationship has all of the variables and intricacies of a marriage, which in fact it may also be. Since such a working situation is frequent among puppeteers, one would hope for more guidelines than are possible because of the individuality of the relationships. Rarely is the actual direction of the show a shared task. Usually one person is the more talented craftsperson and the other more gifted in performing, so that their responsibilities to each coproduction are weighted accordingly. The only real guide toward successful coproduction is that you both understand exactly what you expect of each other in the beginning of the partnership. If you each respect the other's contribution and are able to talk over differences, you are well on the way to a successful working relationship.

Ultimately, then, it is the role of the director to interpret the script by drawing forth the best possible performances from his players in such a way that they fit his overall concept or style for the production. It is vital to any puppet production that not just the puppeteers and the puppets themselves harmonize with the chosen style, but that there is unity in the mise-en-scène as well; lighting, stage design, music, and costume must all contribute to the unity of the production, and each must add to the total effect within the chosen style. In order to tie all of these theatrical elements together, whether or not he executes each of them himself, it is vital that the director know something about each area of artistic input. He may not design the scenery or costumes himself, but he will surely have to understand the designer's problems and the technical practicalities involved in order to request modifications (and to argue) until a unity of style is reached. If, like the majority of directors of puppet theatre, he is "on his own" and responsible for all aspects of the production himself, it will behoove him to keep working at the areas in which he feels least competent, learning as much as he can about each, until he is finally able to bring all of the many component parts of the production to an equal level of artistry. Only then will he be fulfilling his role as director and giving his audience the quality in puppet theatre that it deserves and which will develop the potential of the puppet theatre in the Western world.

# 7
## Costume Design for the Puppet

Just as acting and directing must be modified for the puppet stage, so too must costume, makeup, scene design, and lighting be specifically geared to the special requirements of this special genre of theatre. Of the arts of design, we shall consider costume first, not because it is of greatest importance, but because it usually presents the first hurdle as the puppeteer begins to create original puppets and to mount his or her first productions. Assuredly, costume design must harmonize with set design and lighting in order to produce the unity of style already posed as the director's challenge, but to consider all the elements of design at once would be confusing. Let us in this chapter consider costume as though presented against a black or neutral (perhaps deep blue or turquoise) drop. We will assume white lighting. Indeed, your first shows may well be presented this way, and there is no reason they should not be. There will be time enough to grow into the intricacies of stage design and the effect of colored light upon both costume and design. If you are to become master of all of these arts as a puppeteer, give yourself enough time to master each, before complicating your life to the point that you forget to build upon the skills you have already acquired. If you feel confident acting with your puppets and have launched into directing your show, there will come a point when you will need a new set of puppets, and you will need to know something of costume design in order to create them, or even to be able to tell someone else exactly what you want executed for you.

When you first began to act with puppets, you found it necessary to alter some of them for movement and learned some basic principles of constructing a costume so that it did not inhibit the puppet's movement. Now, let us explore the areas of color, line, and texture to find out how you can utilize them all for emphasis, to establish a puppet's character, and to gain unity within your production. For purposes of example, we will use the human-character hand puppet, but the principles can be applied to any animal or wild sort of abstraction you wish to create.

Since the most obvious and easiest to isolate of design elements is color, we will consider it first. Much has been written on the psychological effects of color, and there are a number of theories on the use and mixing of color. We won't get into these theories; rather, what is presented here is purposely basic and workable. Think about the effect that color has upon you. Unless you are color-blind or already an accomplished painter, you can sharpen your awareness of and sensitivity to color, and doing so will greatly enhance your work. What does blue mean to you, many shades of it, bathing an entire scene? To most people it is peaceful, sometimes spiritual, usually contemplative and restful. It is a cool color and tends to quiet things down. Examine the effect of red. It can be startling as an accent color and, if dominant in a scene, gives the effect of excitement, passion, intensity, often of anger and sometimes death (as in the image of blood-red). Red is very tricky when used on puppet costumes. Any large area of it commands the audience's attention and can tire the eye. How about yellow? It can evoke a happy feeling, a sense of comedy, gaiety, and youthfulness. These three, red, yellow, and blue, are the primary colors. If mixed with the neighboring color on a color wheel, they will produce the secondary colors: orange, green, and purple.

Green makes us think of forests and trees. It has a connotation of health and well-being. In contrast to fiery orange, it is restful. Orange, the blend of red and yellow, borrows from each of its primary components, as each of the secondary colors do, carrying modified connotations of each. Orange can be comic; a dash of it will wake up a costume. Purple, last of the secondary colors, connotes the regal, the wise, and the proud.

There are, of course, individual reactions to color. (Someone hates lavender because her great aunt who treated her sternly frequently wore it, and another feels that lavender has cleansing qualities.) Nor is it true that when you wear red you necessarily feel angry or passionate or make others feel that way. Utilizing color involves both recognizing differences in reaction and realizing that there are some basic usual psychological reactions to colors. Interestingly, the variations in reactions are much greater when we deal with variations in intensity of color and in subtle intermixes of colors to form tertiary shades, such as blue-green, blue-violet, and yellow-orange.

So much for the way color affects you and what the basic colors may suggest to your audience. Now, let us see how the colors affect each other. Take another look at the color wheel. If you choose any neighboring colors and shades in between, they can effectively be used together in a costume and will appear to be in harmony. Neighboring colors are said to be "analogous." After you have chosen the color that best expresses a scene for you, look at the color wheel and pick the colors that are on either side of it. Now, examine the characters in the scene. Is there any one main character or group

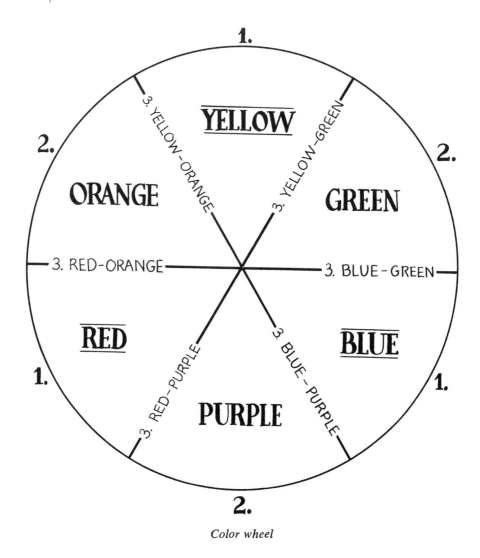

*Color wheel*

of characters to whom you can assign this "theme" color. Whole shows have been designed in this way, using one set of analogous colors to express one scene, then another set of colors, then another. The effect can be particularly striking in a revue, when color can afford to be strong and will not distract the audience.

There is one catch, however. If you use only analogous colors, the effect can become boring. You will need to pick an accent color, and this you do by locating the color directly opposite your predominant color on the wheel. This is the complementary color, and a dash of it will "wake up" your predominant color, making it appear much brighter. If you juxtapose complementaries in equal parts, they almost seem to vibrate: orange and blue, for instance. You won't want to use this effect without purpose or for very long appearances.

From painting and the mixing of colors you can borrow an interesting effect in the creation of grays. If you use a sheer fabric of a color over a fabric of its complement, you will create a vibrant gray, the intensity of which will depend on the shade of the original colors. Why not just use gray fabric? You can, indeed, but occasionally the "live mix" of an overlap of complementaries can give just the interest you need to what would otherwise seem a neutral color. Which brings us to the subject of black, or the absence of color. All that need be said is that whenever you can, avoid it. Use dark brown, dark green, dark anything, but stay away from black. It tends to go dead on stage. White, on the other hand, can be used very effectively. Being the presence of all colors, there are many "whites," and one has to watch dye lots and choose the appropriate white that seems analogous because it contains the other colors used in a scene, but it can work very well for you.

Color conventions can be set up by the designer for a whole play. Perhaps all costumes are in like or nearly like dark shades with an occasional red accent. Perhaps the whole show will be monochromatic, like a pen and ink drawing, perhaps sepia against a muslin-beige. Perhaps soft ochers in many shades are used for all costumes and all are given accents of red-orange. These arbitrary color coordinations do work, but it is better to leave them to the practiced hand of the expert, and to begin your work by sorting the colors you will use from the meaning of the script at hand. Assign the various colors chosen for a scene to its characters according to the feeling you get from each character.

Generally, the strongest character will demand the most commanding color. Villains almost cry out to be dark, while their heroic opponents give the audience a clue to their character by appearing in the complementary lights. One need not be arbitrary. Play with the colors. Paint swatches on papers and move them around, experimenting with their relationships and their effect on you and upon each other. When you have chosen a basic set of analogous colors and color accents for a scene and have assigned colors to different characters, make up a color chart. This will help you immeasurably in seeing the show as a whole, especially if there are several scenes. Simply list each character in the scene, attempting to group those that appear together, and paint a splotch of the predominant color it wears next to its name. Do this for each scene, and make it large enough to post on the wall for easy reference. When you have finished, you will have a color plot for the entire show. Does the progression of color seem pleasing and as though it will express both the central idea and the dramatic progression of your script? Fine. Then you are ready to proceed.

You are almost ready to rough out renderings, which are simply drawings of what you want the costumes to look like. However well you draw and paint, getting down on paper what you think a costume should look like will be of immense help when you come to construct it. You may make changes as you go, but you need to clarify your ideas. You may or may not want to detail faces or leave them blank; do whichever helps you most. Drawing the costume will help you to get a sense of "line" which is the companion to color in making your costumes express your chosen style and individual characters. Line is the arrangement of outlines and shapes that expresses the overall contour of your composition—in this case, a costume. Some characters are best expressed by round shapes, others by sharply angular ones. Related shapes tend to complement each other, pleasing the eye because they create the illusion that the whole costume "adds up." You will want to consider the shape of the puppet's head. If it is triangular and has pointed ears and nose, how can you pick up the triangular shape and echo it in the costume? Does your costume need a flowing, unbroken line from shoulder to head, giving a sense of dignity and grandeur? Or should it be a broken line of patches of color and pattern, indicative of a comic character? Is the script set in a historical period? Then you will need to research the costumes of your chosen period and figure out how to modify the prevailing line for the puppet. (Some suggestions for modifying period costumes for hand puppets are given at the end of this chapter.) Sometimes a historical period covers a fairly broad span of years, early, middle, and late periods having quite a different line, and you can choose the one you like best for your play.

With the hand puppet especially, never underestimate the power of a headdress! The lovely Gothic peaked hats with flowing silks worn by Medieval ladies can spare a hand puppet princess from appearing short and stubby; another pointed hat can give a wizard sufficient mystery and allow him to dwarf a prince without altering the proportions between the puppets. You will want to take care never to attach to a costume something bound to get caught on the scenery or on other puppets. You want to preserve the "purity" of line, too, so don't forget that byword of puppet theatre: simplicity. Try to get to the essence of the line and leave off anything fussy that may clutter. Large collars can give male puppets real dignity; gentle fichus at the lady's neck can help her short arms seem longer and her body to appear better proportioned. But that fussy ruffle that is just a little too large and obscures the face has got to go! You have already learned to construct a costume for movement; now you must incorporate both line and color for the effect to be pleasing and in character.

Try not to "cut your characters in half." Since hand puppets appear short and stubby, you will help them and give a more pleasing proportion if you don't make the lower glove and skirt almost equal in size to upper body and head. Often you can lengthen the upper body a little, perhaps by using a smock instead of a shirt, by lowering the waistline, or by adding a longish apron thereby making a three-quarter break in the line. Consider plumes on hats and the line of the hair in the overall picture.

There is a technique of blocking out the costume in terms of basic shapes that immediately reveals how the eye is led over the costume and if the result is pleasing. Many people like to use this technique when first thinking out a costume design; others find it helpful when they are "stuck" and need to find out why a costume doesn't look right to them. When a costume is blocked out in terms of simple shapes, it becomes obvious when the line is clumsy or top-heavy or not expressive of a given character. Below, compare the drawing of a puppet Harlequin and the same rendering given in terms of basic shapes.

Copy or trace the basic shape drawing of the Harlequin several times so that you can illustrate for yourself some guidelines in making line and color complement each other. Get out some crayons, or whatever coloring medium is handy and easy for you to use, and get ready to make a number of sample renderings. First, note that the triangular detail, traditionally clear red, yellow, and blue, has been left off the shape rendering. On your first drawing try coloring in this detail (roughly—this is not meant to become a finished picture). Keep all of your colors of equal intensity. Now notice how the basic shapes of the design have been obscured. With that much detail you must do something to bring the line back into focus. Take any dark color and accent the line down the center of hat and vest and also the lower edge of the V below the waist. It all comes back into focus, doesn't it? You have just learned how to subordinate busy detail so that it is not distracting.

Notice how the face in the drawing, even if you have not colored it in, stands out. Color the hat a dark color or medium shade and you will heighten this effect still further. Do you see how the white ruff calls attention to the face? Color it any light color and the effect will be intensified. Take another drawing and reverse the process: color the ruff dark, the upper body in a medium neutral or dull color, and make the pants or lower glove a bright, light hue. Where is your eye led to go first as you look at your drawing? Remember that the lower glove is the least interesting part of a hand puppet; you want to draw the eye away from the fact that your puppet has no legs

*Harlequin with basic shape rendering for tracing and practice*

and lead the audience toward where interest lies—in the face and hands of the puppet. Take any combination of colors you like and make another drawing, keeping the lower glove dark or medium and neutral, the upper body medium, the ruff light and bright. Notice how the darker the color is, the more it tends to recede. Light colors tend to come forward and call for attention. Keep this last drawing you have colored as a reminder that light colors should be used near the face, moving toward the deepest tones in the lower body.

If the colors you have used are complements, notice how they seem to vibrate. Gray one of them by overcoloring with its complement. Isn't that more pleasing to the eye? If you used widely opposing colors for jacket and lower glove instead of analogous shades, your puppet probably looks "cut in half" and you will need a very strong accent on that vertical center line to help your drawing tie together. Experiment with groups of analogous colors in hat, jacket, and lower glove, varying their intensity. Don't forget that puppets don't have to be realistic. Try the effects of green, lavender, and orange skin! Examine the effects you have achieved and find out what pleases you.

Now make a drawing and exaggerate the size of the hat. The puppet looks top-heavy, doesn't it? You have drawn attention to the head, but the effect is uncomfortable to look at and appears almost deformed. Learn to bring the size of hats and wigs and headdresses into harmony with the size of the other shapes in the costume unless there is a character reason for the exaggeration. A head that is already just a little too large, coifed with an ample wig, can make the puppet look "all head." Accessories like hats and jewels and interesting trim can be marvelous accents, giving character distinction and the sense of a historical period, but you must learn to bring them into scale for your puppet. You will find that it is again a process of selection and exaggeration. A puppet simply can't wear all the detail a human actor can. Select the detail that says the most about the character and best complements your design and forget about the rest.

In order to accent the hands, you have already exaggerated their size in proportion to the puppet body. You may want to sew a ruff or a cuff of a light color to draw attention to the hands. Do not underestimate gloves, either. They can be any color you like; the lighter the shade and brighter the color, the more commanding they will be. Gloves are simply the hand itself, painted. A cuff of matching felt can be attached, which gives a fine illusion of a longer arm. The cuff is cut in a circle, slit, and the center cut out to fit around the hand. Try it on the puppet, adjusting the fullness of the cuff by cutting out part of the circle and slip-stitching together when the proportion pleases you. If you are using felt hands, the whole glove can be made in one color, but an exciting effect can be attained by using different colors for the top and the bottom of the glove. With the felt glove, the cuff usually looks best when it is cut in a separate piece in a color matching the top half of the glove.

When it comes to costume details and accessories, puppeteers become veritable pack rats, keeping buttons, costume jewelry, old Brillo pads, and heaven knows what because it might come in handy someday, and usually does—if they can find it when they need it. Tremendously helpful is some sort of filing system for your fabric and useful junk. Get yourself a collection of sturdy boxes. Cardboard files are great if you can find them. Boxes with tops necessitate shelves. Label your boxes either according to fabric type (felt, wool, silk, et cetera) or color (not being too specific, that is, reds, greens, browns) and sort your pieces into them. Reserve some boxes for jewels, hair, fur, and whatever categories of junk suit your collection. Now, when it comes to building a new show, you will be able to "pull" what you need, usually finding you have more on hand and less to buy than you had thought.

Just as in filing you found that family groups of colors and variations on colors "belonged" together, so too, in design, you will be able to take advantage of color "groups." Let us suppose you have a group of peasants whom you wish to appear related to each other and in contrast to, say, a little prince. You can use shades of browns, grays, and accent colors that are a component of the earth colors on your peasants and set them off from the young prince by dressing him in a clear, light blue. With a little experience you will be able to spot the kind of brown or gray, that is, is it a red-brown, yellow-brown, or does the gray seem cold and predominantly blue? By relating the lines within a character group as well as the colors, you will heighten your effect. Go back to your color chart for the show and see if related characters have analogous colors. Check your renderings and see if the lines of the costumes are similar.

When line and color are brought into harmony in your renderings, there is one more consideration before you are ready to "pull" all of your fabrics from stock, and that is texture, which can do much to define character and period and can either bring out or destroy line in the actual creation of a costume. Think first of obvious textural differences, say of fur (or fur cloth) and of satin and of burlap. All fabric has a texture, some of it appearing quite different from a distance than when you actually feel it. Become aware of the subtle differences in texture so that you can choose the one that best suits your characters. Take advantage of the excitement you can create in a costume by contrasting textures, again being careful to retain a harmony of line and color.

Suppose you have chosen to dress a princess in satin. What *kind* of satin? There are many different types and they perform in as many different ways. Never forget those early rules: the fabric must stand up to wear, and it must drape consistently with the line of the costume design in the small scale of the puppet. Many beautiful renderings for puppet costumes have been a flop when executed because lovely and possibly expensive fabric may have been used, but it did not "move" well or drape in a convincing manner. The princess with the stiff satin skirt is never going to look as though she is walking. Her sister, dressed in flowing soft lingerie satin, will look alive. Jerseys of many kinds drape well. Experiment with any you may have on hand. Try the effect of hanging the fabric from the bias as against the straight (as the threads are woven) of the material. Find out how you can pleat the fabric so that it creates different types of folds.

Expensive fabrics do not always do the best job, so do not be carried away by the fact that because of the puppet's small size you can probably afford most any fabric for its costume. Do not underestimate duvetyn, an inexpensive flannel available in any theatrical fabric house; it has all the properties of velvet from a distance. Or obtain your "velvet" by dyeing or painting on white cotton flannel. Sometimes the colors you want, even with the tremendous variety of fabrics on the market, just can't be found, and then those colors are worth dyeing for! It is a messy job, but well worth doing, if you are in search of just the right colors. You can get many subtle shadings within a color grouping by dyeing your fabric. Muslin (unbleached, all cotton) dyes beautifully; earth colors, especially, are hard to find in subtle gradations and can be created by dyeing. Just remember that nylon and most polyesters resist dye. Cotton works best, but wool and felt can also be dyed. The lighter the original color of the fabric, the more true your final result will be to the color of the dye you have mixed. Always allow for lots of shrinkage, and never cut or sew before you dye. It is a good idea, too, to dye more fabric than you think you will need, since it may be difficult (extremely) to duplicate a dyed color exactly. Occasionally, white fabric will appear "too white" and attract too much attention, a problem that can be remedied by dipping the fabric in tea.

Sometimes you will need a certain small pattern in proportion to your puppet, and instead of running your feet off looking for it in stores, you can accomplish as good an effect or better by choosing the appropriate weight of muslin or of cotton jersey (what undershirts are made of) and painting or stenciling on the pattern with textile paint. Acrylic paints can also work, if not too thickly applied. Consider, too, dyeing fabric and *then* stenciling on a pattern. Extremely unusual effects and often ones that evoke a period effect can be obtained in this way.

Now that you have taken stock of what fabric you have on hand and thought about what fabric you want to dye or decorate yourself, it is time to go shopping. Take your costume drawings with you. And don't be put off by an impatient fabric clerk. Stores do not like, understandably, selling you twenty or more small pieces of fabric, but they will. Ask first what is the smallest length you can buy (often one-fourth or one-half yard), and warn the clerk that you will be buying many small lengths. If you go at a time when the store is not too busy, have your renderings with you, and are pleasant (very), you may even get the clerk interested in your production. However, even if you have the misfortune to encounter a hostile clerk, *take your time*. Prop the fabric bolt up and view it from a distance. Play with the fabric. Is it *really* wrinkle-free? How does it drape? And how does it compare with the color in your rendering? If you are in doubt about a fabric or want to look further, ask for a small (it may be minute) sample of the fabric and pin it to your rendering. Do *not* depend on your memory in matching color or judging the color's faithfulness to your rendering; color is extremely difficult to remember—especially blue, for some reason. Do have pinned to your rendering any swatches of fabric that you intend to use from stock on hand. Remnants can be a saving, but often aren't, because you may end up having bought more than you need. But do search out upholstery samples, which are inexpensive and often are woven in interesting textures and with good, exciting mixes of color. Do look at the wrong side of fabric, which often works better than the right side. Who says you have to use the fabric as the manufacturer intended? The wrong side of foam-backed lining can be useful for anything from seals to space suits!

With fabric pulled and bought, mount your renderings, with swatches attached, where you can see them in your work area. You are ready to assemble, or have assembled, your puppet costumes. A few sewing hints can save you lots of time. Do sew on the machine any seam that will bear strain. Careful hand sewing will hold costume parts to the glove, but don't hand sew the whole thing. Don't ever hem when you don't have to. Most knitted fabrics and so-called stretch fabrics need not be hemmed and drape better if you don't. Overperfection of sewing in hems can ruin the movement of your costume. Many light fabrics can be "hemmed," if they would otherwise fray, by edging them with colorless nail polish. Before assembling the costume, spread the piece of fabric on newspaper and apply a thin line of polish to the end that will be seen when the costume is finished. The polish will stiffen the fabric slightly and discolor it a little, but not so much as to be noticeable from a distance.

If you have designed several costume changes for any puppet, beware. If the change is any more than a cape or hat or other small accessory, make another puppet wearing the changed costume. This may sound time-consuming, for you may have to make several puppets in different costumes, but remember, you cannot make a doll's dress for a puppet! Also, changes have frequently to be quick, and if they are complicated, no one may have hands free to do them. Better to *know* that a different puppet is dressed and ready to go on. If you do make small accessory changes, Velcro is usually a quick and efficient way of fastening capes, wigs, and such.

By now you have an understanding of the principles of color, line, and texture; you know basic construction from making or remaking your earlier puppets; and you now have a few more hints about building successful costumes. Let us move on, then, to a discussion of the adaptation of the costumes of various historical periods to the demands and capabilities of the puppet stage. What follows should in no way be construed as a replacement for research, nor are all costume periods covered. In each period there are several lines favored, often with several styles changing as the period progresses. People dress according to their station in life, in a way that serves their occupations, and above all for comfort, according to the prevailing tastes of their times and the availability of materials. In no way can we cover all of this in depth. Whenever you undertake to design a production set within a historical period, you will enrich your work by steeping yourself in a knowledge of the people, their customs, and their dress. Arm yourself with costume books and also search out paintings of the period and read up on its history. Only a few main periods will be treated here, but it is hoped they will serve as a guide and a spark to your imagination and provide you with the ability to look at period costumes and adapt their lines to the proportions of the hand puppet.

*1. Egyptian.* Line: Garments were often straight and close-fitting, being gathered to fullness in the front and caught just above the waist with an ornament. Large round collars, often very ornate, were worn. These can be simulated with beads and small ceramic tiles glued to a backing of Pellon or other facing material. Decorations tend not to adhere well to felt. Since the garments varied from extremely sheer to linen-weight, you can capture their feeling in a range of fabrics from gauze to muslin. Though much white was employed, the collars were brilliantly colored, and some clothing fabric, among those who could afford it, was woven in patterns, embroidered, and/or brilliantly dyed. Acquaint yourself with the motifs of the lotus, palm, and scarab; see if you can work the beautiful winged disc into your designs. All of these motifs and many more will help greatly to give the feeling of the period.

One difficulty you will meet in adapting Egyptian costume is what to do about the generous amount of bare skin often in view. Male bodies sometimes look believable, especially if the style of design is not too realistic, if they are made of flesh-colored felt. Sometimes you can fashion a felt body over a muslin one, padding with Dacron stuffing in between for more realistic contours. Another solution is to cover the whole body from neck to hem with a simple white or off-white tunic and then apply robes or the draped male skirt over it. Try to stay away from loincloths in their variations, but if you must use them over a felt body, don't attempt legs; just taper the glove. Women's bare or partly bare bosoms present a problem because of puppet proportions and the demands of hand movement. If you construct a molded chest piece of celastic, papier-mâché or plastic wood, it is not only peculiarly foreshortened but is very limiting to the movement of your fingers in the puppet's hands. Applying a flesh-colored piece of felt over the chest can work, but if this piece wrinkles when the puppet moves, the effect is really strange. In general, it is easier and more effective to hide her behind a collar and capture the line in the draping.

Egyptian headdresses of pharaohs and queens are extremely beautiful, and adaptable to the puppet if care is taken that they don't become too large. You will have to make yours smaller in proportion to the puppet than they were in proportion to real people so that the puppet isn't top-heavy. Wigs are among the easiest of all Egyptian costume elements to adapt. Crepe hair, which is bought by the foot tightly braided and is available wherever theatrical makeup is sold, works very well. You must unbraid it by removing the string inside, wet it, and stretch it to the desired degree of curliness, allowing it to dry before releasing from the stretcher and getting to work on it. Most wigs can be made in the following manner, but the Egyptian is especially easy because it frequently employs bangs. Cut two strips a little longer than you think you will need and lay one straight piece at right angles to the other, longer in back than in front, where the "bangs" will be. Stitch the "part" on the machine, using a long stitch with tissue paper underneath along the part. Also stitch across the strip that will lie underneath, stitching just above the line of the bangs. Now, pick up the hair pieces and position them on the puppet head to try the effect. It is often helpful to rest the puppet on an armature or small-necked bottle during this process. Now, remove the wig, paint the scalp fairly thickly with white glue, and reposition the wig as you want it. Wait until the glue dries to make details, but get the general line now. Extra braids and curls can always be added later. When the rough wig is dry, it can be cut to shape and tacked with thread to hold the shape. For the Egyptian look you may want to spray the head (cover the face to protect it) with lacquer to give it sheen.

*2. Greek.* To design in any of the Greek periods, you will need to know how to make both a chiton and a himation, the two basic garments.

The chiton was the basic women's garment, though also worn, especially in short form (bare skin again), by men. The himation was a draped shawl; though it was frequently worn by statesmen and orators, you can use it with a good bit of freedom to vary the stage picture. Bear in mind that despite the impression given by surviving Greek statues, Greek clothing was *not* all white, and lovely vegetable dyes were freely used. Motifs such as the key, the wave, and the egg and dart were colorfully used for borders and are very adaptable in scale to the hand puppet.

The chiton begins with a rectangle about a third larger than your puppet's width at the broadest point of the glove. It can fall straight (Ionic) or be caught up in irregular gatherings at the waist (Doric). Either type works well if straight across at the neck, loose at the armholes (how nice for the puppet!), and caught at the shoulders with some handy gilt ornament. Borders may appear at neck and hem. In order to achieve the Doric drape, simply gather the rectangle, which must be cut at least six inches longer than the puppet, in two uneven rows in pleasing lines above and below the waist. Size to the puppet glove. Matte jersey drapes very well, but you may want to consider acquiring the vertical Grecian folds in the following manner. Take fine unbleached muslin dyed any color or left plain, cut your rectangles an inch or two too long, wet them and twist them into a vertical "rope." Tie at both ends and hang by one of the strings to dry, preferably stretching the rope until dry. The more tightly you twist the fabric, the finer the folds will be when the fabric is released.

For the himation or long shawl, cut a rectangle about three times as long as your puppet and as wide as the measurement from your puppet's underarm to the point on his glove that will be even with the playboard. Tack the rectangle to the center back of the glove and wind around the body in front, across the back, and up over the left shoulder, allowing the ends to hang in folds until it is about three inches shorter than the front length. The real garment often obscured the left hand, but the effect will be sufficiently authentic if you tack the fabric behind the left wrist. The himation was also worn by women, but then it was draped from the right shoulder and brought up over the head, a great style for old women and soothsayers. Short capes and equally short chitons, as well as warriors' armor present problems too copious to detail here. Just remember that just about anything can be adapted, bearing proportions in mind.

*3. Gothic or Medieval.* We are taking a large leap in history to our next period, from which much script material is adapted for the puppet stage. The jewel colors of this period, like those of stained glass windows, and the long, flowing garments are particularly flattering to the hand puppet. You can have a lot of fun playing the bright, clear colors worn by nobility against the drab, earth-colored garments worn by the poor. Toward the end of the period the styles moved toward greater complexity and ornamentation. Examples are given from both early and late Medieval periods, since both so often turn up in fariy tales. The earlier period has a plain, simple, rather ascetic look, in contrast to the highly decorative and almost flippant look of the later period. Mixing the two periods won't do, so be sure to do sufficient research.

Though men did wear short robes with tights, the look is very hard to capture with any grace for the hand puppet, and it is recommended that you stay with the long length. Make a complete underrobe, just a little larger than your puppet's glove, and secure it over the body glove. Over that can go a cape made from a very slightly gathered rectangle, belted or not. It may have its own collar or be worn with a separate fur collar. Save the more sumptuous fabrics for the later period, but some velvets and luscious shades of jersey do serve very well here. Old bits of beading, evening bags, or nineteen-thirties dresses, if you can scavenge them, make wonderful trim. The men often wore the chaperon, a headdress which sometimes had an exaggeratedly long tail. It is useful for jongleurs, dwarfs, gnomes, pages, et cetera. Unfortunately they have got to have short jackets. Just make the jacket and chaperon colors dominant and cut the lower glove in a dull color and fit it as tightly as you can for comfortable movement and gloving.

The lady could wear a complete underglove and over it a sort of long apron, cut very deeply at the sides. Trains were worn but are not recommended for hand puppets. Sometimes, if the fabric has body, you can cut the back of the skirt longer and by catching it back up to the underglove give some illusion of a train. If you *have* to have a train for story purposes, cut the back of the overdress long (say six inches longer than the rest of the skirt), let it hang until you want to call attention to it, then use your free hand to move it at the level of the playboard. Once in a while it is worth the trouble.

Remember that only young girls' hair was worn loose and flowing; after marriage hair was always pinned up, often in two buns at the sides of the head over the ears, and decorated with nets covered with jewels. Wigs for these ladies can be quite a chore to construct. Yarn can work if its feeling is in keeping with the style of the production. Actually, mohair, if you can get it, is very lifelike and often produces just the combination of realism and fantasy needed. There is, as mentioned before, crepe hair, but you will need to straighten it. It can be reset after the wig is formed. Some Dynel switches can be worked with, though they are often too wiry. Human hair is impossible; it simply will not stay put. Doll wigs usually look terribly artificial and are almost never in any usable style. Men's wigs are much easier to construct. Even a fur-covered head can work very well, and fur is excellent for beards. Just be sure to shear it in a believable pattern. Headdresses became very elaborate in the late Gothic period, though young girls' flowing hair, difficult to wig, remained the same as in the earlier era.

In the late Gothic period, a lady's robes became very full (about twice the fullness of the glove body), with long, flowing sleeves. Actually, these sleeves often reached the floor, but your puppet will probably have a more pleasing proportion if you let them hang about three-quarters of the distance to the floor. You can dispense with a full underdress over the glove and simply make inner sleeves, tacking them to the glove. These sleeves should not be full, just a little larger than the puppet glove. The oversleeve will give the desired illusion of arm length. Buckram or cone shapes cut from cottage-cheese cartons are recommended for stiffening the hats. Light cardboard is too likely to become crushed and stay that way. Use as sumptuous fabrics and colors as you can find.

The gentleman wore an overrobe with sleeves cut in a "feathered" pattern. It almost has to be made of felt. You can put a few pleats in the front and back for form and fullness, cutting the robe just an inch or two larger than the underglove. On his head he wore a hat with a soft silk or silklike, gathered ruffle. Under the ruffle, attach the long tail or liripipe. Often, you may want to use a medallion hung on a chain around the neck, since it is both decorative and draws attention toward the face. Do tack it to the costume and underglove so that it doesn't bounce around. The late Gothic is a period in which the richer and more effeminate gentlemen might wear a two-colored glove to advantage.

*4. Peasants.* We need to present peasants, not as a period, but as a group. They turn up so often in puppet stories, and their dress remained pretty much the same from the Middle Ages through the Renaissance. One marked change occurred in headgear: the head wound in muslin on the women of the early Medieval period, graduated to the mobcap shown in Renaissance times and right up through the Colonial era. The more pleasing proportions of the longer apron on the woman and of the smock rather than the shirt tucked in at waist for the man work very well and can be found in any costume book.

Because of the sameness of the cut of peasants' clothing, you will need to put your ingenuity to work on color and texture and subtle gradations of both. Iridescent cloth (in which warp and woof threads are of different colors), tweeds, and small patterns in subdued colors can relieve the monotony. Capes of varying lengths can help a lot, too.

If you are costuming a little peasant girl, do not make her skirt as short as it would be in reality. The illusion of shortness will be conveyed, if you stop the skirt just short of where the glove is even with the playboard and cut the skirt two or two and one half times as full as the waist of the under-gloves so that the skirt sticks out.

*5. The Renaissance.* Be conscious again that there are many periods within this one and that styles varied considerably from country to country, always becoming more ornate and elaborate the closer they got geographically to Italy. Let us discuss some of the general characteristics of line and cut that prevailed in Elizabethan England. Over and over one finds the heart shape repeated, from hairline to shoulder line, and again in the women's skirts, held up by farthingales, and in the puffy pumpkin hose worn by the men.

To adapt the lady's silhouette to a hand puppet demands a little trickery. You simply can't build a hand puppet with a tiny, pointed waist. What you can do, though, is cut believable bodice outlines, ending in the characteristic point, and appliqué them to the underglove. The material for the sides of the bodice should be dark and neutral, but not black. Now make your sleeves quite puffy, perhaps gathering them once at any point you choose, to give one line favored by Elizabeth. Under the skirt you can attach "sausages" of stuffed muslin to hold up the skirt as if by a farthingale. Fabric with quite a lot of body, such as brocade or damask upholstery fabric is needed for the skirt in order to capture the line. If you must construct a French farthingale, bear in mind that they are awkward and hard to proportion agreeably for the hand puppet. The best effect is obtained by attaching heavy buckram in an oval shape to the underglove even before the bodice is applied. Now, gather medium-weight fabric—silk or velvet— over the stiffening at the waistline. Cut it to just longer all the way around than the stiffening. By hand sew to the outer edge of the upper skirt a gathered lower skirt at least two-and-one-half times as full. You may need small beaded drapery weights around the bottom hem to make the skirt hang properly. An interesting effect and a pleasing line for the puppet is achieved by using an insert panel on either or both the bodice and skirt. The insert also helps to give the illusion of slimness to the bodice.

Ruffs were worn by both men and women during the Renaissance, and these can easily be made by gathering a folded piece of organdy or organza to the desired fullness. A more stylized ruff can be made by sewing satin ribbon in loops to a twill tape backing. For starched collars, simply heavily starch a piece of lace cut to the desired shape and glue or tack it to buckram. Use the lace on the side toward the head. You can cover the back of the collar with lace too, but the effort is likely to go unnoticed.

The Elizabethan man's costume takes a lot of selection and simplification

*Renaissance costume; abstracted line*

*Renaissance adaptation examples*

to make it suit a hand puppet. Using long capes can sometimes get you past the problem of tights and pumpkin hose. In any case, you will probably have to make at least some pumpkin hose, those short, puffy gentlemen's pants worn over tights, so let us see how they can be most believably adapted. Care must be taken that they be only slightly puffy, perhaps only an inch wider on cutting than the glove base, since it is very easy to make them look out of proportion. As to the puffings and slashings—the manner in which a fabric was cut at intervals to allow a showy under fabric to peek through—these effects are better used on sleeves than on pumpkin hose. Even then, the sleeve area is so small that only one or two slashes will show off well. If you can put your men in outer robes, fine, but there are bound to be young princes and pages for whom nothing will work but to concentrate attention on the upper body, choosing a material for the pumpkin hose that harmonizes with the jacket but is more subdued. It will help vary the stage picture and aid your poor men in pumpkin hose if the latter are companioned onstage by robed figures as often as possible.

Since by now you have probably got the idea of how to select from the line, colors, and details of a period, there is no need to take you through

*Mr. Punch*

the Restoration and Commonwealth and further, toward the present day in costume. Let us end our discussion with what is probably one of the most glorious adaptations of the dress of the day to the medium of the puppet: the incorrigible, indomitable Mr. Punch. With his peasecod doublet, rakish ruff, and pointed hat that nearly reaches his crooked nose, he epitomizes the Renaissance in his dress. His humped back is his own, carried through history from the *commedia dell'arte*. Himself he is, indeed. And what a startling example of purity of line, appropriateness of color, and embellishment of texture!

# 8

## Makeup for the Puppet

Very much a case of which came first, the chicken or the egg, costume design and makeup for the puppet are inseparable. It is an absolute must that they complement each other and that the design appear as a whole when the puppet is finished. It is impossible to tell you which to design first. The best advice that can be given you is to bear costume in mind while working on makeup, and vice versa. You will then be able to create a puppet in which the color, line, and texture of both costume and makeup augment and echo each other.

By "makeup" we do not, of course, mean greasepaint or any other cosmetic, but rather the coloring of the entire face: whatever may be applied to a cloth head in the way of features, or the application of the paint itself to a painted puppet. The relationship between costume and makeup is much easier to see in the case of a cloth puppet. For example, a woolly dog body is going to demand a woolly dog head and face to go with it. A felt head, which has appliquéd features, may have a piece of felt cut in the shape of "eye shadow," and if its color clashes with that of the puppet's costume, the disharmony will be immediately obvious.

Just as you did in making your puppet head and in designing its costume, in painting or otherwise decorating the face, you must bear in mind the totality of the design, being careful that all elements are related, for the whole is indeed equal to the sum of its parts. Sometimes when you attach head and body, you will find that either the costume or the face appears too complicated; one seems to overwhelm the other. Remembering that you wish to draw attention to the face, simplify your costume and remove any details that seem "too much." Look at the head. Is it too "busy"? You may wish to remove those furry eyebrows and just leave the beard. Some of the best makeup consists not in adding, but in taking away extraneous detail. Perhaps your puppet doesn't need a mouth. Look at it from a distance. Would that woolly dog carry best to the last row of your audience if there were a line defining his eyes or if he simply had round jet-black buttons the same shape as his very round self? You are in the final stages of completing your puppet; stop viewing it as a bunch of parts and search for the total effect.

Many of the principles of stage makeup can be applied to the finishing of a puppet face. If you learn these principles, you will be able to use them directly for your painted heads and adapt them, extracting what tips help you, to almost any type of puppet head you may create. In all cases you are deciding what to add in finishing the face. Through stage makeup techniques you can learn both how to heighten the effect of the molding of your head and how to more or less modify the contours to bring back details that may have been lost in casting or sewing. This is known in stage parlance as the process of "corrective makeup."

In order to avoid painting and repainting a head or painting numbers of them in order to learn a few techniques, two easier paths are open to you. One of them is your own face. If you have or can borrow stage makeup, use your own face for practice; if you don't have access to stage makeup, don't buy it, since it is costly, but you may want to purchase some inexpensive makeup from the ten-cent store. If this is your choice, purchase one very light and one very dark "base" or flesh-colored undercoat, a palette of eye-shadows in cream form and in the widest array of colors you can find, and a brown eyebrow pencil, plus one clear red "pot" of cream rouge, and some cold cream and Kleenex to remove it all. If you don't feel like fooling with makeup or going to the expense of purchasing any, you can learn quite a bit with some paint, preferably acrylics because they mix best, and a series of hard-boiled or blown eggs. What we are going to do is experiment to see how we can change the contours of the face with the application of color and the judicious use of light and shadow. The egg is a special challenge, but you will see that you can make it appear to change shape and even make a line-drawn nose seem to stand out when viewed from the front.

If you are using stage or other makeup, cover your entire face with your light-colored base, eyebrows and lips too, and sit in front of a mirror. If you are using an egg, block in eyes, nose and mouth in a light brown or lavender outline, using only the most necessary lines to indicate features. From now on, procedure with the egg or your face is pretty much the same, except that in between demonstrations you will clean your face with cold cream, whereas with the eggs you go on to the next one, finding yourself ready at the end to prepare a giant salad, provided your paints aren't toxic! If using paint, just use a color that corresponds to the makeup indicated below.

Take your darker-colored base and fill in the areas at the sides of the nose, leaving a narrow strip right along the entire bridge of the nose in a triangular pattern. Now vary this pattern by making the strip on the bridge of the nose wavy. Do you see that in the first instance you have narrowed the nose, and in the second you have made it appear crooked? Now, for a more pronounced effect, take your dark base or brown shadow and fill in the area below the cheekbones, again in a triangular pattern. Do you see how you have narrowed the face, making the cheeks appear hollow? Change the shape of the chin by applying dark base or shadow under the jawline. You can make it appear pointed or give the effect of jowls. You have done all this without using a line at all, only shadow in the form of a deeper flesh color.

Don't clean your face yet or go on to the next egg. Let's find out about the effects of highlight on the contour of the face. Mix some yellow or white with your light base tint. Apply it to the bridge of the nose next to your shadow. Lightly place a smear of highlight on the top of the cheek-bone and along the line of the jaw, above your shadowed area. Do you see how the highlight applied to the *high* side of the shadowed areas accentuates the original effect? Remember, dark colors recede; light colors come forward. Whatever you wish to indent or render smaller in a face, color darker; lighten whatever you wish to enlarge or bring forward or make higher.

Try the same technique on the eyes. Shadow above and below the eye, in an oval shape or following the contours of your face. Apply highlight very slightly just below the dark circles and below the eyebrow. Shadow in at the temples near the eyes. You now have the basis of an old-age makeup and are ready to accentuate your effects with line.

Never, never use black liner. For that matter, try to throw black out of your palette entirely. Black will deaden a face; it is not only too sharp, it is flat and uninteresting. When you have a clean face, go wherever there is a crowd of people. Start really looking at lines and shadows in their faces. Notice how many colors really compose shadows and how wrinkles are never, never black. For now, a brown liner will do. (Once in a great while a villain may need black for eyebrows or moustache, but keep it away from facial lines.) Make a brown line on the low side of a shadow you wish to accentuate. Next to it on the high side, apply with a brush a bright, light color. Follow the contours you have blocked in in shadow. You will follow the same procedure when you are painting a puppet head, first blocking in shadow, then highlight, then lining the contours that you have now finalized by shadowing what you previously molded. Take a little rouge and smudge it wherever you want the cheek accented. Rouge applied toward the nose will narrow the face; applied outward and brought down near the ears, it will widen it. Apply thin lines vertically to the lips over *very* slightly darkened rouge.

The quality of lines painted is very important, not only how dark they are, but whether they are broken or smudged, or crisp and clean. In general, the broken line, occasionally smudged, is more realistic. Bright, clean lines will give an effect like that sometimes produced in animated cartoons. Try both, so that you can realize the difference in effect. Which kind of lines you use will be determined by your painting style and also by the style of your overall designs. You may want to use different techniques at different times, but do remain consistent within any given production.

Clean your face or start with a new egg, and repeat the shadowing process on as many areas as you wish, this time trying for new contours. If you made your face thin before, make it fat now, and so on. This time pay attention to the color of your shadow. Don't use brown; try lavender or green. Any cool color or gray mixed of complements can be used for shadowing. When you are working on a puppet head, one of the easiest ways to tie the face and costume together is to echo the colors of the costumes in the shadows of the face. You can then follow through by using a line in the darkened portion of your shadow. By using colors in shadow and line the face becomes markedly more interesting.

If you will look at the paintings of the French Impressionists you will find glorious use of color in shadow. If you can get to a museum, go; otherwise, check out of the library the best print you can. Look at the painting from a distance and enjoy its overall effect. Now, look up close and see how the artist has broken down the colors into components, often using many colors to express one mass. The works of Monet afford especially beautiful and easily "readable" examples. If you look at the work of the mature Seurat, you will find a technique you can adapt with much profit to the painting of puppet faces. Called "pointillism," this technique involves the painting of many tiny dots of color within what appears from a distance to be an opaque area of a solid color or colors. In scene design and makeup we call this technique of painting with many dots or color "stippling," and it is extremely useful in enlivening the rouged or shadowed areas, as well as in the painting of a puppet's eyes. Experiment with it.

Obviously, you cannot paint out your own eyes, so if you are using makeup, turn for a moment to paper or an egg. Outline the eye area slightly. Now fill in the round or oval shape with stippled color. Try blue and green or brown and red. Shade the area toward a deeper hue near the center. (If you make the darker area near either corner of the eye, be sure that you do the same to both eyes, or your puppet will look cross-eyed or as though his eyes don't focus.) As a matter of personal bias the author avoids painting in irises at all costs; eyeball puppets stare and look pop-eyed. The puppet is not a doll, and his expression will be more likely to appear to change in light if he does not have eyes statically focused by a fixed retina of paint. Sometimes an accent dot of white or light blue or yellow at the outer sides of the eye will "awaken" the eyes, if you are afraid they will look blind or if they cover an unusually large and/or flat area. Placing a red dot in the inner corner of the eye is a holdover from old-fashioned stage makeup and was thought to make the eyes carry better. It is doubtful if it makes any real difference.

Proceeding to the general treatment of the eye in stage makeup, let us return you to your mirror with a clean face or back to your supply of eggs. Again, cover your face with light base or draw in the basic lines of features on an egg. You have learned how to correct the contour of a face, how to change it, and how to produce the effect of age; but what of "straight" makeup for the many juveniles and young persons you will create among your puppets? As you discover your style, you will make up your own rules within a few basic guidelines.

Usually you will need no shadows, unless contour needs correcting, and then care must be taken to keep the shadow light, probably a deeper tone of the flesh tint. You will probably want to shadow above the eyes, since color there makes the eyes carry farther. The effect is more pleasing if the shape of the shadow follows the contour of the eye and if its color is analogous to the eye color. Since the shadow should also relate to the costume colors, you may look to the costume to determine the color of the eye, unless you have a character reason for using a certain eye color, and then you must bring the costume into harmony. It is extremely hard to make very light-colored eyes appear natural. Unless you want a "made-up" look for your puppet, you will shade the shadow off gradually, blending it into the skin color. Try it on yourself.

Now, line around the eye, heavier above than below and keeping this line slender and unbroken. Sometimes a light line next to this liner on the side away from the eye can give the illusion of extraordinary brightness. The only other line you will need will be the eyebrows, and they should be feathered, that is, composed of many lines rather than one harsh, crisp line. In making up your own face experiment with brow shapes, notice how different you or your egg looks if the brows almost meet over the nose or if the brows are widely spaced and arched.

The last detail you will need for straight makeup will be rouge. It should be blended outward from the point on the cheek that you wish to make most prominent and faded off until its ending is indiscernible. Experiment with the Coppelia effect of round red circles, and you will determine never to use them unless that specific effect is called for. (The same can be said for "doll" eyelashes painted on.) Rouge can be painted on chin and forehead very lightly for a look and glow of health and youth.

In transferring to the puppet what you have learned with makeup or painting on an egg, you will need to add to your repertoire a very few painting techniques and a knowledge of the properties of the paint itself. Acrylics are highly recommended, principally because they produce a depth of color and have a dull finish. Never use oil color; it will never dry completely. Tempera can be used if it is coated after drying with a dull varnish; otherwise it will rub off. Do *not* use shellac. It will shine, and shiny puppet heads are distracting and doll-like. Acrylics dry very fast, so you must learn to work rather quickly. A piece of aluminum foil serves nicely as a palette for mixing and is inexpensive enough to be disposed of, eliminating cleanup. Do clean brushes thoroughly and immediately after use. Acrylics are mixed with water and colors mix with each other as we discussed in the previous chapter.

You will need tubes of red, blue, and yellow, *and* green, purple, and burnt sienna as basics. Try to stay within a color family (such as cadmium, or phthalocyanine), but the difference is never as critical as on paper or canvas; they just mix to a more chromatically true tint. Orange mixes easily, purple will almost never be true if mixed of blue and red. Green is equally unpredictable. You will need a large tube of titanium white.

You will find a good half-inch water-color brush with tapered end a fine investment. It will enable you to get a smooth finish impossible with cheap brushes that streak your paint and deposit hairs over your puppet. Two fine water-color brushes are plenty for lining, and one small oil-painting brush comes in very handy for stippling and broken lines. Acrylics do not wash out, so be advised to wear old clothes or a smock.

Now that you are using paint and don't have a previously prepared base, you will have to learn to mix flesh tones. Caucasian skin is a mix of yellow, red, and white in an infinite variation of proportions. The color for your puppet with its age, stage of health, and character is best reached by your own experiment. Do go easy on the red, since one of the commonest faults is that of erring toward a deeply pink flesh. If it looked right when you mixed it but doesn't look right on the head, repaint it; no amount of shadow is going to change the basic color. Do mix enough paint at the start; flesh tints are very hard to duplicate exactly. Bear in mind that you will have to color the whole head; you don't want a white scalp peeping through the wig. Even when you know you will employ a hat that will cover most of the scalp, it is advisable to paint too far to be on the safe side. Don't forget the neck, both front and back; it will look very strange if it doesn't match the face.

Don't try to be too realistic, even when you are using flesh tints instead of lavender, blue, green, or fur. When in doubt use the most extreme basic color that fits your character. Skin for black puppets should never, ever be black; look at blacks around you and notice the rich variations in tones of browns. Burnt sienna with added red or blue will give you most of the tints you need. Do remember to shadow and highlight; just because a face is dark doesn't mean you can shirk on contour. Ocher can be very helpful for highlights.

Bear in mind, too, the historical period in which your production is set. During the Restoration very pale skin and pink-and-white complexions were in fashion along with the powdered wigs; but in ancient Egypt there lived a predominantly dark-skinned people, with practically every gradation of skin color imaginable included in the populace. Were American Indians really "redskins"? Even in exaggeration for character and effect you will want your puppets to be pleasing to representatives of the ethnic group they represent, not hurtful caricatures.

After you have mixed and applied the flesh tint all over the head, the only difficulty you are likely to have is in shading rouge and shadow. Thin your paint for blending, overbrushing with clear water if necessary. Be careful, though, that you don't thin through the base coat. With a little practice you will be able to catch the base coat at just the consistency you want in order to blend in rouge and shadow.

When you have finished, stand about ten feet back from your puppet and see if the features all "add up." By extending an eyebrow or the line of rouge or shadow you may be able to tie all the features together. The line of the eye should lead down the nose and naturally into the face. If your puppet appears to have features that are isolated and seem to be floating on the face, you need to go back and pull your design together with high-light and shadow. Usually, unless you have not molded contour into the face or have lost a great deal in casting, your painted face will add up with very little adjusting. When it is dry, hold its body up to it and then make any changes in the painting that seem necessary. Do *not* attach to the body before the head is thoroughly dry, and never before you paint! If there is to be a wig, glue it in place *after* painting and *before* attaching the head to the body.

Though wigs have been mentioned along with costume design, nothing has been said yet about beards. If you have ever seen a man before and after the growth of a beard, you know how much that trim goatee or scraggly thatch can do to alter the appearance, the character, and even the contour of the face. A good beard, well designed for the puppet head it will adorn, can do as much. As with wigging, you will want to let paint dry thoroughly before attaching a beard. In the meantime you can design a beard that carries out the lines of the features you have molded and painted (pointy? squared off? wispy?), and you can choose the medium out of which to construct it that will best carry out your ideas. A beard need not necessarily be made from the same yarn or fur or crepe hair as the head hair, but it should blend in. If you use fur, direct the hairs downward and cut a piece generally the shape of the beard. Fur is best cut from the back with a razor blade, so as not to catch hairs in the cutting and leave bare pelt. After you have the general shape, you can slit darts in and shape it to the face, afterward gluing it into place.

Beards of crepe hair or yarn are best applied painstakingly, strand by small strand, building them up from the lowest point on the neck or chin to the top, most visible layer. Trimming comes last, or next to last. You may want to spray a long, finished beard with Varathane to give it body (shielding the face during spraying). A good trick to make a short beard point is to apply several thin coats of colorless nail polish, shaping between coats. White glue can be used, but its weight will pull the beard downward. Stubble at the end of beards can be painted on or filled in with mere shavings of the hair material and white glue.

Occasionally, you may want to use bits of yarn or crepe hair for eyebrows. The trick is to apply it sparingly, judging the effect as you go along. Fur can also be used. The fun comes in that you are adding a new texture to the face and, along with texture, interest. Just don't overdo it and drown out the good effects of a fine paint job.

It takes a little time, as with your other skills, to learn to finish a face boldly enough to carry from your stage to the last row of your audience, so be patient with yourself. You do not want garish heads, but in the beginning it is usually better to err on the side of boldness. If your faces seem to be washing out at a distance, go over them and see where you can make contrasts greater and where, above all, you can simplify. Will you never stop hearing that word? Simplify, simplify . . . you will hear it endlessly, as long as you work with the puppet, even as you start, soon, to design your stage.

# 9
## The Stage Itself

It can now safely be presumed that you are ready to consider mounting a real production in puppet theatre; if you have followed the work outlined thus far, you are not only ready but champing at the bit to get started! It is time for you to take the time and money to construct (or have constructed) your own puppet stage. You have chosen whether you wish to work overhead or behind a scrim, with other puppeteers or alone, and you have now discovered the idiosyncrasies of your style that will affect the design of your stage.

Since your stage must be as individual as you are, it is impossible to tell you how to construct the perfect stage for *you*. Indeed, puppeteers are like primitive man with their stages, moving from cave to hut to house of stone, seldom quite satisfied with their "puppet house," forever modifying it or building a new one to suit new needs as they grow in their work. You may not be able to avoid rebuilding entirely, but you can make your stage a much more permanent acquisition if you consider both your own style of performance and the functions that your stage must perform.

If you are going to travel at all with your stage, you will want it to be both lightweight and portable, and speed in setting up and striking is of considerable advantage. Not only the number of puppeteers to be involved but where you will perform will make a difference in the requirements of your stage. Indoors, a light framework of wood or aluminum covered by drapery usually solves the problem best; but for use in parks, successful stages have been created in the backs or sides of vans. Drapery will blow in the wind, perhaps taking your whole stage with it, so you may have to resort to a permanent structure of marine ply for a large stage out of doors. (Immediately you would have a giant acoustical problem, but this has sometimes been solved by cutting a panel near the puppeteers' microphones and covering it with gauze painted to blend with the rest of the stage. Well-placed speakers help to solve the problems of voices that seem to dissipate to nothing in the open air or of voices that come from a source too distant from the puppets.)

There are all kinds of unusual staging requirements, and puppeteers continue to come up with ingenious solutions. Puppet stages have been created on the backs of wheelchairs or are even worn by the puppeteer, in the manner of Japanese street puppet stages. Stages continue to be fashioned of old refrigerator cartons, and at the opposite extreme of complexity and sophistication there are the beautiful permanent state theatres in Poland and Russia with seemingly every known resource provided the puppeteer-producer. Despite their differences, however, all of these stages solve the basic demands of a puppet stage. They all adapt to the work to be presented and to the puppeteers who will play in them. All, in different ways, provide masking, hiding from the audience whatever would shatter the illusion the puppets create. All provide ways to mount scenery and lighting instruments. All provide easy access to puppets and props. (One thinks immediately of the inimitable Jean-Paul Hubert of France, who not only wears his stage but hangs his puppets and his props in unbelievable profusion about his waist.)

All puppet stages, even the most open, must provide a "frame" for the puppets in pleasing proportion to their size. Providing some sort of frame is a use of focus in its most elementary form; if the area is not defined, the viewer's eye will wander. You, too, must deal with masking, mounting of sets and lights, the accessibility of puppets and props, and provision of a frame for puppet action. One of the best ways to set about designing your own stage is to consider your own requirements while studying a proven example of traditional staging. You can then adapt what you need from a plan demonstrated to be workable. Two plans are given here. They are by no means meant to be the answer to every beginning puppeteer's prayer, but they are highly workable examples which you can either copy and construct, or modify to suit your needs, style, budget, and performance site.

Let us suppose, first, that you are going to construct a scrim stage. If you look at the plan, you will notice that the overall height is seven and one half feet. Since most ceilings are eight feet or more, you can fit this stage into most homes without difficulty and into almost any school room or comparable facility. The proscenium opening, or the actual stage area, the "frame" within which the puppets play, is forty inches by twenty-four and one half inches, large enough to give one operator freedom to move two puppets with considerable variety, but small enough not to make a one-person show look "lost in space." In the rare instance of a two-person scrim stage, the design given could be widened across the stage by a foot without changing its pleasing proportions or weakening its structural strength. As with the overhead stage pictured, each part of this scrim stage contributes not only functionally to the needs of the puppeteer but also to the strength of the stage. There are no unnecessary parts, and this fact is important, since most puppet stages must be portable.

Our scrim stage was designed to be constructed of three-quarter-inch tubular and right-angled aluminum, but it could also be built of wood. The aluminum requires riveting, but it is both strong and light. Just be careful that you do not use the wide, soft tubing that dents easily; a stage made out of this material is a constant nightmare. If any part of it is dented, the whole structure is thrown out of kilter, and you will be constantly adjusting it.

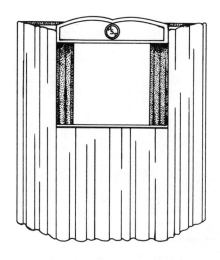

*Scrim stage, front view*

Note that the playboard, prop shelf, and proscenium top are made of one-quarter-inch plywood. The playboard has a quarter-round molding strip on the audience side to prevent props from dropping into the audience. The triangular shape of the playboard and prop shelf at the ends determines the angle of the stage sides and supplies bracing. The proscenium top is decorative, but it also allows a place to mount a traverse

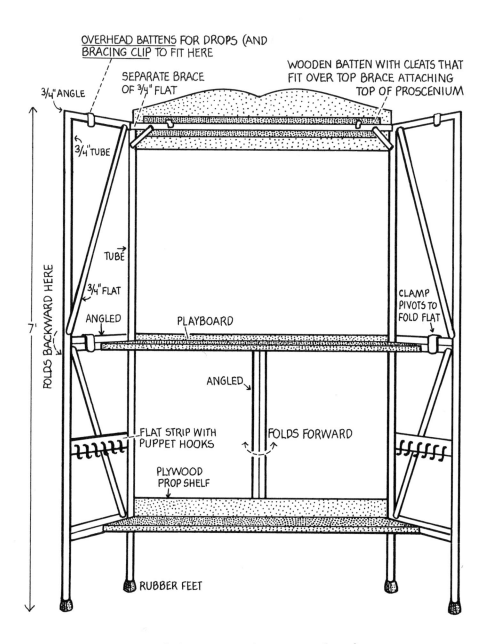

*Scrim stage seen from rear, undraped*

rod which will hold the Act Curtain. At first inspection, this stage appears to be a threefold screen, but do not underestimate the importance of the overhead battens. These battens, which are made of two- by two-inch hardwood, have a metal corner that overlaps the sides of the stage. Always use the farthest backstage batten even if you don't need to put a drop on it, since it establishes the stability of your stage. Threefold stages without some means of bracing are just too rickety for any practical use. The scrim stage in particular, since it is smaller and appropriate to small audiences, is likely to be used on a floor level with the audience, and you do *not* want it to fall over on little Johnny or Mary when they pull on it. It is possible to brace the scrim stage at floor level and then to sandbag that brace, if you load the front with heavy lighting instruments, but you will then have to be on the watch yourself not to trip over the brace. Any bracing at waist level or so will add to the stability of the stage, but it will be awkward for you to have to duck under it to get in and out of the playing area. It is better just to figure that this stage simply will not accommodate elaborate lighting.

Hooks for the puppets are at the sides of the stage because of the limited size of this stage. In playing, this arrangement is quite practical, because your props are readily visible (and grabbable) in front of you, and your puppets are within convenient reach, hung with face towards you on the side of the hand that will use them. Working with two operators, each has his puppets hung on "his" side of the stage. If you work with two people, there is not room in this stage for anyone else to help glove you into your puppets, so plan on doing it yourself.

If this stage is constructed in wood, the folding frame can be hooked together with screen-door hooks when dismantled. The aluminum frame can be tied securely and easily moved. The long pieces all fit together into the prop shelf piece and can be wrapped in canvas and tied for short and simple moves. If you plan to tour with such a stage, then two special boxes should be constructed, one to hold the folding frame and the other for the long pieces. You will still have a light, portable one-person or two-person unit.

One disadvantage of the little scrim stage is that there is no way for the Act Curtain to pull all the way off stage, so the playing area is cut down by folds of drapery, even if matte jersey or some such softly draping fabric is used. You can do without the Act Curtain (that curtain that is seen by the audience before and after your show and sometimes at the close of scenes), but it does have several valuable functions: it is something decorative for the audience to look at before the show, opening it provides a surprise when your backdrop is revealed, closing it between scenes gives you a chance to change scenery, and it signals that the show is over when you close it at the end of your performance. So consider carefully before you do without it.

It is possible to extend the legs of the scrim stage by inserting the leg pipes into just slightly larger tubing and bolting them together through drilled holes. If you do this, you will have an overhead playing area for yourself or, with the extended playboard, for two people. If this area is not sufficient for you, do not try to extend the width of this design. Your overhead battens will begin to sag in the middle. Better to go into building the more complicated overhead stage. Even if you decide to work on moving stools or on your knees (yes, some people really like to play whole shows this way), it will be easier in the long run to adapt the Morrison overhead design that follows than to try to adapt the simple scrim stage.

Our overhead stage stands nine and one half feet high, so that one has always to check the height of the hall before moving in to set up. It has the advantage that if the ceiling is not high enough, the bottom half can be used alone, with a backdrop on poles inserted. When there is no proscenium arch or top, no lights can be hung above, unless they are provided by the auditorium in which you are playing and focused for you. One can, of course, hang lights on trees at the sides of the stage in view of the audience, and methods for doing this will be discussed along with other aspects of lighting. Some puppeteers like to work with this open kind of stage all the time, feeling that the openness suits their style. It does give a freedom of movement, but you can have only one backdrop and no Act Curtain. The half- and fully-open stage is, however, eminently suited for television work, when you must use studio lights, and it would be impossible to slot them into a closed proscenium. The lower half of the Morrison stage can be set up very quickly (in about twenty minutes, fully dressed with drapery and puppets hung and ready to go), which is also an advantage for television, when everything is moving on a time clock and hourly union wages. They will love you better if you get in and out fast and efficiently. It is worth noting that when you march into a television studio, however small and local, you are likely to be told that the stage hands must set up your stage for you because of union regulations. One advantage of the Morrison design is that it looks so puzzling until you understand it (and then it is very simple), that most union stage hands will take one look at it and be happy to have you assemble it yourself, and then you will know that it will all be assembled properly with nothing lost.

Before you opt for the totally open stage, take a good look at our fully

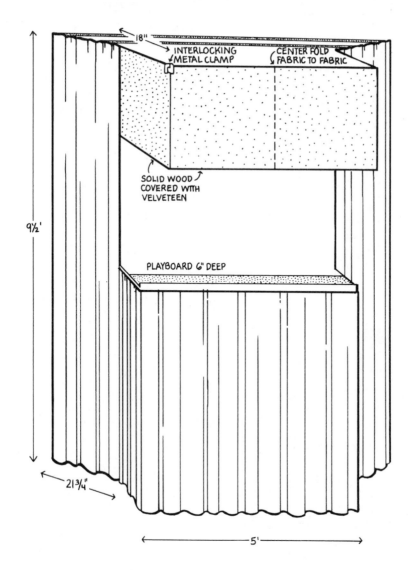

18"

INTERLOCKING
METAL CLAMP

CENTER FOLD
FABRIC TO FABRIC

SOLID WOOD
COVERED WITH
VELVETEEN

9½'

PLAYBOARD 6" DEEP

21¾"

5'

*Morrison overhead stage from front*

assembled overhead stage design. Though it gives the illusion of being a "little theatre," it actually is not as closed-in as you might first suspect. Because the playboard extends out in front of the Act Curtain, good sight lines are maintained at the sides, and the puppets have a lot of depth available for their action. Because the lights are hung inside the proscenium top primarily on a front batten, it is possible to give the illusion of a quite open area by darkening the house as much as possible during performance. It is important that your stage be draped in a pleasing color, but a lot of decoration on the stage front or proscenium top is not recommended, since

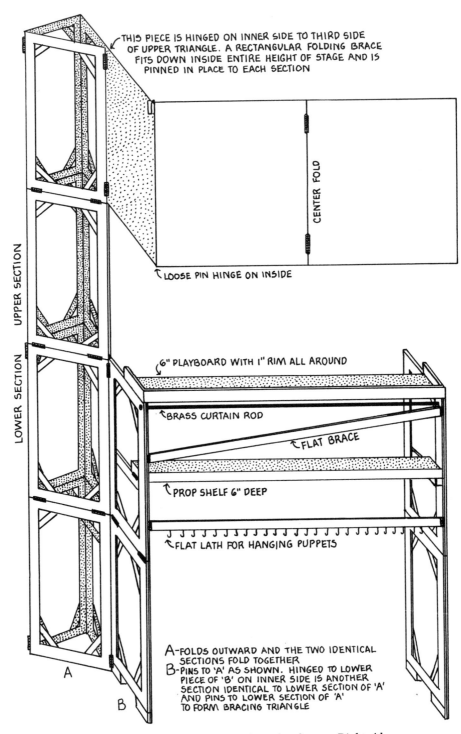

THIS PIECE IS HINGED ON INNER SIDE TO THIRD SIDE OF UPPER TRIANGLE. A RECTANGULAR FOLDING BRACE FITS DOWN INSIDE ENTIRE HEIGHT OF STAGE AND IS PINNED IN PLACE TO EACH SECTION

CENTER FOLD

LOOSE PIN HINGE ON INSIDE

UPPER SECTION

LOWER SECTION

6" PLAYBOARD WITH 1" RIM ALL AROUND

BRASS CURTAIN ROD

FLAT BRACE

PROP SHELF 6" DEEP

FLAT LATH FOR HANGING PUPPETS

A-FOLDS OUTWARD AND THE TWO IDENTICAL SECTIONS FOLD TOGETHER
B-PINS TO 'A' AS SHOWN. HINGED TO LOWER PIECE OF 'B' ON INNER SIDE IS ANOTHER SECTION IDENTICAL TO LOWER SECTION OF 'A' AND PINS TO LOWER SECTION OF 'A' TO FORM BRACING TRIANGLE

A

B

*Fractional front view of overhead stage. Right side is identical to left and omitted for simplicity.*

if there is any light on it at all during performance, it is likely to compete with the puppets for your audience's attention.

Velvet, velveteen or waleless corduroy are recommended for draping your stage and covering the proscenium top, though any fabric that resists wrinkles, is lightproof, and drapes well can be used. Remember when you are seaming the curtains to check, if your fabric has nap, that you have it all going the same way, preferably down (smooth to the touch when you stroke it downward). The extreme front curtain is attached by threading a brass rod through three-quarter-inch casing. The sides of the front curtain and long side curtains are attached by Velcro, one side sewn to the curtain, the other glued to the stage itself. The strictness of fire regulations varies according to location, but it is highly recommended that you always fireproof drapery, especially when it is of any substantial size, of highly flammable fabric, or anywhere near your lights. If you can get the fabric you want from a theatrical fabric house, it is worth paying a little more to have it fireproofed by them. Allow for a lot of shrinkage, and take their advice as to how much. It can be up to six inches per yard. Fireproofing somewhat alters the color of a fabric and can affect its wrinkle-shedding qualities. A theatrical fabric house knows which fabrics work well and which don't. You can, however, call your local fire department to find out your nearest fireproofing facility (often a dry cleaner). Sometimes, you can purchase the dry compound yourself and take it to a cleaner and have him spray it for you. You can spray it or dip it yourself, but you will need a place to hang it to full length and must be sure it is thoroughly saturated. In any case, keep your "calendar number," the number of the fireproofing compound. Carry it with you whenever you perform. You can then produce it immediately as proof that your drapery is fireproof if you are questioned by a local fire marshal. It is no fun to lack proof and have him light a match to find out. If you are building your stage of wood, it is recommended that you paint it with a fireproof black paint and attach the label to the prop shelf.

If you must do your flameproofing yourself, an acceptable compound can be made of one pound of sal ammoniac, one pound of borax, and three quarts of water. You can brush or spray it on, but you should dampen the fabric first. Anything sheer should be dipped. It is a messy job and the mixture is highly corrosive to brushes, spray cans, and such, so wear gloves and wash all utensils thoroughly and immediately in cold water.

Our overhead stage playing area is approximately thirty-nine inches high and five feet wide. The proportions are pleasing, and the area is adaptable to many frame sizes and types of puppets, up to a twenty-four-inch rod puppet (though several of these would appear crowded and in need of a larger home). For small puppets it is possible to bring the Act Curtain in at the sides and lower the proscenium by attaching a "teaser" or short drape to an overhead rod. You can also hang backdrops simultaneously. Up to five puppeteers can work comfortably within this stage, provided they are good at staying out of each other's way.

The stage collapses into three sets of pieces, lower stage, upper proscenium, and a unit composed of playboard, rods, and other long pieces. Mr. Morrison designed special cases for these three sets of pieces. They are made of marine ply and lined with carpet pieces so that the sections all fit snugly. The boxes are strengthened with metal cornerpieces and covered with fabric painted with white glue. They are extremely sturdy and portable, really capable of being shipped anywhere.

Note that the puppet hooks hang across the front on a special batten. There are two hooks at the side, but with several operators it is impossible to hang puppets *all* at the side and have them quickly accessible. The hook batten is high enough above the prop shelf that a twenty-inch puppet hanging upside down and facing the operator still allows room for access to the props.

Note, too, that the back braces are high enough to allow reasonable comfort in entering and exiting from the playing area. We do say reasonable comfort, for as noted before, no stage can be designed for the height and comfort of every puppeteer that may ever work in it. Five feet from the floor was chosen as a height for the playboard, since it is one of average comfort. If the playboard is raised much higher to accommodate, say, a six-foot puppeteer, the sight lines may not be agreeable for the audience. Just remember that the higher you raise the playboard, the farther back you are going to have to seat your audience, and since you may be playing on a raised stage, this is, indeed, a factor to take into consideration. Even with a five-foot elevation for your playboard you may find that in some halls or theatres you will have to rope off and not use the first couple of rows of seats.

There is absolutely no way that you can be protected from the evils of balcony sight lines except to make an agreement with the theatre not to use the balcony. It is some help to move your puppet stage upstage in the theatre, but even then and with clever lighting, you can usually see the operators' heads from the balcony, and it is distracting in the extreme. Black scarves or skullcaps help some.

Before making any alteration of the overhead stage here given, it is suggested that you contact the designer.[1] Since each part serves as a brace

---

[1] Mr. Al H. Morrison, Box 75, Old Chelsea Station, New York, New York 10011.

for the entire structure, no part should be omitted and stability assumed. The dimensions and placement of parts are strategic. One demand that this stage places upon the owner is that it be assembled and disassembled in the exact order that the parts are numbered. Departing from the planned system can cause the stage not to fit together properly when assembled or make a large portion to fall upon one's head while disassembling.

The front of the proscenium top is so calculated that it will counterbalance the weight of four baby spotlights and two PAR floodlights in baskets at the side top, UL and UR. Weight should be added with care, being careful not to put undue stress on the inner corner hinges of the upper proscenium. If you are sure the stress can be borne by the top pieces, but are afraid of too much forward weight, consider that the depth of the stage and the back braces help to offset the front weight. If you are still concerned, sandbag the inner side triangles at the floor.

This stage is really very stable, but because of the number of cables necessary to run lights and sound it is inadvisable to invite an audience of more than five backstage after a performance. This rule of protection is true of almost any stage. Unless it is bolted to the floor, several small bodies *can* pull it over. And people do manage to trip on cable on the floor (you can alleviate this problem somewhat by taping cable down). It is usually a good idea, even when you have checked out your equipment and are sure that it is safe, to consult a reliable insurance agent. Find out where you are liable. Find out if a hall you are playing in covers you in case of accident *before* it happens. Usually a hall will be covered only for its own equipment (for instance, a theatre seat falls in). All of this may sound paranoid, but as in the case of fireproofing, it is far better to be safe than very, very sorry.

Don't let this note of warning scare you away from building a stage. If you build the overhead stage as pictured here or alter it with the help of the designer or some other highly skilled craftsman, you will have a flexible, portable, durable unit. The only disadvantage to the design is the time it takes to erect it, and this is cut considerably by familiarity with the assembly. Under normal working conditions with puppeteers familiar with the job, two people can erect this stage in forty-five minutes. Always, however, allow extra time for the jack that won't fit the house sound system, or the forgotten cable to be replaced, or whatever emergency can sometimes arise. You don't want to be putting up the stage as your audience enters the auditorium.

There are so many possibilities for stage construction, even when we limit ourselves simply to the hand puppet. You may well think of one that hasn't even been tried yet. But go ahead and build or find someone to build for you, because your puppets can't perform, nor can the set be put in place and lit, until the stage itself is done. Whatever you build, do keep it simple (that word again), practical, and adjusted to your needs and those of your puppets. If you choose one day to direct a show in which the operators are sometimes seen and sometimes behind masking, you will certainly need to create a stage that meets the needs of that production. We do not mean to limit you in the manner of staging or to stunt your creativity in designing the type of "puppet house" that best suits you. Two highly workable plans are given which incorporate portability, aesthetic demands, and safety. The variations are infinite; build what suits you and your style, bearing in mind that you may discover a new style only after working for some time in one of these more conventional stages.

Very often staging that appears "new" is really an adaptation of very old workable methods. One thinks of the brilliant staging of a Pushkin tale by Sergei Obraztsov at the State Central Theatre in Moscow, in which a series of "stages" appears upon the "live" stage, the entire area of which frames the production. Live actors are seen manipulating the puppets; at other times ingenious forms of masking are used, and sometimes the actors actually become the puppet stage. In one scene two young men hold a puppet proscenium frame at either of its sides. Three women stand behind the frame, operating the puppets; their skirts, seen below the playboard, are all of matching color and form the lower portion of the "stage." In another scene the women lift their aprons to form waves, a "stage" upon which sails a puppet boat. Later a high wall conveniently masks a puppeteer, and a puppet king appears above it. He talks to a swan whose female operator is in full view of the audience and who moves with such grace that she and her puppet appear one. Ingenious, yes, and apparently very new, but really a beautiful adaptation of familiar staging and satisfying all those basic requirements met by an "old-fashioned" puppet stage. In every scene, though the entire stage is used, the puppets are in some way "framed." Here lighting helps tremendously, as do elements of the set design, and as we move into greater areas of complexity in staging, a greater demand is placed upon our knowledge of both lighting and scene design. Even in the simplest production, they will be important, and since your familiarity with these tools and your decision concerning the complexity you will need to provide for in both areas will affect the type of stage you build, it is time to turn to a study of these important elements of the mise-en-scène.

# 10
## Scene Design

Though many pantomimes, revue numbers, and short playlets can be most effectively staged in front of black or neutral curtains, there are many other productions that are greatly enhanced by an environment provided by stage scenery. If you wish simply to define a "limbo" in which your puppets set the mood and place, then blacks are your best scenic answer. They are unobtrusive, and your puppets will stand out well against them. If, however, your puppets are enacting a story which would be helped along if the audience knew locale, mood, and perhaps even something about the characters the minute the curtain opened, then you will want to turn to partial or full setting. Because the puppets must always be the center of interest for the audience, you must choose the elements of your setting carefully, bringing to your design what you have learned in directing about the composition of the stage picture and in costume about your ability to choose and relate line, color, and texture. Together, the costumed puppet, lighting, and setting form the total stage picture. Though we must isolate the setting here to study the elements of its design, it should never be thought of as complete in itself, a picture into which the puppets will later be placed. A successful setting will remain in the background, reinforcing the action of the characters in a style consistent with the design of the puppets and in keeping with the overall stylistic concept for the production.

Go back to your initial analysis of your script. Is it bright and farcical, having called for gay color and crisp line in your costumes? Would a stylized setting, perhaps gay poles wound with ribbons arranged against a neutral drop, establish the right mood? It is difficult for an audience not to get the idea that the piece will be a comedy if the first thing it sees is bright colors, exaggerated whimsical shapes, festoons, and flippant curlicues. Or is it necessary to give the audience a knowledge of the place in which the drama is enacted? Seldom will you want to be totally realistic, but you may wish to suggest a locale by choosing certain lifelike elements and forms immediately recognizable to the audience. The tale of "The Three Wishes," for instance, would pull the audience into its story sooner if the poverty of the peasant house were established right away in the setting. In an interior, especially, one can show something about the characters through the detail that is chosen. How much better we know someone when we have been to his home! How realistic or stylized are the puppets to be used? Your answer will tell you how realistic your setting should be. Can you imagine how disturbing stylized puppets would be in a realistic set? It is extremely important when several talents are involved—perhaps one person building puppets, another the set, and yet another directing—to decide on the chosen style at the beginning. A good deal of cross-checking back and forth is recommended to be sure that the harmony of elements remains. Even if you are designing the entire production yourself, you must keep working for consistency in style.

Harmony and consistency of the elements of production do not, however, mean "sameness." A great deal of taste and judgment come into choosing just how much the puppets will echo the setting or vice versa. Too much sameness can be boring, too much contrast, jarring and distracting from the total effect. Can you imagine a setting composed of ominous pillars rising into a gloomy sky as a background for a comic sketch about Buddy the Purple Weasel? You cannot set up the audience visually for one thing, then deliver them the opposite. On the other hand, there are formal settings, composed of nonrealistic shapes that with a change of lighting adapt to almost any mood. Here, lighting and the style of the puppets establish the style of the drama. Sometimes, if the puppets are quite elaborate you will need the contrast of simple forms in the setting so that the whole effect isn't overly busy and lost in too much detail. If you have really established the style of your production in the building of your puppets, it should not be too difficult to figure out the style of setting that will best complement them. Once you have done this you are ready to start sketching. Yes, always make a sketch first. From it you can determine if your design is complementary in style and also to some degree if it is practical. It is far easier to alter a sketch than an unworkable setting built without due consideration for the needs of the puppets and the puppeteers.

Remember that puppets need space for their action. Furniture that looks fine in a sketch may in performance get in the way of the puppets. Try to leave the center acting area as uncluttered as possible. You must allow for entrances and exits. The traditional live theatre "box set" with three solid walls is just not practical for hand puppets. Be very certain to avoid projections on any part of the scenery that can get caught on a puppet. An actor can disentangle himself from a rosebush with only a little embarrassment; a puppet may very well remain "stuck," and have to suffer the indignity of having a puppeteer's hand appear to release him. Bear in mind, too, that the puppeteer's audience has different sight lines than the audience in live theatre. Don't design any part of scenery that will block the audience's view of the puppets from any angle. Last, but by no means least, make sure that planned set changes can really be made and be made quickly and quietly. Pulling a curtain aside should present no problem, but hanging a heavy set piece very well could. Remember the limited space as well as time in which changes have to be made. An example of a beautiful design that did not work, but looked great on paper, is afforded by some heavy cathedral doors that were designed to be hung as a set change between a cut-out wooden drop of pillars and arches in front and another rigid drop behind. If the doors had been hung alone, they would have been fine, but the designer forgot that there was only a four-inch gap through which to insert them and then somehow to secure them overhead. They were lovely, but they had to go.

If your set is to involve moving parts or anything but a simple curtain, make a model after you have made your sketches. You can make it in proportions of one-fourth inch to one foot or any scale that is easy for you to work with. Use three-ply bristol board and cut with an X-acto knife, matt knife, or razor blade. If you have a succession of set pieces, with a model you can readily see how they will hang in the limited space you have available to you. Arrive at a model that works before you even think of construction.

Building a working model will also help you to think in terms of plastic shapes and what you can do with set pieces, that is, masses. By plastic we refer, of course, to that which is three-dimensional, not plastic as a material. It is a temptation for the puppeteer, with his limited space, to stick to just the painted drop for scenery. While there is much, as we shall soon explore, that can be done with line, shading, and color to give an illusion of depth to a painted backdrop, the effect is usually much more exciting if a painted drop is used in combination with some three-dimensional set pieces. These may be furniture, trees, abstract shapes, or even hand props; they all contribute toward building an environment rather than a flat little picture. Unfortunately, the puppeteers who stick to the painted drop alone usually err in the direction of almost photographic realism, and as a result, their productions have the look of the live theatre of fifty or more years ago. There is a place for superrealism in a painted drop, such as in a puppet melodrama or period piece of a time when such drops were used in the live theatre, but then they are really making a comic comment on the action rather than asking it to be believed. (If this kind of comic realism is used, a further effect can be created by painting set pieces and furniture on flat plywood. Such treatment is, of course, not realistic, and makes its comment by trying so hard to be so. Puppets can get away with treating flat pieces as three dimensional and be quite funny). Perhaps this is the only style of production in which the realistic painting of an outdoor scene on a drop can be anything other than a disaster. If we are forced to take the painted realistic drop seriously, we can't; we have just enjoyed too much sophistication in live theatre design to do so.

Let us go back to your initial sketch, thinking in terms of utilizing plasticity in the setting, and examine the effect of several different types of line and composition. Straight lines seem bold and strong; curved lines are graceful and restful. If we oppose one curve in reverse against another, action comes of the opposition. You will want a sense of movement in your composition, all strong lines moving toward the focal point, the center of interest, in the stage picture. Weaker lines lead to secondary points of interest, establishing focus.

If your production is set within a given historical period, the quality of line chosen for the setting can do much to establish the flavor of the times. The lines in costume and in setting are very closely related, because the dress lines and the architectural lines of a given period always echo each other. You have only to consider the fluid vertical lines of the Greek columns and compare them with the same flowing vertical lines of the chiton and himation to appreciate this relationship. Or look at the elaborate drapings and ornamentation of the costumes of the Restoration and then look to the architecture and even the furniture of the times. Often the same motifs will appear as ornament in costume, architecture, and furnishings. Motif can supplement line and tie together your costumes and setting. Consider the lotus and bud appearing on an Egyptian collar and perhaps being repeated in the decoration of a couch or on the setting itself. More subtly, you can learn to abstract the line of the motif and use that as your theme for repetition in costume and set. Obviously you are in for a research job again. You will need to know both the architectural design favored in the period you have chosen and something of the theatrical conventions of the day. Knowing that Greek drama was performed in the open air with masks or that Restoration plays were not only played in front of elaborately painted drops but framed by painted wings could change your whole concept for a setting. When you have done your research, chosen your style, and abstracted the line you will use, you are ready to compose the stage picture.

There are several ways of achieving balance within a scene design. Just as in your directorial visualization of the puppets, you must compose your set so that it has pleasing balance; otherwise one side of the stage will appear top-heavy. The director cannot be constantly offsetting a stage that seems to tip; he has enough problems balancing his puppets within the established equilibrium of a well-designed set. When balance is carefully established, the audience can sit back and enjoy the show; if the stage is not balanced, they will have difficulty concentrating, unconsciously trying to correct the balance.

Take a piece of paper and fold it down the middle. Draw any simple set, repeating on the left side of the center line exactly what you have drawn on the right. You now have a perfectly balanced symmetrical setting, though it may be a little boring. Now try changing the detail of any part of the right side, while keeping the relative sizes of the masses on both sides identical. You have now retained the balance, but the picture is more interesting. Such a balance is called "axial," and you may find it useful in establishing a sense of order, peace, and dignity. Provided that you do not clutter your design with detail, a setting with axial balance can show puppets off very well, since it has an imprint of simplicity and, all things being equal, leads the eye toward the center of the stage.

"Occult" balance, which is most commonly found in live theatre, has nothing to do with séances and spirits, but simply means the balance of unlike objects or masses within the space they occupy. With a little practice, you will begin to sense immediately whether a composition is balanced or not. Take a look at the illustrations given, covering the captions and deciding for yourself which is balanced and which is not. Now experiment for yourself with some indoor and outdoor settings.

Take a look at your sketches and try to imagine how they will look from different points of view in the audience. Unless you are playing in a real theatre where the seats are raked, the lower portion of your backdrop will be lost to people sitting in the back of your auditorium. You will have to design a drop in such a way that the lower portion is unimportant. Any detail that is referred to in the play is going to have to be high enough so that *everyone* in the audience can see it. Look at your design and decide which masses can be made plastic. Eliminate any detail that is unnecessary or distracting.

It may help you to cut a paper "puppet" out of bristol board when you are sketching or constructing a model. If you have been careful to keep your sketch and model to scale, replicating the shape of your proscenium opening, you will be able to cut a paper puppet to scale and find out how he works in proportion to your scene design. Because a hand puppet usually occupies a much larger piece of the stage picture than the actor on the live stage, care must be taken that he appears in proportion to his setting. A two-foot puppet standing next to a two-and-one-half-foot house is going to look like a giant. Perhaps all that should be seen is a doorway. Or you may wish to capitalize on the optical illusion your design is providing in order

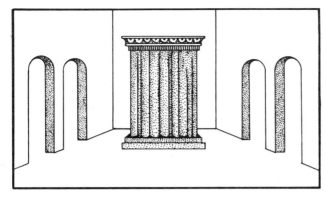

*Symmetrical balance*

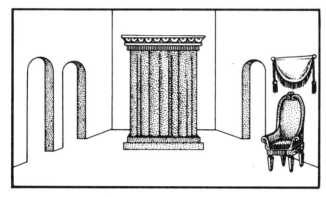

*Axial balance*

*Occult balance*

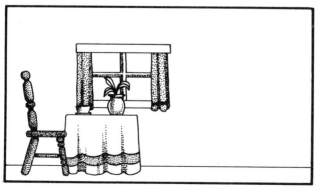

*Heavily weighted left stage*

to *make* him appear a giant. Just be sure that you are creating the effect you want. Suppose that you have a set piece of a very large chair, large in proportion to your stage and your puppet, perhaps twice his size; he will appear to be a Tom Thumb.

If you wish to give the illusion of distance, you will need a working knowledge of perspective, though there is no need to become overburdened by complex theories. Remember the example of the puppet that exited and appeared to reenter behind a higher masking—only it was a smaller duplicate puppet and therefore seemed farther away? The same principle, that shapes appear smaller in the distance, applies to your setting. Distant shapes will also appear closer together. We will discover shortly how color gets into the illusion. Let us see what can be done simply with line.

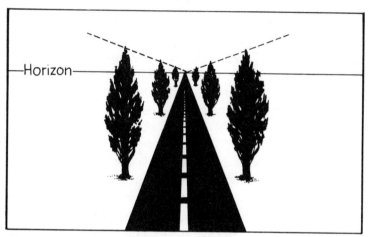

*One point perspective*

Picking the point of view (POV) of the best seat in the house, assume a horizon line at which point everything will appear to vanish into the distance. Generally it is less pleasing to the audience to place your stage picture on the horizon line, where it will seem to be cut horizontally in half. Ordinarily, the higher the horizon line, the farther away shapes on it will appear. We are looking at the road in the illustration above from a frontal position, and so all lines converge at a single vanishing point. This is an example of one-point perspective. Were we to view a scene or object obliquely, we would have a more complex problem. If we view a cube from the corner, the diagonal lines that lead the eye to the horizon would converge in two separate vanishing points. This is two-point perspective.

Occasionally you may want to make use of "forced perspective," that is, when the POV is both frontal and from above, such as in many Japanese

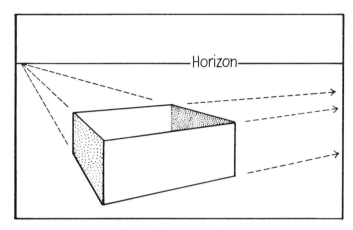

*Two point perspective*

paintings, when we see, for example, both the top and the front of a table. It is important to make use of distortions, but to use them with full knowledge that you are doing so and of the effect they will have on your audience. Ordinarily, if the lines of perspective are not in agreement and taken from one POV, the composition will have an out-of-sync look and is likely to unsettle your audience.

One extremely effective way of achieving the illusion of distance is to hang a series of scrims, on each of which selected details will appear farther and farther away. By casting light through a series of scrims, a mistiness is created, and even if they are hung only six inches apart, a tremendous depth can be suggested. (We do not here refer to the scrim stage, but the use of scrim curtains in the overhead stage.) These scrims can be made of any sheer fabric that will take the dye (preferably aniline) with which they must be painted. Since the dye has a tendency to bleed, a little starch should be added to it, and if you have trouble getting it to permeate the fabric, try adding a little vinegar, too. Scrims should always be made seamless—rarely a problem for a puppeteer since puppet stages are usually small—but should you have difficulty finding fabric that is wide enough, go to a theatrical fabric house, where both bobbinet and sharkskin scrim fabric in a variety of colors are usually available in widths up to thirty feet! This fabric drapes well, is durable, and takes dye. The color usually most effective is a dark blue. Wonderful transformations can be achieved with scrims, because as long as light is kept only on the front, only what is painted on them will show, and they will appear opaque. If light is brought up behind (you will have to experiment with the intensity needed to achieve the effect), the scrim and its painting seems to disappear, and whatever is behind it is revealed.

Before we move on to a discussion of color, one word of caution concerning line. Be careful that you respect the laws of gravity in your setting. Unsupported objects give the illusion that they are about to fall, and leaning shapes seem to lean farther and farther the more one looks at them. Such effects should only be used with an awareness of how much attention they will command.

The only aspect of form we have so far neglected is shading. By the deft use of shade and shadow, you can give the illusion of weight, shape, and even distance. If you do not have much drawing experience, experiment with drawing some simple objects you have in your workroom, attempting to capture their form with shading. Pick objects that have strong, simple contours and try to put them under a single light source. Draw what you see, noting where light and dark fall on the object and also where the object casts its shadow. Sometimes there may be several light sources in a painted setting, but it is always safest to assume that one is strongest, thereby insuring that all shadows will fall on the same side of every object. Careful shading can give plasticity to whatever has to be painted on the drop and will bring the painted scene into harmony with three-dimensional set pieces.

Once you have arrived at a workable sketch and model, you are ready to construct your set pieces and to paint your drops. It really doesn't matter which you do first, as long as you have their relative proportions well in hand, but for our purposes here, we will assume that you are going to start with the painting. Except for scrim or matte jersey drops which require dye, it is recommended that you use scene paint. Acrylic paints, even on the small scale of the puppet stage, can get quite expensive, as can textile paints. Since pigment for scene paint is usually sold in large amounts, you may be able to strike a deal with a local community theatre and purchase the amount you will need from them. (Tempera is definitely not recommended, since it rubs off. It can, however, be mixed with a small amount of white glue as a fixative, with somewhat unpredictable results.) You will also need as much whiting as pigment. Whiting or "size" is added to the pigment and water to give body and opacity to the colors. You will also need rubber or gelatin glue, which has to be boiled—and don't plan on using that double boiler for anything else later! This glue also smells unpleasant, but it is worth putting up with its inconveniences because it will cause your paint to adhere to the fabric surface of the drop without cracking or peeling, if reasonable care is taken not to get the paint too thick.

There are also casein colors available in ready-to-mix form. They cost more than regular scene pigments, but remember you don't need as much as an opera house would, and they may be very useful on some occasion if you are going to be performing out of doors, since they are water repellent. When working with them, remember to clean all brushes and pots immediately, or they will harden and not be reclaimable.

It is good standard procedure to paint a base coat over the entire drop before lining in the shapes enlarged from your sketch. Almost any light color, even one left over from another drop, will do. Some puppeteers like to tack drops to a canvas frame while painting. They then shrink tight with the base coat and offer a smooth surface for painting. If you don't want to trouble with a frame, spread your drop out on newspaper. Painting flat makes it easier to assure that paint will not run. On the other hand, it is more difficult for even the practiced eye to judge the effect of a drop when looking down on it. If you choose, instead, to hang your drops for painting, add enough whiting so that dripping is retarded, and work slowly and carefully. Let the drop dry thoroughly before taking a small brush or charcoal to outline the major areas of the composition. Many people like to use lavender for lining, since it fades out completely at a distance, and nothing is lost if you forget to cover some of the outline. Next, you will want to take a large brush and block in your major areas of color.

Scene-paint colors mix exactly as do the acrylics you learned to mix for your puppet heads, and most of the same principles apply. The only major difference to remember is that they dry about three shades lighter than the color when first applied. The addition of a complementary color will gray a color, and it achieves a better color than addition of black. You may occasionally want to use black for a very sharp accent on your setting, but it tends to attract a lot of attention to itself and does "go dead," except, oddly, in the case of black curtains used as background. Remember that light, bright colors come forward, while dark and grayed tones recede. This is a very important principle to consider when you are painting in perspective and wish to suggest distance. You may want to change the color as well as the intensity of objects as they disappear into the distance, but remember, they will grow less intense and grayer as they approach the horizon line. Lavender is usually favored in painting to give the illusion of distance because of its likeness to nature's distance color, and also because of its tendency to disappear as it becomes lighter.

Just as with line, you will want to make your scenic colors heighten the effect of the puppets. Too much contrast, or the use of bright complementary colors, will be distracting. The most frequent error seems to be sets that are as bright (or of as intense color) as the puppets, so that the puppets get lost in them. Not only must the line of the sets not be overwhelming; color, too, must be more subdued in the setting than in the puppets. You will be able to pick up colors analogous to the costume colors and echo them in the setting, but remember that a puppet dressed in exactly or even very nearly the same color as its background will blend right into it and seem to disappear. Clever use of like colors can make a puppet appear and disappear; unplanned like colors can kill an otherwise good show.

The simplest setting background, after plain black curtains, is the sky drop. It may or may not have set pieces in front of it, and if your stage is deep enough, it may wrap around the wings of your stage up to the point where your puppets need entrance room. In such a way, the sky or any drop hung farthest back can provide valuable masking of the backstage area, which can be critical from the point of view of the audience seated to either side. While light plays a large part in making a sky drop effective, there are also tricks you can play with paint. Do not use a flat light blue over the whole drop; spatter your paints, using mostly your chosen shade of blue and then a fine spattering of a darker blue, and perhaps pink, lavender, and even purple. You may want to resort to an old toothbrush rubbed over screening to get fine enough dots. Stand away from your work periodically, so that you are sure you are not concentrating the color in any one area and getting a splotchy effect. You can, of course, spatter by simply shaking a wet brush, but it is hard to control the concentration of color. Do not paint clouds on a sky drop! That's a good example of the superrealism we spoke of earlier. A well-painted sky drop can be lit many ways, take on many colors, and serve many functions, in the manner of the cyclorama, or "cyc" of live theatre. Use a good heavy muslin for this drop, roll it carefully when not in use, and it will serve you well for many years. Any large fabric store will furnish you with heavy cardboard tubes on which to wind your drops. Hoard them!

You may want to use different methods for hanging different types of drops. Since you will use a sky drop frequently, it is unadvisable to staple or otherwise permanently fasten it to a batten. Most painted drops wrinkle if they are wound around a batten, but matte jersey can sometimes be most easily transported and hung this way. The most durable drops are made in the manner of live theatre curtains, with webbing sewn at the top and grommets attached every four to six inches through which ties are inserted to secure the drop to batten or pole. If a drop is made of lightweight fabric, cotton twill tape may be heavy enough for the top, and drapery hooks can attach it to a rod. A drop that is tied on will not pull aside quickly; drapery hooks, especially the fully round type that cannot slip off a rod, work very well for fast changes. The squeeze type of drapery hooks are very practical, since they can be removed from one drop and used on another, and they are very quick and easy to attach. Hooks work best to attach a drop that hangs in fullness; tying is more secure for a drop, like the sky, that must hang flat. You can insert a brass rod in a casing at the bottom of a drape to stretch it taut, and even full drapes sometimes hang better if a length of tiny drapery weights or light bathroom chain is inserted in a casing at the bottom. All drops, except the scrim in front of the operator in a scrim stage, should be cut to hang at least six inches out of sight lines from any point in the audience. Nothing is more disturbing to the illusion than to see the bottom of a painted drop; anything painted on it will seem to end in midair.

Almost always, anything painted on a backdrop will be grayer than any set piece, since it is farther back. You will learn to trick the eye in interesting ways as you become facile at combining plastic set pieces with backgrounds. Take, for example, the setting for a street lined with houses. Perhaps the face of the first house on either side of the street may be molded of papier-mâché or formed of celastic over a cardboard base. The next houses may be painted on the drop, very gradually diminishing in intensity of color. If the jump in intensity between the plastic piece and the painted one is carefully controlled, the illusion can be very convincing. The plastic piece can be either hung, if puppets must enter behind it, or attached to the drop, but the illusion is more complete if the gap between the two units is kept as small as possible.

Hung units such as houses, trees, pillars, and the like cause a special problem in the hand puppet theatre, since there is no floor from which to brace them, and it is disastrous if they swing when a puppet accidentally hits them. They can sometimes be tied off to the stage on both sides, but care must be taken not to block puppets' entrance area. If you are playing in a real theatre that normally accommodates full-size sets, you may be able to fashion a stage brace and secure a set piece to the floor. Be sure that such a brace will not be in your puppeteers' way and also that you have clearance from the theatre owner or manager to screw a brace to the floor. Some school stages or concert stages have treasured unmarred surfaces, so find out first.

If you are lucky enough to have a permanent theatre of your own, you may be able to solve the problem of securing large set pieces, as do most permanent European hand or rod puppet theatres. In these ideal situations, the whole theatre has been designed for optimum viewing from the audience, for the comfort of the puppeteers, and for the flexibility of the stage design. First, the audience is raked, and though the theatre may be quite deep, seating does not extend far to the sides, and there is no balcony. The stage is planned at a height most pleasing to the viewer. But what can be done with the puppeteer, since he is taller than the distance from theatre floor to the playboard? The solution is very simple. The puppeteers are pitted and free to walk their puppets among set pieces secured to the stage floor.

*Permanent European pitted puppet theatre*

Sometimes, the settings may be on wagons, and the stage may be ten or twelve feet deep or more. You can imagine the range of effects such depth allows the designer. A never-to-be-forgotten moving forest of huge bamboo poles secured on tracks both above and below was created by Adam Kilian for the Teatr Lalka in Warsaw. Truly a most gifted artist, Kilian combines live actors wearing masks with the puppets, creating breathtaking effects by the contrast in size and through his imaginative and stunning use of color. Happily, here is the case of a fine artist who is blessed not only with talent and training but also with a performing facility that is sufficiently sophisticated to allow the expression of his ideas. Few puppeteers in the Western world will ever perform in such a splendid, tailored-to-puppets theatre, but we can all learn from the giants in our art and profit from their technical innovations, adapting to our small stages what can be made practical for us.

You might decide to build scenery units as small wagons mounted on casters. Use a large (three- to four-inch) rubber-tired caster, so that your set piece will not squeak as it moves into place. It should roll easily over lighting or sound cables, but it should be sufficiently stable to stay put of itself when placed or be equipped with a stop or brake. It should not roll if a puppeteer bumps into it! Wagons are alluring, since whole interiors, forest pieces, et cetera, can be built on them, but before you plan any, bear in mind that they are going to be cumbersome and better suited to the resident company than to the puppeteer who must fold everything up to tour in a van.

Before we turn to the construction of small set pieces, let us return to the subject of color, in order to examine how the manner of the application of paint will alter both the intensity and the texture presented by the surface. Just as when you shaded your sky drop with several colors instead of painting it all one flat hue, you will find that scene paint is usually best applied in several tones. You remember from studying the effect of stippling on your puppet faces how dots of colors create a more lifelike color than one flat tone. Remember that shadows are colored, and experiment with creating grays by spattering a complementary color. You may want to line the deepest portion of a shadowed area and highlight its brightest point, lining just as you did in painting a face.

Besides stippling, there are several other means of applying paint for texture, and they can be used on drops, or set pieces or even on small props. Spraying produces very fine dots, and thus very delicate shading. Apply in many light coats to avoid drips. If you want a rougher texture, you might try applying the paints with a sponge. If you want lots of depth in color and stippling doesn't create a bold enough texture, try "scumbling," which means applying three or more tones with different brushes, allowing the base coat to show as well as your brush strokes. For a one-color look, brush strokes need to go in several directions with an even amount of color. You can vary this effect by using a dry brush and lightly feathering your brush strokes.

Just as you found it handy to be able to stencil small appropriate designs to cloth for costumes, stencils may help a lot in producing believable wallpaper in a scale for a puppet. Do use stencil paper purchased from an art store. Cardboard stencils soak up your paint and muddy the outline very quickly.

With a little practice and lots of observation, you will be able to use different methods of applying paint, along with your knowledge of color and of highlight and shadow, to reproduce the effect of almost any texture, thereby adding interest and richness to the stage picture. Once again, you will face a question of degree. How much contrast is needed between the texture of the costumes or even the puppets themselves and that of the setting? How much of the costume texture do you want to "pick up" in the setting?

You will not, of course, accomplish the effect of texture solely with paint. There may be times when a silken drop or elaborately draped velour curtain will incorporate all the necessary elements of line, color, and texture in a given scene. Alone or in combination with painted drops, you will call upon a number of different types of curtains, necessitating your knowledge of their rigging.

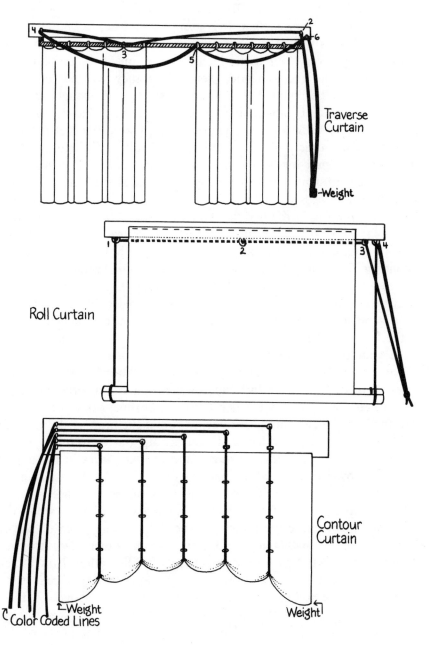

*Three types of curtains*

You can often mount a traverse rod from the hardware store, but sometimes this will not work, for lack of a place to mount the end fixtures or because of too long a span. It is useful, therefore, to know how to "do it yourself." You will need a curtain divided in the center, a rod of wood or brass, rings every four to six inches at the top of the curtain (sewn-on drapery rings are recommended here, since they will not catch on the fabric and can be counted on to slide easily), and enough firm rope to reach from point (1) about six inches below curtain line to the upper left corner (4) and back to (1). Nylon cord slips well, but if it is too fine, it tends to twist on the pull side, making it difficult to distinguish which side of the loop to pull for "open" and which for "close." It helps, whatever rope is used, to wind some colored tape on one side of the pull to code it for you. Screw eyes have to be put into a rigid batten of sufficient size that it will not sag in the middle. You will need three screw eyes at points (2), (4), and (6). Overlap your curtains several inches to the second or third ring, and go ahead and run the rope as shown, tying it off on that second or third ring. Carry the rope on through, keeping it almost taut between points (3) and (5). Tie at (5) and then lead the rope finally through the third screw eye (6) and down to meet the other end at (1). It's a good idea to tie the ends together, and you can weight the bottom of the "pull" to keep the rope taut when the curtain is open and also to make your pull stay in place.

For a succession of backdrops, a roll or "drop" curtain, or even a series of them, can come in handy. When you use a series of drops, instead of closing your Act Curtain each time to mask a scene change, you can simply roll a curtain up or down to reveal the next set. In combination with the drop and provided that you set up the convention at the beginning of your play, gloved hands can place set pieces in the manner of the live Kabuki theatre, where persons dressed in black simply go about the business of changing a scene in full view of the audience.

First, staple your drop to a batten, leaving six inches of wood bare at each end. Then staple the bottom of the drop to one piece of half-round dowel at least an inch thick, and then glue the other piece of dowel to the top of the first. Nail four screw eyes as in illustration. Now attach the cord to the far end of the dowel, tying it securely and thread the cord through screw eye (1), then (2), then (3). The balance of the cord from (3) should be three times the length of the drop. Now tie another piece of cord to the other end of the drop and feed it up through (4), again leaving cord three times the length of the drop. The final stage ensures that the drop will not only roll down, but up again. Roll the drop up and tie it with a piece of cord in the middle. Unwind pull cords from the doweling. Wrap the cord at each end five times, *going the opposite direction from the way the drop rolls.* Now release the drop from its center tie. It should pull up and down easily.[1]

Two other types of curtains can help you give variety to the stage picture. One is the simple symmetrical draped or "tableau" curtain, the other, the contour curtain. The tableau has a formal, stylized effect and should be used when you want its swags framing the action, since you can never draw it completely out of sight. With this drape, small curtain rings are sewn to the back of the drape, and both lines are tied off together, so that the sides will pull evenly. By pulling on only one line, you can open half the stage, but, except briefly, allowing an entrance, the half-swag division of the stage picture is not pleasing. The contour curtain, on the other hand, offers much variety, since each of the lines is tied off separately. You can run as many lines as you like, but it is best not to get carried away with the possibilities and mimic Radio City Music Hall! Remember, you have to keep the lines separate and need space enough backstage to tie them off. It helps to color code the lines with tape wound near the tie-off. A ring at the end of the line can simply attach to a cup hook, but make sure that the hook is angled so that the line will not slip off accidentally.

One other way to vary the stage picture with drapery greatly helps the puppeteer who has chosen to work in a half stage without a proscenium arch. In this type of staging, one is pretty much stuck with one backdrop, but if you build a frame of lath in whole or in sections, braced archways or square "doorways" and "windows" can be invented. Above each can be hung a little drape with rings on a small brass rod or dowel, which can simply be pulled back by a puppet and needs no rigging. The fun of such a background is in having puppets suddenly appear in a new acting area. You can, of course, incorporate this kind of background into any overhead stage, but since the frame is rigid, you are going to have to close the Act Curtain in order to change it, and it will have a good deal of weight.

Finally, the stage picture can be varied by the set pieces attached to the playboard or to a drop. These pieces not only give plasticity to the design, but they are frequently necessary to the action as well, particularly in the case of those attached to the playboard. Even if you are planning only one performance, it is necessary to build these pieces sturdily and on a firm base that can be securely clamped to the playboard, whether with C-clamps or spring clamps. Spring clamps are preferable, since they

[1] After instructions and drawing by Lewis Mahlmann.

are both quick and strong, and one-fourth-inch ply is recommended for a base. Sometimes a base for a set piece can be clamped to the playboard and a chair or table set upon it. This works, especially if the same set piece needs to reappear later in a different position, but care must be taken by the puppeteers not to dislodge the furniture. If the base is cut somewhat larger than the set piece, but not so large as to interfere with the puppets, the piece can slide a little without tumbling down. Units that must be changed but appear as part of the background against a drop can be suspended on black wire that is hooked over the scene batten. Carpet thread is less visible than wire for hanging but you will have to close the Act Curtain to place any unit that does not have rigid hooks. (Climbing on ladders to change scenery takes time and is invariably noisy.)

Try to use wood when building furniture, not cardboard, and be sure to tack or glue well. Puppeteers do tend to lean their puppets on set pieces, and chairs or beds or tables that crumble during the action of your play won't delight your audience, at least not in the way you had planned! If you cut out an oval opening in a chair seat and angle the chair upstage, a puppet can be easily made to appear as though sitting in it. A bed is easier to make believable if seen from the side (and then, of course, it only *has* one side), but you can cut a hole in the "mattress," in the same manner as in the chair. Just be sure to check from all the sight lines the angle at which the piece is to be set and cheat the piece enough to hide the false opening.

When constructing set pieces, never underestimate the versatility of styrofoam and white glue. Yes, styrofoam is very fragile, but if you paint it completely with three coats of white glue, allowing it to dry thoroughly between coats, it becomes nearly indestructible. You can hurry the drying process by putting it in the sun, but even the lowest oven is tricky. You can experiment and see if you can discover a setting that will not melt the styrofoam. If you are lucky enough to have access to a "hot frame" or want to go to the trouble to build one, it will provide quick and thorough drying. To build one you will need an oven-sized (about three-and-one-half- by three-and-one-half-foot) cube with the front side left off. Line the inside with aluminum foil and install three one-hundred-fifty-watt reflector floodlights in ceramic sockets on the "ceiling" of cube and two two-hundred-fifty-watt heat resistant infrared lamps. The infrareds go in the back with one flood between and slightly in front of them. The floods go front left and right, about a foot from the open front. You can install several shelves of wire, if you choose, and gain the ability to dry many small objects at once. Wood used for the frame should be about an inch and a half thick at the sides and top and a good solid three inches at bottom. You may want to position it on a stand.

However you dry your pieces, be sure that you have sealed all the pores with glue, especially if you will use aerosol spray paint on them. Many of these paints contain solvents that will eat away the styrofoam unless it is totally coated. Perhaps this all sounds like a troublesome process, but remember that styrofoam carves very easily into almost any shape you might want. Even large and complicated set pieces can be made quickly, so the drying and glue-painting time can indeed be worth it. It also is very light, so that even large pieces that must be hung are not cumbersome, certainly an advantage when you have to pack, carry, or ship them. Actually, packing from household appliances affords your best sources of styrofoam. Not only is it formed into all sorts of useful odd shapes, but it has a greater density than the styrofoam usually available in art or party shops. Not to be thrown out, either, are those thousands of odd curled shapes (great for snow or leaves) or large and small beads of foam used in packing. The small beads make wonderful snow. Puppeteers are usually the first to offer to unpack *anything* likely to arrive in styrofoam packing!

Celastic can be a very useful medium also in building set pieces. You can drape it like fabric or free-form it into properties. If you need a base on which to shape it (since it is very limp when wet with acetone) try a wire form. The chicken wire used in live theatre usually has holes that are too large except for making massive pieces like tree trunks or rocks; you can, however, buy finer mesh from any hardware store. You may either wrap the wet celastic around the raw edges of the wire and keep the wire as part of the piece or cover the wire with aluminum foil and lift off the celastic as soon as it is dry. Trim rough edges with scissors when the piece is finished. Though celastic is torn in order to blend edges when used for molding heads, it can also be cut into any intricate shapes before dipping it in solvent if you want to preserve its edge. One advantage to celastic is that it will adhere not only to itself, but also to wood or cardboard so that a set piece can easily be attached to a base simply with extra pieces of celastic. And while cardboard is not durable enough by itself, when covered by celastic, it will withstand a lot of use. Just don't try combining celastic (wet) with styrofoam; the acetone will dissolve styrofoam. Dry pieces of both mediums can, of course, be joined with glue, though celastic tends to be somewhat independent and sometimes won't stick. Many glues (airplane glue, for example) also contain acetone or toluene and these will render the celastic back into its wet state. White glue is safest, but it will not always hold if much stress is placed on the joined pieces.

Tree leaves made of styrofoam, celastic, or several shades of felt, or bought ready-made in the plastic flower stall can be inserted into wire mesh for hedges or bushes or trees. Or, if you need to give the illusion of tree leaves overhead, you can do so by cutting and painting a drop and massing a few three-dimensional leaves here and there. (If the outline of the cut-out is extremely delicate, the muslin can be backed with scrim cut in a simple shape.)

Since puppet props need to be so much larger in proportion than live theatre props, real objects can often be used. Sometimes you may need to glue a rough surface to them so that they won't be dropped. Props that must go from hand to hand can be held by the first puppet and secured to the hand of the puppet that accepts the object by means of a strip of Velcro. For obvious reasons, the use of glass props is discouraged; usually substitutes can be found or a "reasonable facsimile" made of painted styrofoam or celastic. For the rare instances when you must give the illusion of glass breaking, you can use sheets or molded shapes of candy glass. All you need is a very saturated sugar and water solution. Bring it to a boil in a double boiler (about 265° F) and then pour it out onto a greased cookie sheet. With a little care it can also be shaped in simple greased molds.

When leafing through scene design and puppet how-to books, don't be seduced by pages of instructions for building elaborate sound-effect machines, such as wind machines, thunder sheets, et cetera. Most of these books, though in the main solid, were written years ago. Today you have a wealth of sound-effect records available to you, and except in rare instances, they will produce any sound effect you need. Another outmoded contraption is the design for rolling scenery from one drum to another to create an illusion of moving from one place to another. Unless a very deliberate naïveté is sought, the television and film saturation of any audience today precludes the use of this device.

By no means have we covered every aspect of construction and scene design. The possibilities for dressing the stage are many, the combinations and variations of techniques, endless. Some methods you will like, others you will abandon, and you may invent methods all your own. What you have here is a collection of workable techniques for construction of your design and guidance for creating a design that complements your puppets and their costumes and adds clarification and even additional meaning to the play itself. Now you must learn how to light the stage in a way that will not only retain the qualities you have built into your puppets and scenery, but also heighten and enrich their effect.

# 11

## Lighting for the Puppet Stage

Of the three aspects of design for the puppet stage—the puppets themselves, scene design, and lighting—it is lighting that usually receives the shortest shrift. Most beginning puppeteers will devote endless hours to the design and construction of their puppets, put some effort but not enough into their scenery, and then figure out how to hang some lights, somewhere, so that the work they have done can (with luck) be seen. If only these new puppeteers realized what a knowledge of the properties of light and its contribution to the totality of the stage picture could do to enliven and literally shape their work! Sometimes, perhaps frequently, a puppeteer has some knowledge of lighting the live stage, but because of lack of space or funds, he allows himself a lack of imagination in adapting what he knows to his puppet work. If the ideal of what might be accomplished with a full light board, many instruments, infinite pre-sets, and dimmer controls cannot be brought to your stage, there are still aspects of the ideal lighting situation that can be utilized in order to enhance your work. First, let us examine the properties and contributions of lighting to stage decor, and then we will see in what ways you can implement this powerful element of design in your own work, not only to make it visible, but to heighten its effect.

It wasn't until the end of the nineteenth century that the dynamic work of Adolphe Appia began convincing directors and designers of the live theatre that there were not one, but two, kinds of light in the theatre. Appia claimed that, first, there must be general illumination (*helligkeit*), which enabled the audience to see what was going on, and, second, there must be specific illumination (*gestaltendes licht*), which gave objects, actors, and decor their form. Together with Gordon Craig, the scene designer who so loved puppets, he catapulted ahead of his time, suddenly lifting the theatre out of the painted drop lit by white light with all its flatness into an era of discovery and plasticity. The live theatre still builds upon the work of Appia and Craig; unfortunately, in most instances, with the exception of the few resident theatres and occasional artists, the puppet theatre has never quite caught up. Puppeteers persist in lighting their productions with white light and too much or not enough of it. In pursuit of a "cure" we shall have to discover how to use the two kinds of theatrical light in the puppet theatre. We must learn not only what can make the general illumination more pleasing, but also how we can employ spotlights and "specials" (separately controlled instruments on individual control used for special effect) for specific illumination to give plasticity and form. Instead of glaring white light we must learn to find the colors in light that bring out the colors in sets and costumes.

Both kinds of light, general and specific, have three properties: quantity, distribution, and color. Though it is often difficult to determine the quantity or amount of light needed, it helps to bear in mind that too much light will tire your audience to the same extent that too little light on your puppets will force the audience to strain to see what is going on. There is an old tradition of bright light for comedy and dim light for tragedy, and while the basic establishment of mood by the brightness of lighting is useful, obvious extremes should be avoided. Since one of the great gifts lighting has to give the puppet is to let him be clearly seen despite his small size, care must be taken to concentrate the light within the proscenium; just as the setting and the stage picture presented by the puppets help guide the audience's eye, so too, lighting defines the area where action will take place. The more you can avoid the spill of intense light onto your stage outside of the proscenium, the easier it will be for your audience to concentrate.

It is a good idea to avoid rapid changes from brightly lit to dim scenes and back again, for this also tires the audience. If you employ one or more dimmers so that lighting can be brought up and down slowly, you will give the audience time to adjust their eyes. After all, if you walk from the sunlight into a dimly lit room, it takes your eyes a moment to adjust; why should you expect your audience to go from a brightly lit theatre house to a dimly lit scene without giving them a moment for their eyes to become used to the change? Sometimes you will need to open a scene with dim lighting in order to establish mood, but if you slowly bring your lights up, you will find your audience will not only retain the mood but become more attentive. It is rarely necessary for modern puppeteers to make their own dimmers. For a small traveling company, the dimmers manufactured for household use are usually sufficient. They are small, light, and inexpensive, and several can be used in one lighting system. Just be careful not to overload any dimmer. Check the wattage the dimmer will carry. If you have too much wattage running into it, it will blow out, so calculate the wattage of all the lamps you are using, and if it is too great for a small dimmer, buy a larger one or run two lines to two dimmers, or more. Should you be using large theatrical instruments, you may need to purchase your dimmer from a lighting house in order to be sure it has sufficient capacity. (For those of you not familiar with theatrical lighting terminology, "lamp" refers to the glass bulb or globe containing the filament; "instrument" refers to the housing for the lamp.)

The second property of light, its distribution, means the manner in which light is spread over the stage area. You will want less light on your background and more on your foreground, where your puppets will do most of their acting; but you will want enough light on the background so that it is related to the puppets. Light literally ties the two together. Most often, floodlights that provide diffused, general illumination are used to light the background and small spotlights or "baby spots" are used to light the front acting areas. Spots provide intense and narrow beams and must be carefully focused so that they give the specific illumination needed to reveal the modeling of the puppet faces and the form of the setting. Care must be taken that the distribution of light across the playboard is even. If the puppets suddenly move into a dead spot, they will seem to drop out of the action, and while you may for some scene wish the accent of light on a given area, maintaining a "hot spot" throughout the show will make whatever moves into that spot suddenly more prominent than any other.

The third property of light is color, which is difficult for most people to understand but also extremely important. It is often hard for a puppeteer to use lighting color to full advantage, since many instruments are sometimes needed to extract the most from its gifts. We can avoid the difficulties and light our puppets always and only with white light; they will be visible. But since white light tends both to flatten contours and wash out colors, much of our work on stage design and the puppets themselves will not be shown to best advantage. The difficulty arises in that different colors in light afford different levels of visibility, the highest being in yellow and the lowest in blue and green. Orange and red are low, but produce more varying results. What this means is that the minute we begin using colored lights, we are cutting down the quantity of light; lighting a scene in blue light is simply going to demand more instruments or ones with lamps of greater intensity. Sometimes blue lamps can be burned above their rated voltage; this practice will bring up their intensity but also shorten the life of the lamps. Often there is not much space in a puppet stage in which to hang lights, and one must be careful about the weight on the proscenium top. When you are designing your stage and its lighting, plan for the maximum number of instruments you think you will ever need. You can always leave plugs unused; and adding outlets, new lines, or rebuilding whole lighting systems is expensive. Find out the maximum wattage you can plug into a house circuit in your area, if that is where you will be performing, and build accordingly. If you plan to play theatres, check the smallest one on your list and find out the capacity of its wiring. If you are traveling, check ahead to sure you will overload no one's circuit, then build for the maximum capacity you think you will need.

Color in light mixes quite differently than color in pigment; the mixing of light is either additive or subtractive, while the mixing of color is almost always additive. For example, we mix red and blue paint together to get purple, that is, we add one color to the other to form a third. In light, if we focus a colored light on a colored surface, only the rays of color contained in the light will be reflected back to us. If we shine a red light on a green fabric, the fabric will appear black, since there are no red rays in the color green. Already you can see what havoc lighting can play with beautiful puppets and scenery. On the other hand, it can also immeasurably enhance their effect. Blue light shone on a blue surface will make it seem to glow with added richness and depth, as will yellow light on gold fabric. The possibilities for ruining your design or enriching it are endless, but with a knowledge of how color in light mixes you will be able to control your effects.

The primary colors of light are red, green, and blue. The complementaries are blue-green (sometimes called "cyan"), yellow, and magenta. The complements joined together produce white light, which represents the presence of all wave lengths in the spectrum. Likewise all primaries joined together will produce white, as will, strangely enough, any secondary with the primary that is not one of its components. Magenta plus green, for instance, will produce white since green is not a component of magenta. If, as is common practice in the live theatre, and usually practical in puppet theatre, we shine two specific instruments on each acting area from opposite sides, one warm, the other cool, they will mix additively in the given area where the beams converge. They will be seen separately on the puppet or set piece if it is in the path of the beam, and this will delineate form by producing shadow and highlight. Obviously, if this method of lighting areas is used, the cool side of each area must remain consistently on either left or right, as source of shadow, and so too the warm, which usually denotes the imagined light source for the scene (that is, sunlight, moonlight).

When we begin inserting a color medium, usually theatrical gelatin or glass, between the white light source and the surface upon which it is shone,

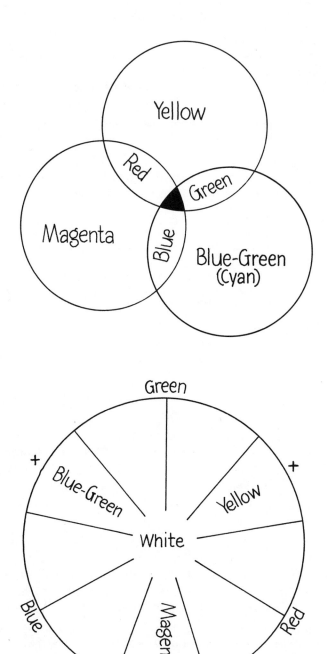

*Color wheels for light: additive and subtractive*

we are filtering the color, subtracting some of the beams from the white light and thereby producing a new color. You can readily see why this process is usually referred to as "subtractive mixing." If you put a green gel over a red gel and place them in front of a light source, no light will pass through, but if you put a magenta gel in combination with an amber gel, you will get red light shining through, since red is contained by both filters. If we picture the secondaries as gel medium, each overlapping, we will begin to understand the principles of subtractive mixing. (Remember that in practice you must refer not only to the filter colors, but also to the subtraction process, sometimes called "selective absorption," of the beams reflected back from the surface upon which they are shone.)

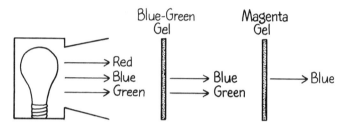

*Subtractive mixing*

Theatrical gelatin may be obtained, of course, from any large theatrical lighting house, but if you need only very small amounts you can probably buy some from a local little theatre, or they may even give you their oddly shaped cuttings. Bear in mind, though, that if you are planning many performances, gelatin fades with use, and you will have to have enough for replacement. Glass filters are only available for standard theatrical lighting instruments, but striplight roundels (colored glass) can sometimes be adapted to home-contrived instruments. Not too many years ago, most theatrical gel really *was* gelatin, and it was extremely flammable; nowadays you will find heat-resistant plastics in almost any color you can imagine. Look in the Yellow Pages of your nearest large city for a theatrical lighting supply house. Most of them will gladly send you catalogs (there may be a minimum order charge), and for a small two- or three-dollar fee they usually have a sample book of gels. Often these samples are about two by four inches, easily enough to gel a baby spot. Yes, you may have to order for floodlight gels, but remember, you may need just basic colors, so order by the sheet. One use for sample gels is for color testing, so that you will only order the actual colors you need and find most effective, even if you need a larger piece than a sample provides. You can mount the sample in "super" size slide mounts and use a slide projector to test them, but you have a much more accurate reading if you can "throw" them with the instrument you will use at the approximate distance it will be reflected and with the type and wattage lamp that will be used. You can "think" a color test by knowing how both light and pigment mix and interact, but do test your fabrics under light as you go along, and take a look at your painted heads and wigs. Fabrics, especially synthetics, and even some pigments can surprise you under light, and it is much better to be surprised before construction is completed. Test a large enough piece of fabric under light so that you can see the shadows in the folds. If it doesn't look right to you, change gel frames to correct the color reflected. Now try testing all fabrics to be used in a given scene. Though it is generally easier to adjust a light than change a fabric, sometimes material just doesn't "take light" well. All the more reason to test all fabrics before you sew them so that the worst that can happen is an investment in another piece of yardage. Pigments tested should always be applied to the surface upon which they will be used. Both texture and absorption of paint can change the quality of light reflected.

It cannot be too strongly stressed that though we have saved lighting until last of the three design units and we are isolating it for the purposes of study, it must be considered from the start of the production as the third part of a totality. Your lighting, puppets (including costumes), and scene design must all complement each other, the light modeling and bringing out colors and contours as originally intended. Perhaps the best way to plan your lighting is to begin with a "light plot" as soon as you have settled on your production outline script.

First, you will go through the whole show, determining the moods to be established and the environments to be created. Write each one down, describing carefully each effect you want to create. Try to determine a mood for the whole show, one that complements the style you have chosen for direction and scene design. Then, go through the play, analyzing each scene for mood and tonal quality. Determine where lighting can help to establish emphasis. As soon as you have a model for your set design, you will be able to take the colors from your tonal light plot and determine where instruments may be hung so that the modeling of the set will be preserved; enough, but not too much, emphasis will be placed upon it; and, within the mood established, the modeling of the puppets and the color and texture of their costumes will be brought out. Though mood will change from scene to scene, try to avoid many abrupt changes, remembering they will fatigue your audience.

Now that you have a basic descriptive light plot, which, if such were the case, you would be able to hand to a lighting designer who would work out the specifics of execution, you are ready to figure out those specifics yourself, assuming that, like most puppeteers, you are in charge of every aspect of production.

The number and type of lighting instruments you use will be determined not only by the kind and complexity of effects you want to create, but also by the size of your stage, its type, and your budget. Safety is well worth a small investment, so don't get involved with truly "homemade" instruments. For the overhead stage, you will need at least two (though four is better) floodlights, one hung on either side of the stage, so that you can crosslight two areas. You are already, in effect, "cheating" by not lighting each acting area with two instruments, but floods cover a large area and most puppet stages will be adequately lit by focusing one warm and one cool on UR and UL areas. To cut cost and weight you can buy the basket floodlights available at all large hardware stores. The ones with reflectors work best, since the reflector measurably increases the intensity of the light, but it is wise to paint the outside of the reflector with a flat black heat-resistant appliance paint, since these units are in no way cooled. PAR two-hundred-fifty-watt lamps in white and in colors are readily available. The pink is quite useful and mixes well, but the red, green, and especially blue do not mix well. The blue is also extraordinarily low in intensity.

If you use basket floods, you will have to make your own gel frames. These can be square-cut a little larger than the instrument and cut of flattened tin cans (round off all corners, bevel edges, and tape all around with electrical tape) or of cardboard heavy enough to stand some use. Cut the frames double and fix the gel inside with masking tape. Tape the frame closed with electrical tape. One way [1] (and you may devise others) of fixing the gel to the reflector is to glue four pieces of wood to the top, bottom, and sides of the reflector. Glue a strip of Velcro to the front of the wood. Glue the other half of the Velcro strip to the back of the gel frame after positioning it. If the wood sticks out about a half inch in front of the reflector, you will be allowing valuable cooling space. It is very difficult to gel floods in wire baskets, so you may have to use them only when the colored lamp is sufficient for your needs. In buying any clamp-on hardware units, look for ceramic sockets, if possible, and also for instruments that will hold the angle in which they are focused. Some simply become limp with use, especially the ones with a ball and socket swivel, and they are very difficult to tighten. Your alternative to these instruments are those available from theatrical lighting houses. Their advantage is sturdiness and

[1] Betty Polus, *Why and How to Light the Puppet Stage.* See Bibliography for information on how to obtain this pamphlet.

longer life, but their weight and size is usually prohibitive for overhead hanging in most puppet stages. If you have sufficient depth to allow you to light a cyclorama (or sky drop) from the floor, the commercial floods are certainly your best answer. Two to four will light most puppet theatre cycloramas efficiently. They are cumbersome for travel but sturdy, and they do come equipped with gel frames.

For spotlights definitely turn to your lighting catalogs. Four or five baby spots, which begin in price at twenty-five and thirty dollars, are well worth the investment. They have a nice sharp beam, a good plano-convex lens, a slide at bottom that enables you to focus the beam; they are cooled, and they come with their own gel frames. Lamps are usually seventy-five watts, so you can run four or five plus two floods on one dimmer (but *check the wattage listed on your dimmer*). Remember, it may be necessary to install several dimmers to carry the load you need. Or you may want to dim floods and spots separately, a very good practice, since it gives you separate control of general and specific lighting. An even more sophisticated approach that is available even to the smallest scale puppet theatre is an additional dimmer or dimmers to which is run a line for "specials" like sudden light on a genie's appearance or a red brought up on a devil while other lights are dimmed. Puppeteers have worked out all sorts of control panels, many with foot control switches so that one person can work lighting effects and puppets simultaneously. What matters is that your lighting system fit *your* needs and that its controls be within the reach and capability of whoever will handle them. You may wish to locate a control panel directly in front of you or on the floor and to the side. The choice is yours. Just make it accessible during the show.

Yes, it is quite possible to make a reflector out of a coffee can, but even with a ceramic socket and vents cut in the sides and a careful covering of heat-resistant paint, this instrument is going to get quite hot, and *must* be kept away from all drapery. Also, if you plan to do any even semiprofessional work, such homemade instruments look like exactly what they are to the fire marshal, and they are not Underwriters' Laboratories (U.L.) approved. Another dangerous cost cut is the use of photo floods or photography bells when you need free-standing light out front, such as in the use of the half-stage with no proscenium arch. These lightweight stands are *very* easily knocked over by even one toddler, and you can imagine the danger and legal implications involved. If you need light out front, invest in a good, heavy commercial stand. You may be able to acquire some stands or "trees" secondhand from a local little theatre or drama school. Do use commercially built spots on them. Two or three instruments to a tree should be sufficient.

Both backstage and certainly in front of the stage, for both safety and aesthetic reasons, bundle your cords and tape them down to the floor so that they don't offer an immediate tripping hazard. Cords all over the place betray the amateur very quickly, and they may betray you, if you are trying to find one for repair.

The only other type of basic lighting instrument you might need in a hand puppet stage would be a striplight trough hung on chains from your farthest batten as a way to provide backlighting if your stage is not deep enough for floods on the floor. A piece of gutter stripping, some porcelain sockets, several low-wattage household bulbs, and lots of electrical cable can be made to produce such a trough. Commercial striplights are too heavy to be hung, but can be used on the floor instead of floods, and they do come with gel frames. To gel a homemade unit, just block off the trough at intervals with cardboard or metal and insert gel in frames as you did with the basket floods. The light will mix somewhat near the source, but you want a diffused effect anyway. The only problem with a hung trough is that it can swing mightily if hit accidentally, producing very eerie lighting. If carefully assembled and if low-wattage lamps are used, it should present no safety problem and will look professional enough to your friendly fire marshal. Unless you are presenting a period piece, such as a melodrama in a time when footlights were used, forget them. They hide the puppets, cast strange, flattening light, and attract attention to themselves.

In addition to your lighting instruments themselves and their lamps, you will need several long (twenty-four- to fifty-foot cable) heavy-duty cords. If you can't find cords with rubber plugs, buy the cord by the foot from the reel (cheaper), and put on the rubber plugs yourself. Never use plastic plugs on the floor, where they can be literally disintegrated by one foot. Do take more cord than you think you will need (twenty-four feet is usually sufficient, but it is amazing how far away a plug can be in a reasonably sized theatre!). We have found a four-way heavy-duty connection box invaluable, but again, watch how much current you are running through the same line. Remember if you run light *and* sound through one line to add up *all* the wattage.

Learn how to make quick repairs of plugs and wires yourself and always take a tool kit with wire cutters, tweezers, and black electrical tape with you. Take a flashlight so that you can see the light panel during the show. It really isn't necessary to build a "work" light into your system—nice, but not necessary. Pack it all with your light box, so you know where it is. Take a spare of every lamp needed, but don't buy dozens in advance, as they lose some life just in sitting around. A footlocker or heavy wooden box that can be mounted on casters (since it will probably be your heaviest piece of equipment) should accommodate all your lighting needs. Pack spare lamps in foam rubber, excelsior, or styrofoam, and put them in their own box within the large lighting box. If you pack carefully, lamps usually don't have to be removed from instruments for packing, but do wait for them to cool before putting them into the box. All cable should be wound in rounds or figure eights. There's nothing more discouraging than opening your light box to find cable that looks as though the kittens had tangled it.

You now have instruments, lamps, dimmers, and cable to reach an outlet, but you have no way to connect them all, so you might as well be standing there with flashlights. In addition to all the rest of your equipment, you will need enough cable to reach from each instrument to the dimmer (or control panel) at the farthest point it may be hung. Cable should be wound with carpet thread and then bound at six- or eight-inch intervals with black electrician's tape, female plugs hanging out of the bundle as needed. By attaching metal hooks about an inch long to your proscenium, you will be able to hang the cable quickly. Do put in more lines and plugs than you think you will need. And don't be like James Thurber's aunt who worried that electricity was surreptitiously leaking from unused electrical outlets! The whole bundle should lead to a control panel, where each cord attaches to an on/off switch. This panel then feeds into a dimmer or dimmers and the panel is plugged into a heavy-duty cord and then into the electrical source. Even with a scrim stage and the need for fewer instruments, it is well worth going to the trouble to do your wiring properly. Even a few one-hundred-and-fifty-watt PARs clamped onto your stage deserve better treatment than being straggled together from one household extension cord to another in a gaggle of short and often dangerous connections. Periodically, check all plugs and cords and replace whatever is worn. Replace any plug that gets hot. Tape over *any* exposed wires.

Floor or clamped floods present no mounting problem, but commercial spotlights may have to have their mounting adapted. They usually come with a screw clamp, similar to a C-clamp, for mounting on a pipe. If you need to mount them on a wooden batten, you may wish to change this mounting to a spring clamp. Just be careful to observe, with commercial theatrical lighting, that you burn the lamp in the position for which it was constructed. Lamps are meant to burn "base-up" or "base-down"; if you don't play by the rules, your lamps will burn out quickly. Note also the life of the lamp, so that you will know when to reorder. The small sizes you will need are sometimes hard to get and you may have to wait for an order.

Except in the beautifully equipped permanent theatres with their elaborate control boards, the problem of where to mount the instruments in a hand puppet stage has never been adequately solved. Ideally, you need not only crosslighting, but some light on the puppets from above and in front. You can experiment with a puppet or your own face in front of a mirror in a darkened room. Take a flashlight and shine it from each side, then from directly above and from below. You will see the need for light from both sides, because when it comes from only one side, the other half of the face is in deep shadow. Light from the top casts very heavy shadows, and you quickly see the necessity of some front lighting. Shine the light from directly in front and you will see how it flattens all the contours. Light from below shows you why we don't use footlights or specials from below unless ghouls and spirits are onstage. Where can we place the instruments for optimum efficiency and effect?

In the overhead stage described in this book, the top of the proscenium front juts out to allow about a thirty-five-degree angle of throw downwards and inwards onto the puppets. It was felt that bringing the proscenium front and attached light batten even farther forward would destroy the stage's balance. In order to achieve the optimum of about a forty-five-degee angle of light from in front and above, one would have to devise some manner of tilting the proscenium top outward at the bottom. We have solved the frontal lighting problem on occasion with an assist from beam light in the house where we played. Difficulties arise with this technique in that the light on the puppets may be very pleasing, but usually a great deal of spill falls on the stage drapery and is distracting. Once in a while you will find a theatre or museum equipped with a follow spot in the center back of the house. These spots can usually be shuttered down to light only the proscenium opening. Since this is very little work for the house technician during your show, you can generally get such a person to produce the effect you want. Focusing of beam lights can present a real problem if they are set for a live theatre show, have to be reset for you, and returned to their original focus when you leave. With a center-rear follow spot, especially in a large theatre, you will have a valuable boost to your lighting, but your system must be able to function adequately without it since the available assist is the rarity rather than the rule. Do not, however, accept an assist from a carbon-arc spot. These are extremely powerful instruments and will flatten contours and wash out any effects of your own lighting. It is also best to accept help from resident theatre lighting only if it can be left on throughout your show; expecting a house technician to cue a light up and down for you, probably without rehearsal, is asking too much.

Obviously, you are best off if you can always take care of all of your lighting yourself. Some puppeteers solve the front lighting problem by extending gooseneck or angled black poles attached to the front proscenium top, usually one light at either side of the stage, though more could be mounted, even on separate poles. It is true that with the advent of the thrust and arena stages, of off-Broadway and "off-off-Broadway" staging, today's audiences are increasingly tolerant of exposed lighting instruments, but you must be extremely careful that there is no spill from the back of the instrument and that it is so positioned that it will not glare at the audience from any point in the house. Light trees, even sturdy ones, at either side of the stage, also present problems, since they must be so positioned that they give optimum light to the puppets and still do not interfere with sight lines. These trees are, of course, necessary when there is no proscenium top.

We have found hanging lights the most pleasing solution in the overhead stage, providing optimum light within the playing area. Puppets must avoid the extreme front of the playboard, since we cannot avoid dark spots there, but otherwise our lighting is adequate in a house with seating up to six or eight hundred. A suggested light plan is shown for basic crosslighting in specific front areas and for general illumination of the scene. Each light can be controlled separately by an on/off switch, and all front spots and floods are on separate dimmers which can be dimmed to black, leaving on a special, if we so choose, at any intensity, since it is fed into a third dimmer. More lines for more specials could, of course, be employed, provided that the capacity of dimmers and the available house circuit are observed.

Lighting the scrim stage, because it is smaller, is somewhat simpler. You

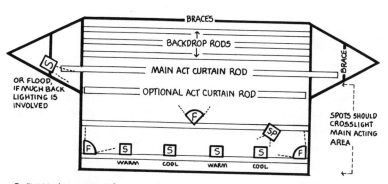

F = FLOOD (ON DIMMER 1)
S = SPOT (ON DIMMER 2)
SP = SPECIAL (ON DIMMER 3)

*Overhead view of overhead stage with a possible light plan*

can use perhaps only four baby spots, or, if you don't want too specific a beam, you may be able to get away with four-hundred-and-fifty-watt clamp-on PARs. The lighting will be improved if you mount your instruments on the front wooden panel, but if you can stand the strong shadows created, you can clamp them on the sides. If your stage is constructed of aluminum, use only clamps covered with rubber, or insulate them yourself with inner-tubing wherever they will contact the metal. Wherever possible, secure lights to wood. Your aluminum stage is a giant conductor, so do not run any wires over it without double-checking insulation, and never attach outlets to the stage itself.

Care should be taken also with aluminum ladders. They are light and convenient for travel, but they are also dangerous. If you use them, do all your hanging of cable and lights and all plugging *before* you plug into the house circuit. (You may want to test just to be sure that the power is on first, but then unplug it while you rig.) Since you will need to make the final focusing adjustments of your instruments with the lights on, wear heavy gloves when touching any burning instrument. Can you imagine the hazard of a puppeteer standing on an aluminum ladder placed on damp grass, adjusting an instrument with a frayed cord? You may well not want to return to the heavy old wooden ladders, now almost extinct, but do take proper precautions. Be aware that broken fluorescent lamps are poisonous, and never use them overhead. If you use them as side lighting, treat them gingerly, and pack them separately, and carefully. If broken, dispose of them immediately, without touching the filaments.

Strobe spotlights and floodlights are also dangerous if broken, and can be harmful to the eyes if stared at directly. They are, however, often worth their risks, but be sure that they, too, are handled with care and packed separately. These lamps produce ultraviolet light, often referred to as "blacklight," and cause anything treated with fluorescent dyes or paints to glow brightly when all except strobe lights are fully out. Some of the colors will look the same under both incandescent light and strobe light; others will be different. Some fabrics fluoresce naturally; most white fabrics, especially synthetics, glow lavender to purple under black light. You may want to switch suddenly in a show to black light for its startling and otherworldly effect, or you may want to experiment with an entire show staged under strobe light. This type of lighting has created a whole genre referred to as "Black Theatre." It is fun because only that which is treated with fluorescent paint or dye is seen by the audience. Therefore, puppeteers dressed, gloved, and hooded in black are invisible, even if they are onstage with the puppets, provided there is no incandescent light source. Creatures may be made to float through the air or appear unsupported at a great height. Several operators may be controlling one large puppet and his props, as in the case of Georges Lafaye's billiard player. Or, as in the work of the Czech Black Theatre company and of the Coad Canada Puppets,[1] whole scenes or even whole plays are given a special illusion. Some further discussion of this mode ends our discussion of rod puppets in the next chapter.

A variant of Black Theatre can be produced without the use of strobe light at all. It is extremely effective and worth its difficulties, but since it usually employs rod puppets, we will treat it under that heading in the following chapter.

Out-of-doors lighting is hard to define. In the daytime, you will need little or no light, unless your proscenium area is covered over or, for some other reason, quite dark. You lose, unfortunately, that valuable focusing of audience attention that only lighting can give. For outdoor performances at night you will have to experiment. Your indoor setup will probably be sufficient in intensity, though you will lose focus if there is any competition from natural light or surrounding floodlights. Do make sure that any cable is insulated for outdoor use, and unless every bit of lighting (and sound) equipment you have is U.L. approved for outdoor use, don't play in even the slightest hint of rain!

The use of actual lights scaled to the puppets, such as lamps, candles, or chandeliers, presents a problem in and of itself. Since these lights usually need to be quite a bit dimmer than their real-life counterparts in order not to attract too much attention, it can be an advantage to use small incandescent lamps and wire the prop instrument into your lighting system. That way you can dim them up or down to blend with scenic lighting. The problem here is that you will then have a long cord which is likely to get tangled among puppeteer and puppets and may be difficult to mask as well. Usually, rigging a tiny flashlight bulb or penlight bulb to batteries is more successful. Naturally you will have to check to be sure your batteries are charged, and be sure to keep spares. Take care that the prop is as simple and durable as possible. Explain your needs carefully if someone is building it for you. A clever but intricate and fragile prop can be a nightmare. Explain that you need as few wires as possible to tangle with puppet or puppeteers and that the prop must withstand packing and many performers. Be sure you understand how it works, so that in the event it *does* blow out, you can fix it. You won't be able to dim battery lights during the show, but if you find the little lamps distracting at technical rehearsal, you can always spatter them with a light coating of tempera or acrylic. If a candle must be blown out, a simple switch can be flicked by the puppet itself. *Don't* use real candles. Fire laws

[1] See Bibliography for information about the Coad booklet on Black Theatre.

will allow them in many instances in live theatre but puppet theatre is just too small, too full of drapery, and the candles are too near the puppeteer's hair to take the chance. Besides, do you really want candle wax dropped on your nose?

You now have most of the basics for lighting your puppet stage, but there is one area of special effects you should certainly explore, that of projected effects and even scenery. It is doubtful that you will be able to manage the incredible number of projections used by the Czech Laterna Magika company (in some of their productions, live actors appear in front of moving film scenery), but you can still employ projections from time to time to enhance your shows. They have, indeed, a magical effect and can be used alone or in combination with plastic scenery.

The simplest type of projection is called a "gobo" and is a gel frame cut irregularly or in a chosen design and set on a spotlight. If other lights are dimmed, the projected spotlight will appear in the shape of the gobo. In order to prevent distortion of the shape, the spotlight has to be mounted at the center of your overhead batten. Distortion, on the other hand, may not matter, or may even be desirable, as in the case of a shooting star, so you can adjust mounting according to your needs. Gobos are good mostly for sudden effects that then fade, since little other light can be used on acting areas while they are clearly visible.

The next type of projection is rarely used in puppet theatre; used well, it can be most effective. This is what we call front projection, and it involves placing a projector out in the house and projecting slides carefully slotted into the puppet proscenium. Front projection works best when there is no overhead proscenium to catch spill or block projection onto scenery. Only rarely can front projection be used in combination with action on the stage, since anything projected will fall not only on the stage and scenery, but also on the puppets. It is also best to set it up as a convention early in a play, since the sudden appearance of projection from the house calls a good bit of attention to itself and it takes the audience a while to stop watching the projector. It is advisable to have someone out in the house running the projector; remote switches are available, but slides can easily become jammed and require immediate and direct human attention. Sometimes puppets can be briefly banished from the stage and a slide sequence used to convey part of the action, perhaps interspersing slides of the puppets themselves with related scenes. This technique offers a unique shock value by juxtaposing the real world with that of the puppet. No doubt you are familiar with the rapid, sometimes subliminal, flow of slides shown from two or more projectors. Our experience has been that without the use of the very best technology and equipment—and probably scores of projectors—

it is impossible to keep the slides in order. Somehow one projector throws the other out of sequence. If you really need this kind of effect, you are probably better off filming it, frame by frame, a tedious but fail-safe process.

Rear projection, in which the projector is placed behind the stage, offers more versatility to the puppeteer, but you can only use it when you have a deep backstage area of at least twelve to fifteen feet. When the space is available, rear projection, done well, would enhance any puppeteer's technical repertoire. One other requirement: you will have to eliminate any cross bracing on your stage behind the drop on which you wish to project. You then need a plain backdrop or cyc, stretched flat, if you want your projections recognizable and without folds. It is a good idea to experiment with a number of different fabrics. Light muslin works well, also silk (if you can afford it) or lightweight synthetics. Remember, you don't want the bright light source of the projector to be seen, just the projected image. If you wish to use projections as a backdrop for action, extreme care must be taken in lighting the puppets, and it's usually best to light them mostly from the side. Use as little front light as you can, since any light at all will weaken the intensity of the projection. Abstract shapes or effects of clouds, stars, and such, indeed anything that is basically atmospheric rather than sharply pictorial, is likely to be most successful. A commercial slide projector can be used, or you can make your own Linnebak projector, directions for which are found in most good stagecraft books. It is really a large hood housing a high-wattage incandescent lamp and fitted with a frame for slides. Its advantage is that slides can be painted on glass or be wooden cut-outs, not limiting you simply to the thirty-five millimeter or even superslide size. Even with a commercial projector, however, you can obtain considerable variation on your slides. You can paint on film, altering slides or using plain exposed film or plain slides taken of different color grounds. Scraps of gel make excellent slides. You can buy special projection paint, but you can also use felt-tip pens. For moving effects, such as clouds, rain, or snow, you can mount your slide in a continuous circular wheel and position the wheel in front of the projector, to be hand turned or rigged to be automatically operated. Color wheels, such as were used in vaudeville, sometimes are used in puppet theatre. Just partition off sections of your slide wheel and change the colors in each. The only problem is that you can't get one color to fade into another; the changes will be abrupt. The most pleasing effect for a general wheel comes from using the colors as they appear in the natural color pigment wheel, primaries interspersed with secondary colors, or a wheel composed of shades of analogous colors, say blue shading to blue-green to green to blue-green to blue again. Note: projecting the lighting primaries just doesn't have the same pleasing effect.

Rear projection upon a scrim offers still another variation for your stage. If you paint scenery on a scrim, light it from the front and keep absolutely all back light off it, even a work light, and it will appear opaque. If you then dim to dark the front lighting and project a slide from the rear, your painted scene will disappear, and you will have a breathtaking scene change. Bear in mind, though, before you start buying or building projectors, that not only must you keep all that space backstage dark, you must rope off the area in front of the projector so that no one will walk in front of it when it is in action. No, projections are not for every production or every puppeteer; they are sometimes frustrating and they have their own special requirements that are sometimes difficult or even impossible to meet, but when used with taste and balanced lighting, they *can* give effects that are well worth the work it takes to obtain them.

As your skill with lighting increases, do not let it take precedence over scenery and, especially, the puppets. Remember, this theatre is theirs. Special effects are fun, but it is the total effect of your theatre that you must keep in sight. You now have a knowledge of both the production aspects of creating puppet theatre, of building the puppets, acting with them, directing the play, and "writing" the script, and of the technical design aspects of mise-en-scène, of the totality of design of puppet, setting, and lighting, and how to make them all work together. It remains only for you to frame your work within your own individual concept, design, and execution. Be diligent, never stop at anything less than your very best work. Compliment yourself occasionally, but never cease working. May you become one of those rare artists who will advance the puppet to take his rightful place in the exciting theatre of the modern world.

# 12

## The Rod Puppet

Once one has learned the techniques of production needed for presenting the hand puppet, it is a natural inclination to wish to experiment with and involve other types of puppets as well. Since the rod puppet is such a close cousin of the hand puppet, we will now take a look at him and several of his variations. Let us see what the rod puppet has to offer us and what he demands from us in return in order to perform at his unique best. There are three main types: the hand-and-rod puppet, the marotte, and the full rod puppet.

The hand-and-rod puppet is nearest to the hand puppet in construction and manipulation, but it presents quite a different effect. One of your hands controls the head, while your other hand manipulates the rods that control the puppet's hands. Because your whole hand is free for head manipulation alone, you will be able to create a great variety and subtlety of expression. (One has only to witness the artistry of Bruce Schwarz's rod puppet pantomimes to appreciate the incredible delicacy of expression possible with the hand-and-rod puppet.) The head may have your whole hand inside it, if the puppet has moving jaws, just as in a hand puppet of the same type with no arms or arms that are not manipulated. It is also possible, for special effects, to rig moving eyes with lids that close. These trick puppets, however, are usually most effective in solo performances or on television; in an ensemble production the effect is likely to claim more attention than the play. Another form of hand-and-rod head is made by inserting a dowel in the head for a neck, which is then passed through a shoulder piece. The head is allowed to turn freely, but stops must be glued or nailed to the dowel below the shoulder piece so that the head will not slip down too far and the neck either disappear or grow very long (unless that is the effect you want). The shorter the dowel and the closer your hand is to the head the easier it is to produce forward and back movement of the head.

The rods that control the hands are best made of one-eighth-inch steel rods. You will need to flatten one end and drill a hole in the flattened metal.

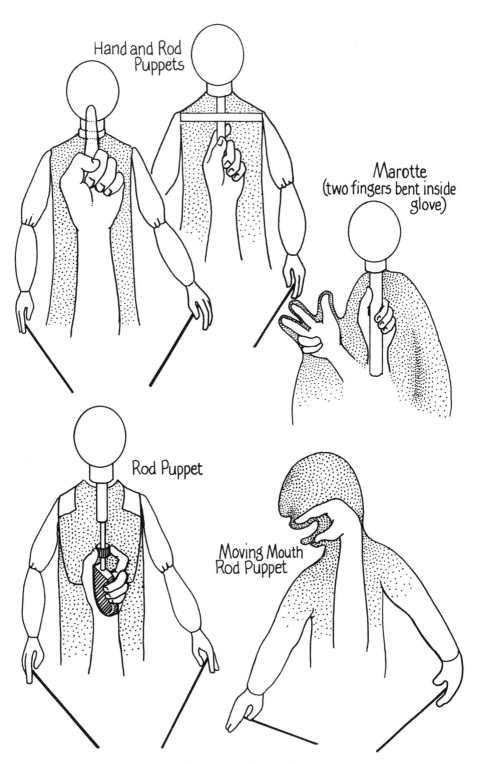

Hand and Rod
Puppets

Marotte
(two fingers bent inside
glove)

Rod Puppet

Moving Mouth
Rod Puppet

*Types of rod puppets*

You can then insert the rod with tiny nails into a wooden hand. Some puppeteers attach the rod to the center palm, but we have found that attaching it into the little finger's edge of the palm produces a finer plane of movement and easier control. If felt hands are used, a pad of felt at least three quarters of an inch square should be sewn to the top of the rod before it is inserted into the underside of the hand and the hand sewn up around the rod and tacked through the pad. Whatever type of hand is used, the bottom end of the rod needs to be embedded in about four inches of half-inch dowel in order to give you a good grip and fine control. All rods must be painted black before attaching them to the puppets, and two coats are usually necessary: a primer so that the paint will adhere and then a flat black metal enamel.

There are several advantages to this type of puppet. Not only is its movement subtle and expressive, when mastered; the hand-and-rod puppet can also be made considerably larger than the hand puppet and therefore will carry to a larger audience. A hand puppet over twenty-four inches is rarely controllable with any ease. The hand-and-rod puppet can be as tall as the operator can reach to control the head. (If the dowel from the head is made longer than just enough to allow a firm grip by the whole hand, much of the subtlety of the head movement is lost; that is, it often becomes desirable to move to the rather complicated controls of a full rod puppet.) Consider also the different type of movement afforded by the longer arm of the rod puppet, contrasted with the short, stubby arm of the hand puppet. You can illustrate the difference yourself by taking up a hand puppet and imagining him to be a stately king commanding a subject to "leave the room." Notice how difficult it is to make a gesture that feels commanding enough with the hand puppet. Now, make the same gesture yourself, using your full arm to point the way to the exit. See how you are able to complete the movement and hold it for a moment to establish its strength. The rod puppet in all its variants is capable of these large and extended movements and of finishing them. Because of the stateliness and dignity of which he is capable, the rod puppet is often thought of as a tragic, at least certainly serious, actor, but he is equally capable of comedy.

Despite the great advantages of the rod puppet, however, he will not always suit your work. Remember, you will need one person for every puppet, since it requires two hands to work each puppet. "Extras" who do not need working arms are an exception. Their heads are mounted on a long stick and the arms allowed to swing with the body movement. In this way, one operator can easily handle two puppets. André Tahon has made glorious use of these simple rod puppets in his fast and colorful folk dances. Most often, however, you will want to have the arms articulating and you will therefore need to figure on an operator for each puppet. Ingenious methods for clamping a puppet to the stage (or even to the puppeteer's waist) have been devised, but they always produce a static effect. Sometimes, it can even require a second person to manipulate one puppet. If the puppet is large and it is necessary that the arms be worked independently, then one puppeteer will operate the head and the more important arm (since he can best synchronize it with the head movements) and the other puppeteer will usually stand behind the first and operate the puppet's other arm. More often, though it does take a considerable amount of practice, one puppeteer creates a lifelike movement for the hands, working both rods in one of his own hands and the head, however controlled, with his other hand. There will be times when one of the rods can be left without control, though great care must be taken never to drop the rod suddenly, and one must pick up the idle rod occasionally, or it will appear a dead limb. Though it is easiest to move both hands in the same direction, the effect becomes boring and obvious if repeated too often. With practice, your digital dexterity increases to the point where you can move the hands independently while holding both of the rods. There is a tendency on the part of the beginner to allow the arm to bend the wrong way at the elbow on occasion. Practice cures this, and it is rarely necessary to build wooden arms with stops to prevent wrong movement; cloth arms jointed at the elbow and wrist with twill tape or leather are quite adequate. Care should be taken that the tape or leather attaching the upper arm to the shoulder piece be both firmly attached and wide enough so that the joint does not tend to twist. If the arm is cloth and sewn twice across at the joint, then stuff not quite up to the seam and allow freedom of movement.

You do not solve the problem of dangling legs by working with rod puppets. Very rarely is it worth it to attach rings to the backs of the ankles and have a puppeteer just to manipulate the feet of a rod puppet in the manner of the Bunraku. Just bear in mind the number of puppeteers required to have legs manipulated in this manner; it can become very crowded backstage, and unless the "leg persons" are very skilled, the effect is often that of calling attention to a fault and away from the production itself. Dangling legs are equally distracting, so the advice is the same as that for hand puppets: avoid them whenever you can.

Not precisely a rod puppet, but closely related because his head is on a stick and his movement is similar, is the "marotte." This puppet's dowel to the head may be quite long, and he may have one hand or two, his hand (or hands) being three fingers of your own gloved hand. Simply take a glove and turn the fourth and fifth fingers inside and sew them there. Put the glove on your thumb, index and third finger, and fold your fourth and fifth fingers against your palm. You now have a puppet hand that can pick up many objects, perform magic, and stroke his face, provoking instant reaction from the audience by the contact of the live gloved hand with the puppet face. Marottes are most effective with large capes, and care must be taken to keep a realistic distance between the hand and head. There are several different solutions to the puppet's other hand, the most obvious being to omit it entirely. If there are many folds in the puppet's costume, the absent arm and hand will not be missed. Alternatively, you can stuff a hand and attach it with or without an arm to the body at about waist height, or you can have another puppeteer operate the other hand. The most drastic solution is to mount the stick from the puppet's head on a skullcap which you wear on your own head, thereby freeing both of your hands for the puppet's hands. It is really difficult to give any finite movement to the puppet's head this way, but it frees you to do anything you like with the hands. Once in a while the overlarge proportion of a whole gloved human hand used with a five- or six-inch puppet head can be effective, but use it only when you intend the distortion. Curiously, the bare human hand used with the puppet head is quite disturbing, a grotesqueness you may sometime want. Obraztsov has used it successfully and achieved the same play of contrasts with quite an opposite and soothing effect: he appears holding his hand puppet baby, the baby's open sacque revealing its back—in reality the back of Obraztsov's own hand.

The true rod puppet has been very popular for years in Eastern Europe and is steadily gaining a following all over the world. This type of puppet permits a greater size, since the operator's hand controlling the head is just below the puppet's waist. A modified control developed by Coad Canada Puppets,[1] leading exponents in rod puppet work, is shown in illustration 30. Their control is much less complicated and easier to operate than either the traditional Czechoslovakian or Russian control. You will need a drill press to construct the control, but it performs very well once you have mastered the fine manipulation possible. You will find at first that it is difficult to keep the head movements smooth, since even lightweight heads have a tendency to slip forward suddenly. At first, also, the demands upon one's index finger and thumb, which manipulate the turning disc, are excruciatingly tiring. Like many of the other demands of puppetry, however, one gets used to it.

Because you will be working overhead with a large figure, the weight of every part of the rod puppet is of concern. The shoulder piece can be balsa or a flat oval of plywood with shoulders built up of celastic, molded free-

---

[1] See the Bibliography for information about their pamphlet, *Rod Puppets*.

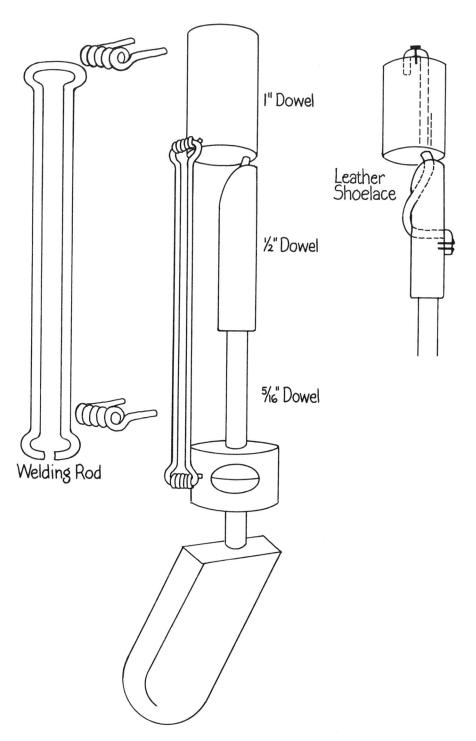

1" Dowel

½" Dowel

⁵⁄₁₆" Dowel

Welding Rod

Leather Shoelace

*Modified European rod puppet control (Courtesy Coad Canada Puppets)*

hand. Celastic can also be draped around the shoulder piece to form an upper body; remember, it adheres well to wood. Care must be taken to keep the celastic away from the control and in form as it dries. Cardboard can also be used for the upper body, but it will be less durable than celastic, though cheaper. Watch that the upper body does not extend *to more than an inch* below the control disc, or it will inhibit manipulation and make repair of the control very difficult. Be *sure* to glue the leather thong in well; movement puts a lot of strain on it, and if it works loose, it is a real problem to repair, necessitating taking the whole puppet apart. If your shoulder pieces are wood such as pine, you can attach arms with screw eyes. Balsa won't hold screw eyes and will need glue. You can glue tape to celastic. Celastic itself used as an adhesive over the tape is not dependable, nor will it hold leather.

The Coads suggest modeling a celastic or papier mâché head over a styrofoam base. We have used both hollow celastic heads and stuffed felt heads (up to six inches) with success. *Whatever* you make your heads of, make sure they are light. A large carved wooden head might be beautiful, but what agony for the puppeteer! Think of weight, too, when initially planning the size and scale of your rod puppets. About three feet is maximum for optimum manipulation and the operator's comfort. Four- to five-foot rod puppets certainly can be constructed, but we have found the size of little advantage and the difficulties of controlling them manifest. Yes, Remo Bufano did create wonderful twelve-foot figures for Stravinsky's *Oedipus Rex*. Undoubtedly this master puppeteer solved all necessary problems created by the grand scale of his work. Be cautioned, however, that with grand scale do come problems, and be sure that added size is worth whatever traumas it brings with it. If the operator or operators are seen, much greater size is possible for the puppet before any problems are caused, but having the operators in view will not always suit your production. This is a directorial decision and one we will discuss shortly, but the choice is certainly one that must be made before the puppets are constructed.

Costuming the rod puppet is somewhat easier than costuming the hand puppet, since you do not have to worry about camouflaging stubby arms. The same principles of line and color and texture will apply, but you have more freedom, since rod puppet proportions more nearly approximate the human. You may even wish to exaggerate by elongating the figure, thus capturing the flowing majesty possible for the rod puppet. Whenever you can, put your rod puppets in long skirts or robes. They can be made to move beautifully and they also circumvent the dangling leg problem. One trick is to cut the robe or skirt about half again as long as the distance from the puppet's waist to the point where you wish the illusion of feet or floor. Then, at the bottom edge gather the overlong garment tightly with heavy thread. Now run carpet or other heavy-duty thread through the gathered end and tie it around the control, just above the pistol grip. To do this you must slit the bag you have formed just at the puppet's "foot" level at the rear "hem." Make a hole just large enough for easy entry of your hand. The folds created in this manner move beautifully, and the added weight of the fabric helps greatly in preserving the illusion of a lower body.

If you must have legs and feet, make an inner glove similar to the hand puppet's, but sleeveless, and attach the puppet's legs to it. They can be made of cloth, stuffed and sewn twice across at joints. Weighting the feet with fishing lead can help to make the swing of these legs believable; how much weight depends on the size and design of the puppet and must be determined by experimentation. One way to avoid legs, especially if you have a scene in modern dress when a sea of dangling legs would be distracting, is to design your puppets so that they are only seen from just below the waist. If all the puppets throughout your piece are seen this way, the convention will be acceptable. Marottes, especially, adapt themselves to this treatment.

There are two easy ways to dress the rod puppet's upper body. Like the hand puppet, it is best not to make a costume and put it on the puppet like a doll dress, but to build it on the puppet. Keep in mind that you must have the puppet retain freedom of movement in the arm joints, especially at the shoulder. Make a sleeve of two rectangles, as you did for the hand puppet, cutting to whatever fullness you desire. Gather and secure the sleeve to the puppet's wrist. Now choose whether you prefer to cut a bodice and fit it to the upper body, fitting in the sleeves last (and allowing a generous armhole) or whether you want to cut a sleeveless inner glove, as you have to do when there are legs, and fit the bodice to it over the sleeve. If you have chosen the inner glove method, you do not need to bring the upper sleeve in as far over the upper body as you did with the hand puppet. If you bend the puppet's arm across its body to the opposite side, you will see exactly how much fullness you must allow in order to permit freedom of movement.

Since rod puppet arms are so basic to the puppet's quality of movement and provide so much of its expression, use your imagination in dressing them. If your historical period or character permits, try billowing oversleeves. Now is your chance to play with the "puffings and slashings" of the Renaissance. Lovely sleeves can be created by forming a puff ending just above the elbows over a tight lower sleeve (which must be of a stretch fabric and not so tight that it restricts the elbow joint).

If, as in Greek or Egyptian periods, you need to show bare arms, don't despair. Felt arms jointed with dyed twill tape in the same shade as the face will work. Or you can use unbleached muslin, cross-seaming it twice at the elbow and covering it (again allowing play at the elbow and shoulder) with a flesh-colored jersey. If you have a solid hand of wood or celastic, you will have to devise a means of attaching it to the lower arm. A screw eye embedded in the hand and sewn to the lower arm will work. Some puppeteers like to use a carved or cast lower arm and hand and omit the wrist joint, but it seems a pity to sacrifice the beauty of flexible hand movement. We have found that a muslin or felt arm sewn to a felt hand that is left unstuffed at the wrist affords just the right amount of play and a pleasing arc of movement.

As for outer garments, think of capes, anything that flows and drapes beautifully. Just as with the hand puppet, a cape will often take the curse off dangling legs by partially hiding them. But keep it simple. Rod puppets have a special affinity for vertical line in their dress. You may also want to experiment with the triangular line formed when the arm is extended fully to the side, then down to the hem. Take care that just because you are working with more nearly human proportion you do not clutter your design with too much detail. Still concentrate on keeping attention on the hands and face of the puppet.

Acting with a rod puppet requires mastering the new type of manipulation to the point where technique can be forgotten and one can concentrate on the character. Just as with a deftly manipulated hand puppet, the actions and desires of the puppet should seem to spring from the puppet himself; because of the difficulty and, often, unfamiliarity of operation, rod puppets all too often appear to be being pushed mechanically through their roles. Nothing can substitute for practice, and a mirror does help.

First, a believable walk must be mastered. Because of his greater size, the rod puppet can afford larger movements than the hand puppet, but he still must capture the shoulder movement and shift of weight of the walking body. Unless it is his character to do so, he cannot glide, nor can he bounce and be believable. Try the same exercise for walking that you learned for the hand puppet. Be sure that you establish a pleasing height for your puppet and that you keep it consistent. If two puppets are playing together, take great care that their relative heights remain the same and that eye contact be established and maintained. If one puppet is suddenly (or even gradually) lowered, he will appear to be walking on his knees. You will have to pick a point on the puppet costume, often a robe, as feet and keep that point level with the playboard.

Bowing or simply bending over must be accomplished believably, again gauging the height of the puppet against the playboard. If you lift him up as he bends over, his "feet" will seem to lose contact with the floor. The length of the rod or of the control will affect the manner in which the puppet bends over. You will have to experiment in order to get maximum movement and believability. Obviously a puppet "extra" with a long rod from head to below his foot level simply can't bend over. Notice in learning these early movements how much more effective the rod puppet is when he completes a movement and then pauses before beginning the next. Pantomimes, like those you did in your early work with the hand puppet, are excellent for discovering the range and subtlety of expression possible with the several forms of rod puppets. Do check out your work with a mirror and with a critical friend, since it is difficult to see from below exactly what the audience is seeing of your puppet. The tendency is to turn the puppet upstage, thereby obscuring his face, since this looks right from below to most beginning puppeteers. It is often necessary to "cheat" a puppet slightly toward the audience rather than keeping him in full profile if much of his expression would be lost in profile. Notice, too, that gestures with the upstage hand are usually most effective and pleasing. Not only do they prevent the puppet actor from covering himself, but if two puppets are acting together, the gesturing upstage arm helps to relate one puppet to the other.

Voice should only be used with the rod puppet when one has become completely comfortable with his movement. Suit the voice to the puppet just as you did with your hand puppets. As is frequently true on the live stage, timing of movement with speech becomes very important for emphasis. Most often, if the puppet moves and then speaks, he will draw attention to his words. You can't use this principle all of the time, or it will call attention to itself, but it is very useful when key information has got to be given the audience. Just so, the most effective exit will be made by a puppet who delivers a line full front, then turns and leaves.

None of the requirements for technique or for the building of inner life disappear when you are using the rod puppet. Even if you are working only the hand of a puppet, you must know and believe in him. Or, if your puppet is an abstract shape, you must particularize exactly what it means to you and why it moves and speaks (if it does) in its own characteristic manner. In fact, the more abstract one becomes, the more necessary particularization becomes. Remember, the goal is to communicate, not to be abstruse.

If it is necessary that you appear with your puppet, you must learn to "drop out" of the scene. You must concentrate so hard on your puppet and what it wants that you literally forget that you are there. If you are concentrating (and it helps if you are dressed in black), the audience will also forget that you are there and become more and more aware of only the puppet. If you like your puppet, you are very unlikely to have difficulty with this technique. Any exercises that sharpen your concentration will help you. Sometimes it is effective if there is an exchange between the puppet and the puppeteer, but great care must be taken that the exchange be an honest one. The puppeteer must really be concentrating on what the puppet is doing and what he wants to do about it; if the puppeteer is showing the audience that he can be cute with the puppet, the effect is embarrassing. This is not to say "Do not use the exchange," but to make you aware that the line between having this technique work effectively or disastrously is very narrow. The greatest clue that the puppeteer is not concentrating is too great a reaction on his part, which often gives way to facial "mugging," always a result of showing the audience what you think they should see rather than letting what is shown come naturally. In case you have been wondering, yes, if you believe in your puppet and bring him to life, the rods will not be noticeable. They will simply be accepted and forgotten by the audience. Nina Efimova developed elaborate means of concealing the rods within long sleeves, but this is rarely necessary.

Directing the rod puppet is an exciting challenge. First, you will want to be sure that rod puppets really suit the script you have in mind, and, of course, that you have enough operators to perform it. Be sure that your puppeteers are fully trained in manipulating rod puppets before you begin blocking. Movement alone is sufficiently difficult that it will be hard for them to concentrate on the puppets' inner life, unless they have first mastered the technique of manipulating them. Most puppeteers, especially when first working with rod puppets, tend to let their puppets "go dead" when they are not speaking. As a director you can make use of subtle small animation on the part of nonspeaking puppets; these little movements help the puppets stay "alive," and they help the puppeteer to maintain his concentration.

Bear in mind, when choosing the script or script material, the inherent quality of rod puppet movement. Though it is, as has been said, perfectly possible for the rod puppet—and especially the hand-and-rod puppet—to present intimate, touching sketches, the general tendency has been to involve the rod puppet in large, often spectacular productions. If the material you have in mind needs intimacy and close involvement with the audience, how can you best preserve these qualities with the rod puppet? If your material has tragic grandeur or colorful spectacle, how can you use the fluid grace and commanding movement of the rod puppet to bring out its meaning? You may wish to combine hand puppets with rod puppets in a production, using the two types to represent, respectively, animals and people; or portraying some regal or perhaps supernatural characters with rod puppets while a small, wistful, or funny character is represented by a hand puppet. Go over your script and see what kind of movement, and therefore puppet, is needed for each character. Provided proportion is kept pleasing, the combination of many forms of puppets can be very effective.

There is a great vogue at present, all over Europe and to some extent in the United States, to mount rod puppet productions on the full live theatre stage with puppeteers in full view part or all of the time. When extreme skill is exercised in all aspects of the production, as in the work of Obraztsov, the effect can be exciting, seemingly releasing the puppets at last from containment in the little box of a puppet theatre. But with what care Obraztsov subordinates his puppeteers at all times; they are often, as has been noted, actually a part of the setting, their own movement never distracting from that of the puppets. Their costumes are in soft, subtle shades, and lighting helps greatly in keeping the emphasis on the puppets. Soft, diffused general illumination falls on puppeteers and setting, while specific lighting precisely reveals the puppets. Puppets seem to appear any and everywhere in profusion; one is tempted to try such a production. Why not? Perhaps one can best answer that if you feel that a panoramic, almost pageantlike production best suits your material, and if you are willing and able to apply the keenest of directorial skills in visualization, focus, emphasis, and every aspect of design, then go ahead. If, however, you are simply charmed by this new and seemingly different approach and want to give it a try, you are not necessarily destined for successful puppet theatre. You may simply be destroying that special smallness and intimate involvement that the puppet theatre supplies. When one has seen many of these productions by companies scattered over the world, one realizes that the "full-stage-with-all-puppeteers-seen" approach is at a point of development that can be likened to the early days of modern dance, when seemingly every company was trying to imitate Martha Graham. There is about many of these "new" puppet productions a self-conscious imitation, which comes from a lack of maturity in the company's own style. In the words of Marshall McLuhan, let "the medium suit the message." Be sure the open-stage approach really fits your script material, your skills, and your own style; don't just mount a production in this way to get on the cultural bandwagon, to the detriment of your own development and expression.

The stage itself, even if you choose to mount a rod puppet production in a more traditional manner, will not be quite the same as for the hand puppet and will play a large part in the success of your production. If you use more than two rod puppets you are likely to need more width than the overhead stage described in this book offers you. Depending on the size of your cast, you may also need more depth. The problem has sometimes been solved by dropping a cyc on a batten in the theatre and backlighting it with floodlights on the floor. This way, you can go back to the depth of your choice, perhaps using several scene pieces on different levels so that the puppets appearing over them give the illusion of distance. Though you may not wish a formal proscenium arch, it is a mistake not to limit the viewer's picture in some way. You can, of course, help yourself with directorial visualization. Make certain that your figures enter and exit upstage and do not simply drop down at the sides of your masking. It is possible to set up the convention, which can be quite amusing, of puppets going up or down stairs to exit and enter. Generally, it works well to have some sort of scene piece at either end of the playboard area; these, along with carefully focused specific lighting, will help your audience to concentrate on the action. The upper end of your cyc may be enough to define area above, but you may wish to lower a "teaser" or small drape to limit the eye, establish proportion for the puppets, and, perhaps, mask lighting instruments. You will have to suit the stage to the size and scale of the production. Most often, instead of constructing a full puppet stage, you can do with front masking and then bring in drapes and battens from the live theatre itself to supplement. For performances out of doors, a front masking or several of them in different heights for depth may be sufficient. Remember, since rod puppets can't pick anything up, you will not be likely to need a playboard. (They can pick up a prop if there is a strip of Velcro on a puppet's hand and another strip on the prop, but they can't put it down again. They can enter with a light prop that can be gently caught between fingers, especially if the fingers are wired inside, and hand a prop to another puppet, this time with Velcro on the hand of the receiving puppet and also on the prop.) Marottes are another matter, since they are forever handling things; for them the playboard is all-important.

Lighting will not vary in principle from that used on the hand puppet stage, though there may be special call upon your ingenuity when working with the rod puppet. Because you have more space and probably more depth, you will need more instruments, but you will also have more flexibility in lighting areas, since you have more space to hang instruments. You still face the problem of providing front lighting from above, if you retain a traditional proscenium at all. Perhaps you can set your teaser or proscenium arch forward of your puppets in order to gain an angle of overhead front light. Otherwise you are going to have to depend on light trees at the sides. If you have only a backdrop and an open proscenium, perhaps simply a masking for the puppeteers, and have no way of gaining beam light in the theatre in which you are playing, you will have to work with side light from trees. You will increase your difficulties measurably if you widen your stage, since focusing side light on your most important area, stage center, becomes more and more difficult. Before you construct an open stage of great width, consider carefully the assistance available from instruments in the theatre in which you will play, however tempting the increased acting area may be.

One interesting variant of side lighting gives us the whole genre of Black Theatre, which is especially suited to rod puppets. In order to produce this rather magical style of puppet theatre, one needs a platform, which will be the puppet's stage floor and behind which the operators will stand. The puppets are operated from behind instead of below and must be constructed so that access to their controls is from the back. Several different controls have been developed, but we have found the hand-and-rod construction easiest and most workable. Rods to the hands must be angled so that one operator can control both without his own hands being seen, since the whole illusion depends on keeping *only* the puppet within the light path. Operators are dressed head to foot in black (velvet preferably, since it absorbs most light). Hoods are made with black net facial screens. Robes must reach below the puppet platform and black gloves must be worn. Light trees are placed at opposite sides of the platform with strong spots crosslighting the narrow platform (about two feet in depth). Black velour drapery surrounds the puppets and puppeteers. Unless you can hang a striplight across directly above the puppets, it is doubtful that the illusion will be complete. A scrim (seamless, of course) hung in front of the platform greatly enhances the illusion, tending to hide the "ghosts" of operators. The effect produced by Black Theatre is exactly the opposite of that produced by an open proscenium; Black Theatre invites us to view, indeed to enter, a strange and wonderful, totally enclosed world, completely in and of itself. Creatures magically fly through the air or appear unexpectedly at odd levels. If the illusion is complete, it is a real experience in theatre. It is, however, an expensive mode, since you will need all those black robes, hoods, and gloves, to say nothing of your lighting instruments, pipes on which to hang them, and, above all, the scrim. Before you venture into this enticing mode, do not only balance your budget, but really question yourself as to whether the approach fits the content and style of your anticipated production.

Closely allied to Black Theatre is the illusion created when only strobe light or "black light" is used with fluorescent figures and props. Much cheaper to achieve than Black Theatre, black light will work if operators are head to toe in anything black, including leotards and tights; and a scrim is not at all necessary. Black drapery behind, as with Black Theatre, obviates any use of scenery. Although these modes are especially effective for supernatural effects or magical scenes, one questions whether whole productions mounted in this manner are capable of involving the audience to the point where we can accept them as "theatre." We have previously discussed the use of strobe light for special effects, and for that purpose it is very useful; but if a whole show is done this way, no matter how cleverly, the novelty of the effect wears off, and the nature of the effect itself distances us from the puppets or the development of real character on their part. Are we, perhaps, too removed from the characters by the medium for us to become involved in them? It would be interesting to see someone try for real character and plot development using black light throughout a production. Possibly it can be done. Certainly one can fulfill both plot and character demands in *short* skits, as so ably demonstrated by Georges Lafaye's billiard player. Black light has been around a long time and is certainly an effective addition to one's bag of scenic tricks. It is also eminently suited to the rod puppet. It is simply questionable whether it works for or against one when used for an entire production.

Aside from Black Theatre and the use of black light, rod puppets require very little different in the way of scenery than hand puppets do. If you are able to support set pieces from the floor or to use wagons, you will add greatly to the flexibility of your staging. Otherwise, you can hang from above any scenery that you would use for the hand puppet —appropriate in proportions, of course. All the basics of scene design previously discussed will remain constant.

By experimenting and using the rod puppet, you are developing an awareness of the scope of puppetry and of the increased possibilities for expression when several types of puppets are combined. And perhaps, once you have mastered the rod puppet, you will go on to discover the marionette.

# 13

## The Marionette

Though you will find in almost any how-to puppet book numerous suggestions for ways to construct a "simple marionette" using everything from spools to folded paper, from the point of view of puppet theatre and of this book, all of these methods are of little use. This will seem to some a heretical viewpoint, but unless you are able to construct a marionette so that it will move in a believable manner, you may have a useful craft project, but your result will not be able to produce "theatre." A puppet whose legs suddenly bend backward at the knee joint, whose elbows cave in, or who moves in a jerky manner is just not capable of creating on the part of the audience that "willing suspension of disbelief" for which we have been working so diligently with other forms of puppets. If we are going to use the marionette, we must be able to create a figure that describes only those arcs of movement that are believable for him; he must have a control that is simple and efficient; and we must learn to bring him to life by applying previously learned acting and directorial skills to this very different type of construction.[1]

Contrary to popular belief, the marionette, if well constructed, is not more difficult to operate than the hand or rod puppet. It is simply different. If its construction is sound, much of a marionette's movement is taken care of by gravity. Perhaps because it is the only type of puppet from whom the puppeteer is so separated physically, the marionette carries with him an aura of magic. If the illusion of his life is sustained, this magic is the marionette's special blessing; if the illusion is broken or never attained, his magic is never invoked, and he is a mechanical failure dangling on strings. Instead of projecting the illusion of life upward through a hand or rod figure, the marionette operator must project his belief downward through the strings. The audience loves the fact that this feat seems impossible to them and they are delighted when the marionette performs,

---

[1] This stance is excepted in the work of older children for children. See Appendix A. We are here referring to traditional animal and human marionettes. Abstract puppets such as Albrecht Roser's scarf-and-ball marionette can be most effective as well as easy to construct.

seemingly on its own, defying the existence of a being with the effrontery to control him. Literature is replete with references to the marionette show-man as a godlike being, and one can readily grasp this image—when the illusion is complete, which it can be with carefully designed and con-structed figures.

Unfortunately, a chapter on how to fix commercial marionettes or ones that you have previously made would not help you very much. Most com-mercial marionettes are useful only as children's toys. Even the Pelham puppets from England, which are very cleverly balanced and strung, work as well as they do partly because the strings are so very short, and they are, most of them, much too small to act for an audience of more than ten. The rest of the commercial band, and also those you may have made that you would like to make more controllable, need not be thrown out if you love them, but you will find that rebuilding them will amount to taking them apart completely and very nearly starting over to make them conform to the requirements of good working marionettes. It can be done, but it will take you as much time as it would to build a new puppet. Why not build one thoroughly satisfactory marionette first and then look at your old figures and see if you really want to remake them? After learn-ing the basic demands for the marionette, you will be able to see what your old figures need and if they are really worth all the time it will take you to alter them.

The marionette should be viewed as a twofold construction problem, first, the puppet itself, and then the control. To go into the multiplicity of solutions that puppeteers have refined over the ages for both of these problems would fill volumes. Instead, we will present different approaches to the construction of the puppet and of the control, all of which are equally valid and will work for you. You will, after making a puppet with some combination of these methods, be able to stay with your choice or discover, search out, and invent other solutions. Trick puppets are very alluring. It is possible to create all manner of come-apart skeletons, jug-glers, and acrobats along with puppets that have finely articulated anatomy and an infinite number of strings, such as Herr Aicher's famous Pavlova. These marvelous creatures are all hybrid variations of the principles in-volved in the simplest, well-made and expertly controlled marionette. Please be content once again to play the scales. We wish we were able to seal the Bibliography's references to volumes illustrating trick marionettes until you have created with understanding one very basic human figure, but this discipline must be your business.

"It is not possible to reproduce in a marionette all the motions of a human figure—nor is it desirable to do so. As in all the arts a simplified or abstracted presentation is often more vivid than an exact reproduction. The designer watches to see just how a wrist joint moves, for example, and then works out the mechanical ways and means for *suggesting* that motion." So says W. A. Dwiggins in his beautiful little *hand-written* book *Marionette in Motion*.[1] He goes on to describe in detail the mechanics of the Püterschein system of marionette construction, carefully examining the arcs of motion of all the joints of the human body and then suggesting a way of reproducing these arcs in the marionette.

You can discover these arcs yourself, using your own body as a model. Stand in loose, comfortable clothes, barefooted, head erect. Imagine that you are suspended by two strings from your shoulders. Note how your body aligns itself in your best possible posture. Now, move your head from side to side and from front to back, noting especially just how far your head will turn or bend before the movement is stopped. In the marionette, capability to perform movement ranks in equal importance to the ability to stop movement before it goes beyond the range of believability. This is why most "quick and easy marionettes" fail; they simply have no provision for stopping movements. Though you will find many plans for cloth marionettes, it is extremely difficult to build stops into them, and though they may be supple, even when properly weighted it is very difficult to give them sufficient stops for believability, most importantly at the elbow and the knee.

Examine first the elbow joint. Discover for yourself just how far your elbow will bend. Now, find the shoulder axis. Exactly how far can your wrist bend back and forward; how much of its arc of movement can you capture with a string that moves from a vertical pull? You must duplicate the same arcs of movement and axis lines in your marionette.

The axis lines must have the proper relationship to each other. "The arm at the shoulder swings through more extended circuits than any other lever of the body. Motion forward and inward is stopped by the chest, but motions backward are not easily controlled." [2] The upper arm can be fastened to the chest by a variety of methods; two leather thongs (shoelaces) or one-eighth-inch woven cord are two of the most reliable means. The holes should be set far enough apart so that the joint has free play but does not tend to twist. If the holes into which they are glued are not quite horizontal, the front hole lower, the angle of the arm will be more lifelike. You can also embed a leather strip into the upper arm and chest piece. Using two cords, however, does keep the hinge at its ninety-degree axis a little better, and leather deteriorates more rapidly.

[1] Puppetry Imprints, Handbook XII (Detroit, 1939).
[2] Dwiggins, page 312.

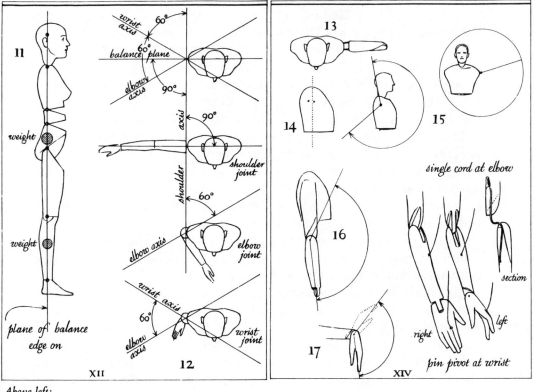

The elbow joint is trickier. It is set at an angle of sixty degrees to the axis of the shoulder hinge. Shown in Illustration 30B is the standard shim joint favored by most puppeteers. It is rarely necessary, except in the case of exposed joints under close scrutiny, to go to the trouble of fashioning ball-and-socket joints, in which the upper arm (lower tip) rotates over a wooden ball fastened by a pin so that the joint is almost invisible. Either joint has the advantage of allowing no motion sideways. The inserted tin shim works equally well. The axis of the wrist joint, which can also successfully be made in shim fashion, is set at an angle of sixty degrees to the elbow hinge. Many different types and variations have been developed by puppeteers, but "any kind of joint will serve, so long as the device holds the motions of the parts pretty much to the one plane of rotation, and stops the swings at the right places." [1] You can readily see why upper arm, lower arm, and hand, if fashioned of cloth and joined with tapes, are not going to supply the proper stops. If you must work in cloth, the joints will be helped if you make the angles of the limb pieces or of cross-seaming (if the limbs are made in one piece) follow the axis lines as shown.

There are varying preferences among puppeteers for casting body parts in plastic wood or for carving them, usually of pine. Either method works, though if the parts are hollow, you may very likely need to embed lead weights at more points than illustrated, especially in the lower legs and forearms. Accurate weighting for optimum movements is your most important consideration after developing a method for stopping the joints. As nearly as possible, you want to approximate the relative weights of masses that compose the human frame, thus grounding your puppet in a believable relationship to the earth and gravity.

Note in the illustration the scale suggested for standard male characters. These scales work well, but if another pleases you, fine; just be sure that you develop a standard scale and stick to it, varying size and shape to meet the demands of your characters. In order for your puppets to appear in the same style and to look like part of the same "company," they must all relate to some sort of given standard scale. Note that the head is larger in proportion to the rest of the figure than in real human anatomy. Pinheaded puppets are a common mistake, as well as figures with too small hands and feet.

The marionette head may be made in any manner we have discussed for other puppets or that you have discovered yourself. The added weight of a carved head can be an advantage, but you can easily embed a small lead weight in the forehead of a cast head before joining the halves. Even

[1] Dwiggins, page 312.

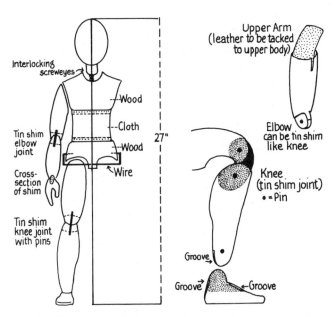

Interlocking
screweyes

Wood

Cloth

Wood

27"

Wire

Tin shim
elbow
joint

Cross-
section
of shim

Tin shim
knee joint
with pins

Upper Arm
(leather to be tacked
to upper body)

Elbow
can be tin shim
like knee

Knee
(tin shim joint)
• = Pin

Groove

Groove

Groove

*A workable scale for male puppet figure with shim type of joints*

a head of papier-mâché over styrofoam can be embedded with a weight just above the hairline. The neck, as shown, must be long enough to fit down into the shoulder piece's cavity, usually joined by linking screw eyes or hand-fashioned linking pins. This joint can be silenced by winding the linking metal with heavy thread. Though the tendency often is to create the head before the body of the puppet, it really makes no difference which you make first, so long as you keep the head in proportion to the body. It will help you, especially at first, to draw out the entire puppet on paper, checking parts against your drawing for size as you make them.

The knee joint is similar to the elbow joint and serves much the same function, permitting no sidewise motion. Note how its carving or molding stops the joint from moving the wrong way, again difficult to accomplish in cloth. The upper leg can be attached to the body by two leather or woven-cord thongs or by a piece of leather glued in slots in upper leg and torso. However accomplished, this joint must hang the leg straight without a tendency to twist. A buildup of the torso between the legs does help to keep them on a straight line along the plane of balance, as does as much width as possible at the top of the upper leg.

The torso is most often carved or molded of two sections, with varying distance left open in the middle. Dwiggins illustrates a beautiful, but perhaps overly complicated, three-piece torso strung together on a spinal

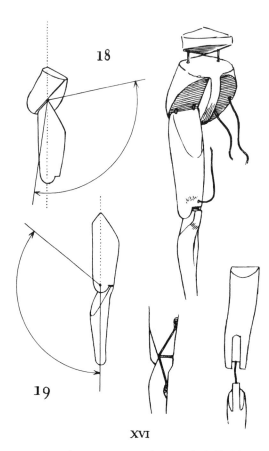

19

XVI

*Dwiggins' leg joints. Note how string is fed through drilled leg. Cord or wire may also be used within the leg. (By permission of Marjorie Batchelder McPharlin)*

cord of thong. It is just as workable to joint the upper and lower bodies with muslin strips or leather, leaving a good distance of air between as Tony Sarg often did. The important consideration should be that the waist joint not tend to twist. You can experiment with the distance between your jointing sections until you arrive at the optimum joint for a given puppet.

The upper torso should be slightly higher at the back and recessed to accept the neck. The higher back behind the neck will prevent the head from tipping too far back but will still permit full freedom for the head to turn. Rounding off the shoulder where the upper arm will join it affords a pleasing line.

We have neglected only the feet. Some puppeteers like to cast them in one piece with the leg, but this gives a very stiff walk. Better to fashion a shim joint (see leg illustration) and attach the foot either with a pin or by means of a string up through the heel and embedded in the lower leg.

The lower leg weight usually obviates weighting the foot, but if you find that it is not making good contact with the floor after the puppet is working, you can embed a small round drapery weight in the ball of the foot. Sometimes it is advantageous to carve the foot of hardwood, since it is heavier than pine.

You should now be able to create a fully constructed and jointed figure, albeit bald, nude, and without strings. Obviously, even when you have the marionette together, he can't go anywhere yet, but you have a little experimenting to do before attaching strings, and also some decisions to make. Take your puppet and let it sit in the palm of your hand. Does it look believable, and does the puppet feel comfortable in repose in your hand? Now take the figure and gently let it fall into a variety of random poses. If the puppet is well made, it will appear absolutely believable in whatever position it occupies. Check out the joints. Are any of them bending out of their necessary arcs of movement? Check their stops. Sometimes you can correct an insufficient stop by filling it in with plastic wood. Check your weighting. The puppet need not be heavy, but it must have a sufficient substance to cause it to fall in definite positions, not fluttering from one pose to another. Correct the weighting. There are no absolute rules, even for a "straight" character. You really must arrive at your own system with the guidance already given, since proportion and materials used will so affect the weighting needed.

You are now ready to set your puppet aside and consider how you will control him. It will do no good to attach strings until you know what means you will use to manipulate them. We cannot possibly discuss all the many controls that puppeteers have worked out (and each usually swears that his is the *only real control*). Three controls are illustrated: the most common, airplane control, the Dwiggins variation on it, and a variety of vertical control. Each of these controls is relatively easy to make, and they all fit well into the hand; which is easiest for you to make and manipulate is a very personal choice. However you build your control, you want it to do its job without getting in the way. As many motions as possible should be under the control of the hand holding the control. The Dwiggins control solves the problem of the strings getting caught on the control itself by offering very few angles or crevices. You will want a method of tying your strings that is simple and won't come undone, and you must be able to adjust the length of the strings, so a place to wind them on the control can be valuable.

As to the string itself, some puppeteers swear by fishline, since it is invisible (nearly) in front of the puppet. Its disadvantage is that it likes to come unknotted unless extreme care is taken. Ordinary carpet thread is

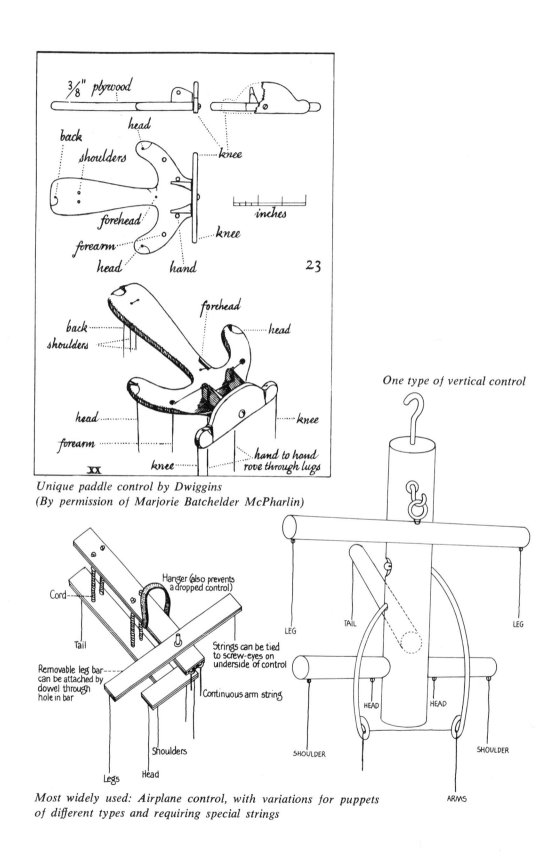

3/8" plywood

head

back

shoulders

knee

forehead

forearm

head

hand

knee

23

back

shoulders

forehead

head

head

knee

forearm

knee

hand to hand
rove through lugs

XX

inches

*Unique paddle control by Dwiggins*
*(By permission of Marjorie Batchelder McPharlin)*

*One type of vertical control*

Hanger (also prevents
a dropped control)

Cord

Tail

Removable leg bar
can be attached by
dowel through
hole in bar

Strings can be tied
to screw-eyes on
underside of control

Continuous arm string

Shoulders

Legs    Head

LEG        TAIL        LEG

HEAD    HEAD

SHOULDER            SHOULDER

ARMS

*Most widely used: Airplane control, with variations for puppets*
*of different types and requiring special strings*

favored by other puppeteers, with a rage of controversy as to whether black or dark green is the less visible. Carpet thread stays knotted and, especially when well rubbed with beeswax, performs well. If the strings in front of the puppet really bother you, you can string from the puppet to just above its head in fishline and then knot (securely) onto carpet thread for the rest of the distance to the control.

If you are wondering why we are not now moving on to a discussion of costuming your marionette, which surely must be done before stringing, it is because you are going to test string your puppet to see if any changes need to be made in its anatomy before you complicate it further and/or make inaccessible that which needs change. Later on, you won't need to test string, except in the case of odd new types of puppets. Now you need to find out how well your puppet moves and also to learn how to manipulate him. It isn't necessary to decide at this point whether you will eventually work in revue style, seen by the audience with your puppet, or from a bridge above and behind your puppet. You are going to clip the strings and restring your puppet after costuming it, anyway, so you can learn to work it now with strings at the length that affords maximum ease of control. The farther you are from your puppet and the longer the strings, the harder it is to control it and to project through it, so let us choose to have you stand next to your puppet with strings long enough to allow you to hold the control just below your waist. Now, let's get the poor thing moving. Call a friend, if you can, since it's a lot easier to string a marionette if two people work together. Later on, if you decide to work from a bridge with six-foot strings, you will need a ladder!

First, knot two strings to the sides of the head; usually screw eyes will be used directly above the ears. The puppet's body weight hangs from its shoulders, so you will want to get these two strings evenly knotted at the desired matching length from the control. Let the body hang relaxed, and be sure both feet make contact with the floor. Now attach the shoulder strings, usually also with screw eyes. As you will note on his control, Dwiggins adds a string to the forehead, a string rarely used. You may find occasion for it or for a chest string later, but omit them now. The "tail" string attaches just where the spine would end, or a little above. You can tell if you have placed it correctly by holding it taut and letting the other strings go slack. If the puppet bows believably, then the string is correctly placed. If his feet tend to skitter as he bows, there is insufficient weight in the lower legs and feet. Now attach the knee strings. If a string is attached to the outside of the foot, attached again at the upper outside calf, and then threaded through the lower portion of the thigh from extreme lower and outer edge to emerge at center for feeding up to the control a particularly fine means of control results.[1] Often the arms of the puppet are strung on one continuous string, fed through either lugs or screw eyes. If the arms are strung to rest just slightly bent at the elbow, their natural hanging position is believable, and the puppeteer is free to concentrate on the movement of the rest of the body. By slipping the index finger through the continuous arm string, one gains control of the arms, though it is usually necessary to nip the string with index finger and thumb in order to make any finite gesture. Those are *all* the strings you need on a basic marionette. More can be added for tricks and special effects, but consider carefully before you add extra strings. And never position the tie-off point on the control of any additional string in such a way that it will impede the action of basic strings. Always work to have as *few* strings as possible do the job. Lots of strings sometimes impress an audience, but they are rarely necessary, and believable movement accomplished by a well-constructed marionette with as few strings as possible is always going to be the most effective.

Now that you have your puppet strung, play with it awhile and see what you can make it do. Always keep in mind the contact of the feet with the floor. Probably the most common fault in marionette manipulation is the lack of ground contact that makes the puppet look as though it were flying or slipping or sliding, rather than walking. Just as with the other forms of puppet, you must first find a believable walk. Rotate the control slightly to get the look of a shift in weight. If you are using an "airplane" control, remove the leg bar and find out in front of a mirror exactly how far you can lift the knees and have the puppet look as though it is walking. How fast does it have to move forward to make the shift in weight from side to side and step to step believable? When you think you have mastered a walk, try running. Notice that when a person runs, the head and upper body lead, the angle increasing depending upon how fast the person is running. No wonder marionettes look ridiculous if their knees are bobbing up and down, bodies moving forward, but with the head vertically aligned to the torso and perpendicular to the floor! Even before you start developing short pantomimes, see how many human movements you can suggest with the marionette.

Make your puppet wave. Notice that the marionette is capable of perfectly isolated movement, as in the technique of the mime. Rarely, however, in suggesting human movement does one part of the body's movement not affect the rest of the parts in some way. Perhaps the puppet's head cocks as he waves; certainly it must be looking in the direction the puppet is waving. Now make him sit down. To make things easier, give him a box

---

[1] Method generally attributed to Rufus and Margo Rose.

on which to sit. Let him look to find the box to be sure it is there before he sits, and when he sits, lift the tail string up slightly and then settle him back and down, watching the angle of the body as he sits. Try laying the puppet down on his stomach. Which part of the body leads in the descent? Make him put his chin in his hands. Now raise him up, carefully noting which part of the body leads. Do you see how much of your work is being done by gravity?

One of the oldest marionette acts (it dates from before vaudeville and is still being applauded when well done) concerns the little clown that is trying to climb up on or into a box almost as big as he is. The act is an excellent exercise in concentration and will help you to begin to motivate your marionette. It is easier if the puppet's hands are shaped so that they will hook over the box, but for the purposes of exercise, this is not necessary. The box can be made with or without a top. The act is sometimes performed with a string to the top of the box that the puppeteer or another puppet pulls to open the box. For first purposes, leave the top of the box open. Now turn your puppet toward the box. Let him examine it, thinking about what might be in it. Turn his head to the audience, and you will see that the marionette is just as capable of a "take" to the audience as the hand or rod puppet. Turn the puppet back to the box. Let him want to look inside it. He tries to climb up the side and falls down. Try to get the feeling of climbing, the various pulls of muscles against gravity, as the puppet tries harder and harder. Remember the magic series of three? On the third try, perhaps the puppet succeeds in grasping the top of the box. Make him look as though he is holding on. Wriggling his legs makes him funny as he tries to climb over the side. Does he succeed in climbing in, perhaps outsmarting you, his manipulator, or does he give the project up in disgust, kicking the box in anger as he stalks away from it. Does he conquer his adversary at last? You decide. You will find that if you are careful in supplying motivations for your puppet as you discover his bodily capabilities, you will have, when you have mastered this exercise, a quite delightful little puppet "act" which should rescue you from any discouragement about mastering marionettes.

Try some other pantomimes, working as you did with hand puppets, holding back on the use of voice until you are totally at home with your puppet and able to bring him alive silently. Though one puppeteer can operate two puppets, don't try it until you have really mastered working one well. Remember how hard it was when you first learned to split your concentration between two hand puppets? Possibly because the technique of operating the strings is so visible and specific, the tendency is to want to master all of the art immediately. Remember how patience with yourself paid off with the hand puppet, whose techniques are more hidden and required you to discover them. Work slowly, and not only will your dexterity immeasurably improve, but also your belief and hence your puppet's "life."

It is extremely important in your earliest work with the marionette that you build its inner life and discover what it wants. Since so much emphasis is of necessity placed on the sheer technique of operating the marionette smoothly, the trap awaiting the beginner is that of becoming so absorbed in technique and in cleverly displaying the puppets that they neglect developing their character or motivation. Because new techniques must be mastered does not mean that they should become an end in themselves. You may well have had the misfortune to see marionette revue shows, in which the puppets go through their motions more or less well manipulated but do not come alive, so that one is very aware of the puppeteer. On the other hand, you may have had the great good fortune to see Albrecht Roser from Stuttgart, Bil Baird, or Tony Urbano solo with one of the "same old acts," or one with a slight variation on the theme, and the puppets seemed alive and almost independent of their manipulators. These artists have combined skilled technique in the most difficult maneuvers (anything done well looks easy) with a belief in the puppet and an absolute concentration on the task at hand; you, too, must accomplish this blend of technique and inner life, just as you did with the hand puppet, if you are to bring the marionette into the realm of true theatre.

If you work to define both character and inner life with your marionette during the period in which you are conquering its movements, you are much more likely to cultivate originality in the development of the script material you will eventually play. If you do choose to do one of the hackneyed acts left over from the days of vaudeville, try to give each act a new twist. A favorite with marionette revue artists (and nonartists) has for eons been the stripper, and for Sid and Marty Kroft's *Poupées de Paris,* Tony Urbano rescued this timeworn act from banality by introducing a very funny salacious bat who claimed the lady's discarded clothes. Bil Baird's piano player is a triumph of character development, with his half-lidded eyes and cigarette dangling from his mouth as he nods into his jazz beat. One of the greatest performances of marionette revue is a variation on a European "stock" character; she is Albrecht Roser's Grandmother. As she sits and knits and prattles on, it is not even necessary to understand her German to become totally engrossed in her actions. She is a fully evolved character, utterly at home on the stage and completely in command of her audience; it becomes doubtful if she really needs Roser at all. That is the kind of suspension of disbelief for which you are working. It will come, slowly, and not by copying someone else, but through your own invention and belief. There is nothing wrong with the revue format; just go over what you learned about it with the hand puppet before you are seduced into building trick puppets just to show the audience how clever you are. Trick puppets are a lot of fun but like any other puppet, they need a reason to be onstage other than just to show (you) off. Unfortunately, since inventive artists in the field of marionette revue have been few, most people's audience experience with this type of entertainment has been with a triumph of mediocrity, leading to the popular misconception that puppets are "just for kids" or an antique curiosity piece. You will, we hope, be among those who will pull up the marionette by his strings, showing the audience that he can, indeed, perform real theatre. Just let originality be your guide.

Before we deal with your choice of whether to do a revue or a story type of marionette show, and whether to perform in view or hidden by staging, let us go back to that first puppet of yours, who is shivering bald and nude, waiting to be wigged and costumed. Having worked with the puppet awhile, you now know much better what you want him to look like, and you also know his movements. You will now be able to plan makeup and a costume that will bring out his character and will not inhibit his flexibility.

Little changes in makeup when we move from hand or rod figures to the marionette. Again, the most frequent fault is that of erring in the direction of photographic realism, probably because the puppet's proportions are more lifelike. Marionettes with eyeballs stare just as blankly as hand puppets with eyeballs do. Even with wigs you should encounter no new problems. Do, by all means, finish the puppet head completely before you attach it to the costumed body even if the head wasn't finished when you attached it to the body for test stringing.

Most puppeteers find it helpful to sketch out the marionette costumes, but if you work better directly in cloth, there is no reason not to drape the costume on the puppet without drawing it out. The marionette is much easier to costume than either the rod puppet or the hand puppet, since proportions are pleasingly like the human, and it is not necessary to mask any distortion. It is difficult to build an armature for a rod puppet so that you can work on its costume as it hangs in an upright position. Not so for the marionette. You simply build a gallowslike "costumer" and hang the puppet from it on a hook. Either hang the puppet headless, using the screw eye to which the head will be attached, or fasten two short strings from the head.

All of the material covered earlier on line, color, and texture as well as the adaptation of historical costume will hold true for the marionette. It is usually a temptation to use too heavy fabrics in an effort to capture certain

Adjust length
for each puppet →

WEIGHT

*A costumer*

textures. Learn to fake textures with light cloth that drapes well and moves easily. It is especially important to build the costume on the puppet, making absolutely sure that none of the joints you have so carefully crafted are restricted by the costume. You may find it a temptation to go into too much detail; the marionette is more like a human than other types of puppets, but it is still *not* human.It is usually small and will drown in a superfluity of detail. Remember that simplicity carries.

With the marionette you can capture the flavor of many historical periods and give a wealth of character information through flowing veils, formal trains—and at last you have a puppet that does not look ridiculous in tights and pumpkin hose. Care, however, must be taken in constructing tights so that they allow play at the knee without being baggy.

In a marionette costume avoid anything that might catch on the strings. Disaster can lurk in protruding jewels, hats that catch head strings, sometimes even in fingers. Beautiful but string-catching hands can be rescued by running thin fishline from finger to finger, sewn or glued, depending upon the material of the hand. Be especially careful when trick strings are added to plan the costume so that the extra movement won't be impeded. If Pinocchio has a string to his nose to enable it to grow, you will endure endless frustration if the string gets caught in his hat every time it is pulled. Keep testing the puppet as it hangs, and you build its costume for movement. Stretch each limb to its farthest point in its arc of movement; if the costume is holding it back at all, ease out the fabric. Most frequent trouble spots are at the back of the shoulder seam and the rear of the upper leg, so always cut these costume parts a little longer than you think you will need. If you costume the limbs first, you can tape them to the torso until you have the body costume draped. Then, trim off excess fabric on the limb costuming and baste it into the body costume. Final seaming of the sleeves into the coat or bodice, or tights into pumpkin hose is always best done by hand. Remember, no doll clothes that you slip on a puppet as a finished garment! Men's trousers should be cut a little loose and fitted several times so as to be loose enough for movement but not baggy. When you come to stringing the dressed puppet, take care that you feed the string through costume parts such as capes and skirts at the points that allow the costume to fall to best advantage.

Though it is possible to change small accessories on a marionette, if any major costume change is required, it is best not to get tricky with intricate cuts attached by Velcro, enabling costumes to be removed around strings. Take the extra time and build another puppet with the full costume change. One of the commonest "time-saving" gimmicks puppeteers fall for is that of leaving the legs off ladies with long skirts (or men with long robes). This practice is a shortcut to disaster, since such puppets cannot give an illusion of walking, but always glide, bounce, or float. There is no way puppets without legs can sit down in a believable fashion. Now, if you have spirits floating through the air, that is quite another matter; leave out any body parts that are inessential to their movement or design. Since flying through the air is something marionettes do excellently, by all means capitalize on their ability. Time their flying so that it is slow enough to register with the audience's eyes, and if the character is supposed to alight somewhere, make sure that it makes contact with its "perch," just as the foot of a walking puppet must with the floor. Mounting puppets on a tandem or chorus control can be another shortcut to losing your audience. If you really want a chorus line of some sort in which all the characters must move at exactly the same time, then the tandem control works beautifully, but if you are mounting several characters together because there are not enough hands to manipulate separate controls, the puppets will most often appear silly moving in unison, and you can make the situation even worse by hanging the control onstage with the puppets left to dangle lifeless from their strings. Once in a while one can get away with hanging a puppet "extra" onstage in a lifelike position, if great care is taken to animate him occasionally, so that he will not appear dead.

Animal marionettes—those that are not anthropomorphized creatures with near-human two-legged bodies and an animal head—can be approached in the same manner as the simple human marionette. All the principles of arcs of movement and weighting apply; your only problem is in discovering them, and here your best friend will be any good book on animal anatomy. Once you know an animal's skeletal framework, you can quite easily figure out how it moves as it does and which movements you want to preserve in your marionette in order to catch the essence of a creature's quality of motion. First, draw out a simplified skeletal drawing to scale. Now go over the drawing, marking where weight will be needed. Simplify body parts over the skeleton. If you are carving in wood or molding, you will be able to cover the whole body with one of the many light-weight fur fabrics just before attaching limbs. (Cloth animal marionettes, if well weighted, can be very effective for floppy, cozy creatures whose movement need not be at all realistic or finely detailed.) Sometimes, if you are undecided about what the arcs of movement really are or what type of joint you want to use, it is worth it to string together approximate limb lengths of dowel—even macaroni isn't too foolish—and play with the "limb" until you have discovered what you want it to do. Remember, you are trying to capture what it is about the animal's shape or movement that says "cat" or "elephant" or "dodo." Get up and pantomime the creature yourself in order to get its "feeling." Finally, before beginning to build, check the scale of your design and its relative proportion to your human figures. Quite often, particularly in the case of the smaller animals, your puppet will be much larger in relation to human puppets than it would be in life. You have quite a range within believable artistic distortion. The range, however, is not infinite, so check your characters and be sure that they appear in pleasing complement to each other.

For an animal, follow the same test stringing method you did for the human marionette. We have found the vertical airplane control (in many variations to suit the special creature) to work easiest and best for animals. If the vertical length of the control is slightly longer than the animal, you gain leverage. You will, of course, need two crossbars, for front and hind legs; either one or both can be pegged and thus made removable. A special *real* tail string can be attached to the end of the control through a hole and tied to a curtain ring for easy access.

Do be sure that each marionette you make has its own drawstring bag cut just a little larger than its owner and labeled. Always bag the puppet when putting it away. In order to avoid tangled strings, hold the control in one hand and with the other hand swing the marionette gently around to twist the strings within a few inches of the control. Now grab the twisted strings and wind them around the control over and over, winding crosswise over any removable control bar. When the strings are wound almost up to

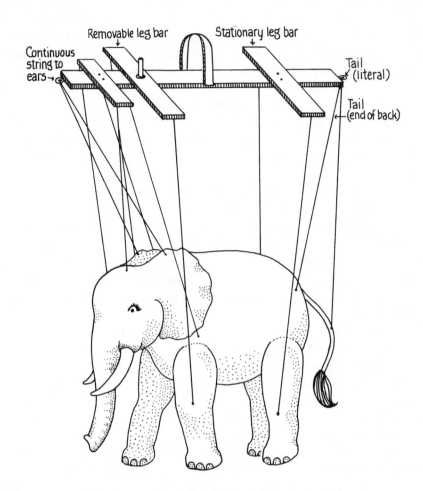

Animal controls must be as long as the animal

*Airplane control for elephant*

the puppet's head, you can lay it gently down for storage with no fears of a rat's nest of strings.

We have left you, though, with a costumed human puppet and perhaps an animal. They are waiting for their final stringing, and before you do that you must decide whether you are going to retain the short strings and appear with your puppet, or operate your marionettes unseen from a "bridge" above and behind them. Both modes are equally valid; the choice depends upon the personality of the puppeteer. Some people absolutely hate to be seen by the audience; others enjoy being the "magician on view." You will probably want to try out both methods, and you may even switch from one method to the other as you progress in your work, since each mode suits a different type of material. Having the puppeteer on view is usually chosen for a revue format. Being seen with a marionette affords more finite control, because of the short strings, but introduces the same problems you had to handle in being seen with a rod puppet; one must learn to "drop out," using judiciously and with taste exchanges between the puppet and puppeteer and at all costs avoiding "mugging" to the audience.

Staging for the revue may be as simple as having the puppeteer step out into a theatre spotlight. Though you are an eminently portable act if you have no stage of your own at all, you may wish to opt for the more sophisticated approach of a slightly raised platform on which you will work with black drapery behind you. If you intend to travel or work extensively, you may want to consider building a platform that supports housing for your own lighting, since you will then be spared coaxing theatre managers to refocus lighting, or working without sufficient light, or most importantly having the light focused on the puppets with too much spill on you. There once was a vogue for puppeteers stepping out into a spotlight in tuxedo or ball gown to operate their marionettes, but somehow, this mode has become passé, and today's audience more readily accepts and certainly more readily surrenders its disbelief if you, the operator, are visible but appear in light of far less intensity than that illuminating your marionettes. You are still the magician, but the effect is much less self-conscious.

If your choice is to present a play or "story" show with marionettes, you will need to consider what story material is most appropriate to the string puppet. Keep in mind the general puppet axiom, "Can it be done better or as well by people?" Then ask yourself what the marionette's special qualities can bring to the script you have in mind. Some material can be presented equally well by hand, rod, or marionette; other material seems almost marked for a certain type of puppet. The special, small-scale intimacy of the hand puppet demands that we accept him as not human; the rod puppet, in humor or grandeur, again is obviously not quite "real." The nearness of the marionette to a likeness of mankind is both his special gift and his bête noir. If he is made to photo-copy the real world, the marionette becomes at best a poor imitation. We must capitalize on his fantasy, the magic of transformations, the movements he can easily execute that most human beings cannot. The marionette can be funny, serious, or even tragic. He is as at home in Greek tragedy with its heightening of tension and abstraction from day-to-day realities as he would be performing an adaptation of a fairy tale. One cannot imagine marionettes presenting *A Streetcar Named Desire*, but one can readily accept *Peer Gynt* with all its brooding characters from the outer reaches of man's dreams. Actors in animal suits are seldom believable; the puppet *is* the animal, and the marionette is eminently capable of capturing the essence of animal movement. Not only can the marionette fly, come apart, or stand on its head for hours without complaining, it also dances beautifully. Quite intricate choreography becomes possible. Choose material that takes advantage of the unique capabilities of marionettes.

Bear in mind, however, the limitations of your marionettes. Though props can be hooked or attached to a hand with Velcro, their use should be limited, because marionettes just can't handle them easily. They are not capable of the small, definite manipulation of objects that you accomplished with either hand puppet or marotte, nor can they make the sweeping gestures of the rod puppet. Almost any strong downward motion, except foot-stamping or sitting, becomes very difficult or impossible with the marionette. Physical contact with other puppets usually looks awkward. Anything from a handshake to an embrace becomes a difficult feat, and marionette fights are rarely convincing. Because elaborate scenic effects are possible, stories that demand them adapt well for the marionette. You will still want to keep your play shorter than in live theatre, but marionettes seem to be able to hold the audience for a longer and more intricate show and for more scenes than other forms of puppets. Still, you must keep the action flowing, and avoid intermissions or at least keep them brief. It is not necessary to keep the hero on stage as much with the marionette; for some reason the audience just doesn't become confused as easily when marionettes are used.

Most marionette shows are fully scripted and most often taped. Most marionette shows also sound "read" or "canned" for these very reasons. Even with a very good tape, one loses, to a great extent, audience participation. Time cannot be allowed for varying audience reaction and, yes, the audience *does* know the show is taped, unless it is all music or at least has very little voice. Sometimes you will have to tape a show with dialogue, but please, at least try playing a marionette show "live." You will need to become very skilled at manipulating the puppets in order to talk for them as well, but you *can* do it. Though it is not the usual approach to marionette theatre, the type of script offered earlier in this book—see chapters 4 and 5—is just as suited to the marionette as to hand or rod puppets, and the vividness of the performance is worth the added effort.

Few differences in directing come up when one switches to the marionette, though it becomes even harder to participate as both actor and director. The most frequent problem for the director of marionettes is to get the operators to a point where they will cease holding the puppets all in a line parallel to the Act Curtain. The natural tendency is to hold the control at the most comfortable distance from the rail, and you will have to do a considerable amount of reminding in order to achieve variety in the line of positioning. Gradually you and your cast will overcome nightmares of control bars dropped in attacks of nerves as the puppeteers begin really concentrating on the puppets' goals and communication with the other puppets.

If you have chosen to use marionettes in a story show, you can use most of the guidelines already given for lighting and scene design. Because of the small size of the marionette stage, elaborate staging that would cost a fortune in live theatre can be built with a modest budget. The greatest new problem you face is designing scenery so that it will not catch the strings. The illusion of a traditional live theatre box set is possible and it may even be composed of small theatre flats of wooden frames covered with muslin and painted. You must, however, split your flats above any scenery at doorways or any other entrance spot to allow for strings. By placing one flat slightly behind the first, the illusion of an unbroken line of wall can be preserved. The depth of your set will depend on the type of stage you build. Obviously, if you are going to operate your puppets from a bridge above and behind the figures, the stage can only be slightly deeper than the distance you can reach comfortably and walk your puppet. If, however, you plan a stage with a front bridge as well, you can operate on a platform as deep as operators on both sides can reach. The complexity can grow to magnificent proportions, as witnessed by the large grid built by Bil Baird for a television production of *Art Carney Meets Peter and the Wolf.* Though Baird admits that such a stage would rarely appear in the theatre,[5] it illustrates both the possibilities and the problems inherent in supplying depth to the marionette stage. The stage was sixty-five feet wide and forty feet deep. Though both sides of the bridges were used by the five puppeteers, a leaning rail was provided only on one side of the bridges. A precarious occupation, indeed!

Obviously, even if he had wanted them, which would be unlikely on television, Baird could not have mounted drop curtains or any other type of drapery in such a complicated hybrid stage. If you are working with the more traditional marionette bridge, you will be able to use drops, as long as they don't conflict with the strings. Act curtains can easily be made

<hr />

[1] Bil Baird, *The Art of the Puppet* (New York: The Ridge Press; Macmillan, Inc., 1973), p.238.

to close or roll up or down in front of marionettes, but remember that you must be able to reach out in front of whatever drop you use to operate your puppets, and don't forget to plan for exits and entrances. As with hand puppets that pop up through the floor, string puppets that are dropped down into the setting for lack of wing space always look deplorable. With the exceptions of ghosts and other fantastical types, they should definitely be avoided.

A wagon stage can be used very effectively with marionettes. It is placed on the puppet stage floor and can be set with two or three scenes, rotating quickly to reveal the next scene and making the closing of the curtain and loss of audience interest unnecessary. House sets that first reveal a flat exterior and then open like a book to reveal the interior are breathtakingly effective and require only the hinging of flats, or even plywood if you are not concerned with traveling weight.

Because there are *so* many variations to the marionette stage and many of them have been well documented by others, we will confine ourselves here to a discussion of the basic requirements, illustration of the most basic stage, and a caution to consider your own needs and production requirements thoroughly before embarking on the considerable investment in time and funds that building a complicated stage requires. Convertible stages that can be used for either hand or rod puppets or marionettes can be made practical. Or you can solve the whole problem, if resident in one theatre, by constructing your bridge of parallels and step units, attaching a leaning rail and dropping blacks around perhaps the full stage width and to a height in proportion to your puppets in order to create a proscenium.

Here, then, are the basic requirements. You need a *sturdy* bridge with leaning rail. If the bridge is narrow, a rail at the back is a fine safety precaution. Some sort of steps or ladders are needed to give operators access to the bridge. A hanging rail with hooks behind the bridge holds puppets ready for use. The puppets need a stage floor, raised to create good sight lines and wider than the actual area seen by the audience in order to permit smooth entrances and exits. You will need a frame to support curtains, if they are to be used, and provision, perhaps on that frame, for lighting instruments to be hung. Light trees or striplights can also be used at the sides. If you are going to travel, weight, portability, and setting-up time need all to be considered.

Lighting the marionette stage usually presents many fewer problems than lighting the hand or rod puppet production. Instruments can easily be hung to throw light from front and above. You should be able to crosslight all six stage areas with no problems, hanging specials where you need them and being limited in effects only by your budget and what

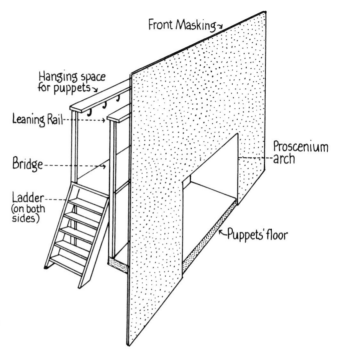

Front Masking

Hanging space
for puppets

Leaning Rail

Bridge

Ladder
(on both
sides)

Proscenium
arch

Puppets' floor

*The simplest type of marionette stage. The masking may be changed,*
*but then must hang from a suspended or supported batten. Rigging*
*behind the masking must be provided for lighting and curtains.*

the circuitry will carry. You can even floodlight a cyc from the floor, provided that you mask the instruments with a groundrow (a piece of scenery placed on the floor). The number and type of instruments will depend upon the size of your stage and the complexity of your production. You are more likely to have trouble restraining yourself from attempting yet more of the wonderful effects available to you than in creating the effects themselves. Try small "specials" to backlight set pieces. An unoccupied puppeteer can even operate a follow spot on a certain character.

The world of the marionette is full of technical challenges, but if you will enter it with a spirit of originality and imagination, it offers great rewards.

# 14
## Shadow Puppets

Despite a rich and ancient heritage, the shadow puppet has fared less well than other modes of puppetry, especially in the United States. Though a permanent shadow theatre exists in Moscow and Dr. Professor Jan Malik regularly presents shows in Prague, an American is lucky indeed to catch a shadow performance—and still luckier to witness a fine one. Despite the horrendous number of puppet shows I have seen over the years, I have rarely had the good fortune to witness quality in shadow work. There are the beautiful films by Lotte Reiniger, and if one is lucky enough to see him, there is the comic genius of Australian Richard Bradshaw. Otherwise shadow performances are usually confined to demonstrations of ancient Wayang or Chinese shadow theatre or to dismal failures. One wonders why more has not been done with this interesting aspect of puppet theatre in the United States.

The shadow theatre throughout its history has possessed a mystic quality. An aura of mystery surrounds that which is not seen. Lotte Reiniger explains the phenomenon in this way: ". . . a shadow always depends on the source of light it comes from; it really does not exist on its own. That is what makes it mysterious." [1] She goes on to draw a distinction between the shadow and a silhouette, since the latter can cast a shadow and it cannot be distorted. Why then do we call it "shadow theatre"? The flat, articulated figures held by rods against the translucent shadow screen do exist on their own, and they can appear distorted as they are held at an angle or moved toward or away from the screen. Whether they are silhouettes or detailed, painted transparent figures, they are an extreme simplification of reality, and they do *appear* through the screen as shadows. Much of their fascination, I believe, whether the artist's intention is symbolism or fun, is with what is *not* seen, what has been selectively left to our imaginations.

Even the shadow puppet's history is shrouded in mystery. Existing in

[1] Reiniger, Lotte, *Shadow Theatres and Shadow Films* (London: F. T. Batford, Ltd., 1970), p. 11.

many parts of the world in related but different forms, the shadow theatre has baffled experts, none of whom agree on its exact time of origin. Let us not join the controversies, but simply state that China records its existence at fairs by the eleventh century and at the same time shadow theatre was thriving in Java and probably Bali. Shadow theatre in India may predate both. The shadows survived the Moslem commandment not to make graven images because the articulated shadow figures were considered exempt from the prohibition: holes had to be pierced in it to joint it, and this let the spirit out. Precaution, however, was taken in Turkey with the Karagöz shadow theatre, which played its bawdy romp during the Ramadan; it was always played out of doors or in a coffee house, since after a performance indoors an angel could never inhabit the building.

The Indian shadow figures are among the largest of the historical types and are made from goat, deer, or calf hide, intricately cut and treated to render them transparent. Puppeteers can draw a moment of fun from the fact that plays still take place outside the temple of Shiva, who is the patron god of puppets. How many of us wish for the eight arms of Shiva!

The Wayang figures are of two types: the three-dimensional Wayang *golek* and the flat Wayang *kulit*, which are made of buffalo hide often very intricate and delicate. Much symbolism is involved and every cut, every color, every cast of the head has its meaning. The holy myths of the *Ramayana* or the *Mahabharata,* recited by the *dalang,* or puppeteer, comprise most of the material for the plays as they do also in India, but comic characters abound. If you are ever able to see an authentic performance, do go, but unless you are an Asian scholar, do not expect to grasp the incredible complications of the symbolism, let alone the plot. And be forewarned that traditionally performances go on all night!

I have witnessed a quite authentic reproduction of the Chinese shadow theatre which was beautifully dull. Many of the traditional Chinese shadow plays were taken from live theatre or opera because, according to one theory, women were not allowed into the theatres but could witness the plays performed at home by the shadows.[1] Even so, in the incredible delicacy of the figures a pure religiousness pervades. The figures are held up by a "rod of life"; each cut made in figures and delicate scenery is made with reverence. It was this theatre that gave inspiration to the twentieth-century salon silhouette theatres in France and Italy, the most famous of which was the *Chat Noir.*

Despite its bawdy nature the Turkish Karagöz is never irreverent. Though its characters represent a cross section of the populace of Istanbul

---

[1] Reiniger, p. 16.

and satire is the meat of their interaction, a religious invocation commences each performance. Karagöz "is a figure of ridicule in his own milieu—but he always has the last word, and invariably winds up triumphing over all adversity." [1] Together with his educated friend Hacivad, Karagöz (and his Greek cousin, Karaghiozis) joins the long line of world puppet heroes—beloved of their audiences and passed on from generation to generation.

But what can *you* do with this strange and wonderful form of puppet theatre? Its aura of mystery and seeming elevation beyond reality make it eminently suitable to dream sequences within any other form of puppet play. Since its staging is so simple, merely requiring a translucent screen and a strong light between the figures and the operator, you can fit it into almost any kind of puppet stage. The frame itself can be made of wood and corner-braced in whatever size you like. Its covering can be silk (if you can afford it) or any white or light-colored opaque but sheer fabric. Do try to avoid seams in the screen; they will be even more distracting than in a scrim. The shadow screen need not be as large as your backdrop; if you mask off the unused area to be lightproof, the shadow screen can appear as though seen through a window or between trees. Since the shadow figures suit themselves so well to depicting large numbers of figures moving across the stage, you may want to use them to show travel scenes or for processions. If you choose to represent characters both in three-dimensional puppets and in shadow figures—a device that can be very effective—take care that scenes involving strong character motivation be handled by the three-dimensional puppet. When the two types of puppet are used together, the shadow figure can handle very well physical movement "from here to there" or dream thoughts, but his impact is diminished when he is seen in a play with a three-dimensional counterpart, and central scenes of the play will not carry if entrusted to him.

Why is it that when whole plays are presented by shadow puppets they so often fail to dispel our disbelief, even when the characters are beautiful and the manipulation clever? There seems to be something about the shadow theatre that leads puppeteers to abandon the disciplines of good playwriting and sound acting technique. Almost invariably they fail to give their puppets strong "wants," seldom projecting through the puppets, but rather "speaking lines" while executing movements. The result is empty, talky, and generally overlong. If you will follow the same disciplines you did in acting and playwriting for other forms of puppets, there is no reason why you cannot successfully present puppet theatre with shadow figures. Once in a while, you can even get away with the usually boring

[1] Siyayusgil, Sabri Esat, *Karagöz* (Ankara: Turkish Press, Broadcasting and Tourist Department, 1955), p. 12.

device of having a narrator throughout. He or she will seem like a "story-teller" and can complement very well the "once-removed" nature of the shadow stage. If, however, your characters have singsong voices and your scenes go on endlessly without building to a climax, your play will be no more successful than it would be with any other form of puppet.

The shadow puppet itself is a relatively simple construction, though you can increase its complexity with the number of parts you choose to animate. Basically, it is a silhouette, transparent or opaque, jointed where movement is needed, and moved by rods. Bristol board works well, cut with a matt knife or X-acto blade. The ply you choose will depend some-what on the size of your figures; the board must be heavy enough so that the largest mass to be cut will hold its shape when the figure is moved. The shadow puppet can be so simple that only an arm or a tail is articu-lated, or it can be made to somersault or dance, with many parts jointed in a torso, leg, foot, or even the fingers of a hand. Your principle should be the same as that you follow with any other type of puppet: you want to capture the *essence* of the character's movement. Carefully analyze with your own body where the pull of gravity and muscles exists in a given movement. Get out your animal anatomy book. Crawl around or leap or trot like each animal you choose to portray. What parts of the body must be articulated in order to capture the movement as you feel it in your own bones, the movement that gives the essence of each character or animal?

Sketch the figure you have chosen on paper in the size you want to work (shadow stages and their figures can be very tiny and still be effective for a small audience in a living room). Work out the overlapping parts and decide which parts must be articulated. You may want to make several different puppets to represent one character, each capable of different movements. A good trick can be borrowed from the Egyptians. Sketch the feet of a person or two-legged creature as though it were standing in absolute profile; then imagine that you twist the torso, so that both shoul-ders are seen from the front. In this way the character is "opened out," and much more articulation is possible. The face, of course, remains in profile.

For fastening the joints, simple wire brads from any stationery store (sometimes also called "shank fasteners") can be poked through punched holes and then opened out. Number 01 will fit even the smallest figures. If you wish to strengthen the area around the holes in bristol board, apply those little gummed circles with holes in the center that are used to strengthen binder paper. Always put the head of the fastener on the side of the puppet that will press against the screen, since you want to keep that side as smooth as possible.

You may want to use black card or bristol board for an absolute silhouette effect, or you might wish to experiment with figures cut from sheets of acetate and painted with aniline dyes. The dyes will work even better if you rub the figures lightly with fine sandpaper before applying the colors. Extremely beautiful effects can be created with these colorful and transparent figures. Here, for once, in the painting of a puppet, you will need black to outline and "tie together" the elements of your design. Do have at least a practice screen set up as you paint and assemble your figures and keep testing them as you go along to be sure that the effect you want is being produced by your efforts. A strong sense of line will aid you greatly, since the tendency is to see the figure chopped up in all its component parts. If you can visualize the whole continually as you work, you will be able to use both line and color to bring out the desired effect of the design.

Shadow figures can be controlled by rods in either of two ways. The rods can be attached so that they push the figure against the screen at an angle, as in the Asian shadow theatres. In this way the operator's hands are below the puppet and will not be seen, but the rods will usually be at least partially visible. Often the "rod of life," which runs up the central portion of the figure and may attach to a clamp or fit into a groove just below the proscenium opening, is visible, especially if the figures are translucent. If the visible rods bother you or defeat the effect you wish to create, use the Chinese method later borrowed by the salon silhouette theatres of Europe. A central rod is attached to the figure, just below the neck in front. All rods are attached at right angles to the puppet, so that none are visible to the audience. Very thin steel rods work best, with the end to be fastened to the puppet flattened and drilled, just as you did for the rod puppet, and painted black and also fitted with a handle in that same manner. The length of the rods will be somewhat dependent upon the size of the puppet, but you must always make them long enough to keep your hands out of the light path, in other words, behind the light source. If you wish to attach the rods at right angles, simply bend the rod above the flattened area; naturally, you can bend the rod at any angle you wish.

Very elaborate scenery can be worked out in either silhouette or translucent style. You may wish to contrast the scenery with the puppets. Take care that the elaboration of the scenery complement the puppets and not compete with them. In the case of the marionette, the possibilities for elaboration are both a source for imaginative enrichment of the production and a lure toward overdecoration and drowning out of the puppets. All forms of puppet, and the shadow is no exception, call for the line of the scenery to complement the line of the puppets; style must complement style. Focus is just as necessary in the shadow theatre as in other forms of puppet art, but it is often lost and the loss helps the shadow theatre to become boring. Learn to use line and mass to guide the audience visually, and if you are using translucent figures and/or scenery, vary the intensity of the color. Since this mode of theatre is absolutely two-dimensional, you can give the illusion of depth only by line of perspective and by decreasing size of the figures.

Scene changes present a problem since one setting pressed against the screen must be gotten out of the way before another can be put in its place. Dimming your light and playing music is going to result in that undesirable break in your audience's attention. Often the scene change is set up as a convention at the beginning of the shadow theatre performance, as the first setting appears, dressing the black screen. The audience will then usually accept the fading of one setting as it moves from the screen and another's appearing in its place, but care must be taken to execute the change with as much speed and finesse as possible. You don't have an Act Curtain to close, and so nothing can go on in front of the screen. You will have to find a way of adapting your performance style for continuity in this restricting but fascinating form of theatre.

Lighting for shadow theatre is so very simple—often just strong white light. Why not experiment with colored light and dimmers, however? The only restriction is that your lighting intensity must be great enough for the shadow puppets to be visible (and you may want their images sharper in some scenes than others). If you dim to very soft light and gently perceived images, the effect can be quite marvelous, but do not stay too long with dim light, or your audience will fall asleep. Though you cannot use specific and general light to mold forms, you can, indeed, employ color and intensity to lend mood and variety to the performance, and all the principles of general stage lighting hold true. Probably you are best off using colored light projected directly on the screen and not trying to cross-light areas. It could be done, but might simply be unnecessarily complicated.

Principles of directing will not be different for the shadow theatre. If you attempt a full play, fewer operators will mean fewer directorial challenges, but there is no reason why, given the space and skill, shadow theatre must limit itself to one or two operators. If you are directing yourself in a one-person show, do check out your work in a mirror, so that you are sure of what the audience is seeing. Just as with the marionette, figures that are fixed to guides at bottom and left untended for long periods of time without animation will appear dead. Occasional subtle animation of secondary figures will keep them "in" the scene. Your greatest problem as a director will be in guiding operators to develop their puppet characters. Any kind of improvisation to help them identify with their characters will be useful. As with other puppets, the development of a believable walk comes first and foremost. Inner life must be kindled if the shadow puppets are to come alive; the operator must not only conquer a new technique which can easily become a total preoccupation, but must imagine a full characterization for a two-dimensional figure (and one that is often not very interesting from the operator's side). Sometimes it helps to alternate roles, so that puppeteers can see what their characters look like in action. In short, do anything that helps to bring the characters alive for your puppeteers.

Choice of material for the shadow stage is really quite open. Many adventure tales suit shadows: fairy tales, the beloved *Just So Stories* that are so hard to adapt for the other forms of puppet theatre, even science fiction. You might look at fables as well, since this "storyteller's" medium does not have quite the necessity for dramatic conflict that the other forms of puppet demand. Do not be misled, however, and pick a story that goes on at a droning level; shadow theatre is still theatre, and as such must be dramatic. Keep in mind the struggle inherent in the material and what you can do to make the conflict visual. Look for material with flying creatures, underwater scenes—as always, things that can be done better by puppets than people, and in this case, by a specific form of puppet.

That shadow puppets can perform adult revue material has been brought happily to our attention by Richard Bradshaw, whose comic sketches seem to have walked right off a superb cartoonist's drawing board. He has not only the ability to capture the essence of a character, but a wonderful sense of the absurd and, most importantly, the ability to say a great deal with the ultimate simplicity. It would be difficult to forget his hippopotamus on a seesaw. Why not experiment with what you can do with satire and with the relation of comical shapes—what they *do* to each other.

The shadow puppet is as much a mask as any other form of puppet, and you may just find that it is the mode that suits you best. Perhaps you will be one of the few to step forward and give some life to this resplendent but long undervalued mode of puppet theatre.

# Conclusion

You now have an overview of the various modes of puppet theatre. You have some general guides to construction, but more important, we hope that you have gained insight into the many theatre arts necessary to the presentation of successful puppet theatre, that you appreciate the value of each, and that you will continue to refine the contribution of each element to your work. Your work will grow; you will develop your own style and methods. You may branch out into animation or film or television, but the essential demands of your art will remain constant. It is our hope that whatever you do as you continue in puppet theatre, we have given you a strong foundation on which to build and modify and experiment.

We hope that you will keep the disciplines you have learned, while constantly looking ahead to new areas of challenge. No art form survives without quality. It is our hope that through your awareness of the possibility of quality in puppet theatre, through your disciplines acquired in order to achieve it, and through the inspiration of your own invention, you will be one of those who will remind the Western world that the puppet theatre has much to say to the child and to the adult in its very special power to capture its audience's "willing suspension of disbelief." Respect your audience, give them your best, give them *theatre*; they will then not only be willing but amazed and loyal, and you will be joining the long chain of those guiding the puppet theatre back to its rightful role, reaching directly to the hearts of the people.

# Appendix A

## Puppet Theatre in the Classroom

Please reread the title of this appendix. It says puppet theatre, not puppets. All too often, usually for lack of a few useful bits of information, puppets in the classroom become craft projects rather than performance projects. Now, it is quite obvious that you can provide a class or classes with puppet theatre by booking a professional company to come in and perform (and it is hoped that when you do, you will book quality, having seen the artists' work, and pay the price for excellence). It is also possible for you as the teacher to use puppets to capture young children's interest, dispelling their disbelief as well as their resistance to a particular subject by having a puppet or puppets "teach" it.

But what if you wish to have the children create puppets themselves? Why is it that so often these projects get bogged down and never reach completion, or that a child makes a puppet to take home but never experiences performance with it at school? Usually, the craft end of the project was designed to take too long, or else the teacher never intended to get involved in performance at all. Let us take a look at some of the values the child can draw from puppet theatre in the classroom, what suits the child at different ages, and finally, how to take the fear out of these theatre ventures for the teacher.

The most obvious value inherent in any children's theatrical endeavor is that of learning to contribute to the value of a group effort. As important as this experience in cooperation is at all levels of child development, there are other more subtle values to be gained. Live theatre experience allows the child to "be" someone else; he not only experiences another personality, but he often allows himself much freer expression than is his usual wont, simply, as Alice said, "because, I am not myself, you see." This release of not being oneself is intensified greatly by the use of the puppet, literally giving the child a mask to hide behind. The more the child identifies with his puppet and projects through it, the more valuable—and often surprising —his experience will be. In fact, one must handle the child's often very deep empathy with his puppet most carefully. It is not unusual for a child who is very shy and speaks rarely to become even garrulous with a puppet. Always the puppet will represent some aspect of the child's personality that has been wishing expression; at first it may be tentatively let out to play, and it is extremely important to the inner child that you guide gently. You may not wish him to keep in a performance everything that is expressed in rehearsal, but with a little sensitivity you can usually feel what a child needs to play out at least once and then suggest *to the puppet* what might be changed in order to make a performance more effective without directly criticizing the child. If the expression of the child through the puppet differs markedly from the behavior of the child as you know him in the classroom, you are dealing with a very naked and vulnerable ego. Note, here, that we are speaking of the "normal" child in a "normal" classroom situation. After one has worked with children and puppets even briefly, the values of puppet theatre experience in different types of therapy become patently obvious. We shall touch on a few of the applications in therapy before closing, but direct ourselves here to the guidance of a children's project geared to graded age levels in a classroom situation.

Coupled with the experience of expression and cooperation, puppet theatre offers the child and the teacher a chance to bring almost any material in the curriculum "alive." How much more a child will learn about the Gold Rush, or life in Egypt, or of Indian lore, if he has to search out material for a puppet play! He will not be reading and memorizing, but finding out how his puppets must dress, what would be important to them, what would be exciting, and what would be fearful. Almost any age can start with a myth or story from a given period in history and locale; the wealth of detail in historical accuracy that they are able to bring to their "production" will be only part of the benefit they will derive. By the time they present their play, they will have used their imaginations to empathize with another people in another time. They will be just a little closer to empathizing with "different" people in their own time.

Nor are you limited to the transfer of social studies information. Can you imagine a child forgetting the struggles of an inchworm who is having a terrible time learning to "go metric"? You can capitalize on the examples of beloved folk puppet heroes and make the children's puppet hero the one who has trouble learning whatever subject needs to be taught. If the "villain" is intolerant of his mistakes, or if his mistakes cause a chain of disasters, the other children will love correcting the hero, setting themselves on the right learning track as they tell the puppet what to do.

There is naturally a limit to the amount of educational content one can expect children to convey in a production they mount themselves. As with the "message" show performed by any puppeteer, it is best to use a light touch. Far better that the children become excited about the subject than that they be turned off by a demand for too much educational content. Children respond very well to requests for reasonable accuracy in the historical or factual material they wish to include, but they are rightly concerned first and foremost with the story content of their show, and the less you tamper with their dramatic ideas, the better the production is likely to be, both in terms of performance and in educational transfer.

If you have difficulty, as many teachers do, in envisioning your knottier spots in the curriculum as dramatic, try turning the playwriting task over to the children. This does not mean, "Let's do a play about spelling," which is a far too broad and singularly undramatic idea and which is therefore likely to be met with groans. But, if you draw a character on the board and say "He (or she or it) can't spell . . . It's in real trouble because of . . . and having a real battle with the . . .", you can let the children fill in the blanks, and soon you have the beginnings for a play. It never ceases to amaze me that what frequently prevents a teacher from involving a class in puppet performance is his own inability to appreciate the dramatic in classroom material; and so, I suggest to you, if this is a problem you share, let the children show you what is dramatic. They will rarely disappoint you.

If you have a degree of bravery, you might like to try the "open-ended" script. In this situation, you give the class the beginning and middle of a story and let them work out the resolution. You must be prepared for almost anything and accept it. Obviously, this plan is best suited to a performance confined to your classroom, or when part of a class performs for the rest, but *not* when parents or other classes are to be invited. Its value is in that it releases so much of what the children feel about the material, and if several groups are performing the same story beginnings, they learn that there are a number of different possible outcomes or solutions. Some may be violent, some may be socially unacceptable, most would get a negative Nielson rating if shown on TV. Do not, however, underestimate the value of post-mortem discussions of why endings worked or how the rest of the class felt about them. All of this ferment of imaginative activity is helping to free your class from a mesmerized culture in which entertainment is fed to them on screens and through boxes. Puppet theatre can give them a chance to get involved imaginatively without the complications of a full live theatre production; it can kindle interest in areas of your curriculum at levels in accordance with their own growth and development; it enables children to discover what "entertainment" is all about. It is not unusual for this type of project to stimulate discussions of dissatisfaction with TV and movie fare. Something formative is happening to the grown-up viewer who will emerge from these children. Let us hope it is awareness and that each one of the few whose standards are raised will help later to raise standards for the many in years to come. Idealistic? Perhaps. But what happens if no one sparks the curiosity of the young? What happens if they are allowed to sit mesmerized and never to become truly involved either as viewer or participant in the imaginative mystery of theatre?

If you will refer to the chapter "Acting with Puppets" in the body of this text, you will find that most of the techniques can easily be applied when working with children. The more they believe in what the puppets want, the less likely they are to become preoccupied with the puppets hitting each other. Point out to them that there are other actions for a puppet to do and that it isn't necessary for a puppet to touch another puppet whenever it speaks. If you supply a goal for each puppet, children will quickly drop the tendencies toward constant movement and solution of every problem by a fight. The transfer of that learning process need not be detailed!

Well, you say, I can see the children might benefit in several ways from an experience in creating puppet theatre, but there are so many problems and it takes so much class time. In a way, you are right, but there are ways of cutting down on the class time and controlling, if not eliminating, the problems. Step one is for you to have a highly organized project and know beforehand just how much time you will allot to it. Step two is to choose easy construction methods in keeping with the age level and abilities of the children. Step three is to divide your class into groups.

Grouping can be done in a variety of ways, again suiting the age level with which you are working, but also your own convenience and resources. Teachers of K-3, especially K-1, often panic at the idea of several groups working separately, particularly if they do not have a teacher's aide and must somehow oversee all of this seething young humanity alone and un-protected. It has been our experience that even the very young, who are just learning to work together, can successfully combine efforts. The trick is to keep your groups small, no more than four or five, and if you have pairs, or even one or two children who wish to work alone, to respect their wishes and allow them to do so. If you have one or two real trouble-makers, you will know where to group them so that they will be under your watchful eye. Usually the youngest fare best if kept in the same group right through the project, from construction to performance. Older chil-dren, about at the third grade level, tend to stratify according to abilities. You will find certain persons who will want to work backstage and not perform, others who will perform or die. Again, respect their wishes. As long as everyone is contributing, all are gaining. What about the person who makes a dreadful puppet or hates his puppet himself or doesn't finish it? You can find something else for this small person to do in the production, but it always works best to have everyone go through the construction phase. Groups may shift slightly according to what gets finished and who decides to belong to another group, but usually the shifts are minor.

Young groups (K-2) will not work at an even pace in the craft phase, but you can get one group on its feet rehearsing while the rest are half-watching and half-crafting. Yes, an aide helps, but the lone teacher experiences little difficulty when the children's enthusiasm is kindled from the start. The greatest service you can do yourself and your class is to turn the nonperforming groups into critics. Let them tell the rehearsing puppeteers what works and what doesn't. If you always guide toward constructive criticism, making sure that both the giver and receiver understand what is being said, and that the receiver has the chance to consider and accept or refute the criticism, you are contributing pricelessly to each child's education. All his life he will have to give, take, and assimilate criticism. Learn to refuse comments like "It stinks," but to encourage the speaker (or if the speaker curls into a mute ball, call on another child) to say *why* he thinks something didn't work. Ask for a positive suggestion of what might work better. Always make the point that it was what the *puppet* did that didn't work, and that this was quite separate from the operator's worth. Do you see what is happening here? Often even criticism received by the child at home becomes directed at his or her own worth and is not focused on an act; you really can help to right this balance through your puppet work. And the puppet helps, because, just as in a professional performance, the puppet did it, not the puppeteer.

During the grades four, five, and six you will find a growing sophistication, not only in craft work, but in the child's appreciation of his own abilities. These are the grades where you can have everyone make a puppet in art class and then use the ones that the class fits into scripts under your guidance. Or, if you are in charge of all phases of production, you may want to choose with the class who will be puppet makers, who will be script writers, scene painters, et cetera. You are dealing with an age that can be guided to love research on costume and setting. Your biggest task is in sorting the children so that each child feels involved and appreciated and no one child becomes the "star." At this level, you may want to involve the whole class in one production. This is a personal choice and depends on how well the class works together and how well you work with them as a unit. They are capable of working either way—in small groups or all together.

If you choose to work with small groups, they will always separate into plays that succeed in varying degree. *Never* make a competition between the groups, but again encourage constructive criticism and appreciation of what was successful about each production. Even the worst performance is going to have something about it that you can point to as successful. Whether you have parents attend an in-class production or let other classes see it should depend partly upon how finished a production you had aimed for in the first place. Performance should always be geared toward communication with an audience, whether the audience be the rest of the class, or parents, or other classes. The size of the audience is really not important; it should be composed of those most likely to appreciate the performers' efforts.

Grades seven, eight, and above tend to be highly self-organizing and to decide very quickly who will do what part of a production. The only pitfall to avoid is a half-and-half situation, when half the class is involved in construction and the rest take over the performance. You don't want half your class idle during each phase. Simply assign lighter tasks or an assistance role to any person who is not employed. The experience of adding something to the area of their least talent is often the most beneficial to the student.

We cannot encourage you enough to draw your material from your curriculum, and we refer to the body of this text for information on scripting the play. And whether you use ours or a similar method, we urge you to avoid the written script from the library *at all age levels*. The youngest children can't read anyway and will have great difficulty memorizing. The second through fifth and even sixth grades are going to get preoccupied with words and sound "read" if you use a written script. The seventh grade and older may be capable of a slick production from a written script, but all will gain so much more if the entire project originates with the class and they are allowed a measure of improvisation.

Thus far, the material presented may sound more fitted to the "open classroom" than to the "structured" one, but this is not necessarily so at all. It does require a certain flexibility on the part of the teacher and an appreciation on the teacher's part that it is worthwhile to give up a social studies class in order to do research for a puppet play set in ancient Rome. The amount of juggling need be only minimal. Sometimes the cooperation of several teachers may be needed (art, science, homeroom, for example), but this is rarely a problem. After the third grade the children do not have great difficulty shelving their project after one period and then going back to it in the next time slot. Try to compress the time spent into no more than two weeks for first and second grades and a week in kindergarten or a kindergarten–first grade combination.

But, you say, how can I do this when the children must craft the puppets, write the play, and rehearse and perform it? You can; you just have to simplify the craft end, for it is true that many puppet projects have gone down like the *Titanic*—and without even an iceberg—because the project dragged on long past the children's interest span. All you need to do is fix your goal upon *production* and then gear the type of puppets the children make to their age and abilities and interest spans. This is easier than it sounds. There are only two requirements; the puppets the children make must be as quickly assembled as possible and they must stand up to the wear of rehearsal and performance. One obvious answer is to have the children use a group of puppets your school already has, perhaps adding costume or bits of character color. This is really cheating the child's imaginative expression, however, and it isn't that much more work to let the children design and make their own puppets.

*Warning:* if the children bring puppets from home, you are going to get collections of popular television characters, and it is going to be very hard for you to get the children to make up scripts that aren't copies of what they have seen those characters do.

Without going into a detailed craft manual of puppet making by children (see the Bibliography for a number of books that have already done that), let us review some construction methods that fit various ages. Keep in mind that the teacher's biggest mistake is to become preoccupied with construction to the point that the children have lost interest by the time rehearsals are supposed to begin. You will need to decide whether to let a class construct any character they choose (perhaps assigning older children a certain time period or culture) or to gather the framework of a script first. The latter is usually much more successful since even though you may have to make minor script changes as characters have altered during construction, you will not have the task of evolving a script around eighteen horses and four princesses and a spaceman! Choose your method of construction and have *all* the materials you will need assembled at the *first* construction period. Some children like to draw their puppets before constructing, others hate it—just as with adults, their choice works best.

## Suggested Construction Methods

### Kindergarten, First and Second Grades

The youngest children have not developed sufficient digital dexterity to control even the simplest hand puppet. They will do best with stick puppets, and these can be combined with several types of hand puppets made by the more adept students. Any cardboard cut-out can be mounted on a stick and made to serve very well as bird or butterfly or anything that need not be finely animated.

With *any* type of school puppet, adapt your paint. Acrylics are usually prohibitively expensive. By adding a one-eighth portion of white glue to school tempera and stirring well you lessen the tendency for it to rub off. You can also spray the finished product with Varathane, but this adds a slight sheen. Treat the paint used on backdrops, even if they are painted on brown paper, or the paint will inevitably rub off onto the cast.

Moving-mouth puppets can be successfully made by reasonably adept very young children by joining two empty Jell-O cartons with masking tape, then painting them and attaching a sleeve made of a sock bottom or a fabric glove. (Note: through fourth grade, *any sewing* of seams that must hold is done by *you* ahead of time.) Socks can make mouth puppets with less defined mouths simply by adding features, tongue and hair, et cetera.

Paper bag puppets are favored by many teachers, some of whom actually have accomplished a performance with them and their owners. Usually, however, they just get sent home, which seems appropriate since they are fun but just not durable. No child wants to replace a torn puppet and start over on construction in the middle of rehearsal.

When a real hand puppet is desired, do not start with molding in clay and casting, even in papier-mâché. The process is too involved and takes too long. Papier-mâché is fine, but have the children apply it to a base that will remain part of the puppet. Inverted, empty, and rinsed, school milk cartons are probably the cheapest base, and the children have no difficulty accepting the square heads that their shape produces. Do discourage the making of realistically shaped animal heads or any heads that require great masses of papier-mâché, since they take this side of forever to dry. Unless you like its ugly, pebbly texture, don't use prepared craft papier-mâché; torn newspaper strips with wallpaper paste and a top layer of paper towels works very well. If you are organized, the whole head-making can be accomplished in one class period, painting in the next, and wigging and finishing in the third. Then you glue the puppet to the body.

*You* cut and make the bodies. This is a boring task, but the children cannot do it themselves. Use unbleached muslin and hem the bottoms. You can sew one in five minutes, so the project is really not so awesome. School scissors never cut fabric well enough, so don't decide to develop the children's cutting ability by having them cut them out. You can pass out the bodies when the heads are finished, and the children can decorate them with magic markers and glue on bits of trim, if you like. That way, they have personalized the puppets, and yet costuming is kept to a minimum.

Another good head base is the styrofoam ball. You can have the children cover it with papier-mâché, or, for a superquick head, simply have them cut features out of felt and glue them onto the balls. *You* cut the neck holes in the balls, keeping them on the small side, with an X-acto knife before giving them to the children. With this type of head the body can be glued to it or not, but bear in mind that the interchangeability of bodies and heads may not counterbalance the risk of heads lost in rehearsal and performance!

Do go over the puppets after the children have checked them and recheck to be sure all parts are secure. Don't change their work, but do reglue any loose parts. You must start and finish rehearsal with puppets that *work*. Do not add the frustration of flimsy or overcomplicated or inadequately glued puppets to the new and, to most children, unfamiliar period of rehearsal.

There is no way to give you an absolute time period for rehearsal, but at this age four or five class periods is about all interest will support. Try to keep the script to one scene and one backdrop, which can be painted on butcher paper and hung on the wall behind. Some schools have puppet stages, but it is often more difficult to adapt them to the size of the children than to adopt a simpler solution. If you have a stage that works for you, fine; if not, never underestimate the value of a refrigerator carton. It will hold four or five operators playing overhead. If necessary, you can tape or glue on a corrugated playboard for props (remember to keep those props large and *unbreakable*). If many children must be involved, a cardboard masking can be attached to school desks and made just high enough to mask the students. Just make sure the masking is securely taped, so that it will not come down in the middle of the show. Young children tend to lean on any masking, so you will have to make clear (often) that neither they nor their puppets can lean on it. All sorts of ingenious staging has been devised for classroom use. It need not be elaborate, with curtains and lights. It need only be sturdy enough to get through rehearsal and performance and large enough to mask entirely those who are performing.

### Third, Fourth, Fifth, and Sixth Grades

These children have considerable and growing manual ability, but it is still advisable to stay with simple methods of construction. You may want to experiment with shadow puppets of cardboard, for which you will need to make the screen. Buy heavy enough bristol board or cardboard for the puppets so that it will hold up without tearing or bending and will still be lightweight enough for the children to cut by themselves with school scissors. Experiment with what is available in your area.

What has been said for younger children is still valid with this age group in regard to hand puppets. It is still recommended that you sew the under-bodies, though some of the children may want to fashion more or less elaborate costumes. Give them the materials and see what happens. A box of scrap fabric, another of buttons and trim, another of yarns and fur will produce the most ingenious results. Unless you are prepared for most bodies and/or costumes to return unfinished, sewn so as to be unworkable (in the strangest ways), or deftly crafted by a talented mother, don't send the bodies and/or costumes home to be sewn. Sixth graders *could* certainly cooperate on cutting and sewing them at school, but it is the lucky teacher who has not only good scissors but a sewing machine at her disposal.

These are good years to introduce new textures and methods of crafting. Why not try foam rubber, bonded by contact cement? (See Bibliography for Bruce Chessé's pamphlet on "spong-ees," which are fun and quick to make by his method.)

Rehearsal periods at this level can be somewhat longer than for the younger child, though running over six or eight sessions is courting lost interest. Forty-five minutes to an hour at a time is about all you can ask. If your class production requires more time than that to present it in a finished fashion, it is too complicated. Keep it simple. Your students need the pride that comes of a performance well done. You will need to be the watchdog spotting overcomplicated plot, talky scenes, and impossible business. Suggest alternatives and with your best kind-yet-ruthless manner help them to simplify and then simplify again. Remind them that they must make the audience understand what is going on. (If you really get this concept across to them, they will do most of your job for you.)

While many of these fourth, fifth, and sixth grade students might like a formal puppet stage, if your school hasn't got one, don't let that deter you. An improvised stage such as we suggested for younger children or one of your own devising can be made to work very well. If you are dramatizing social studies, fairy tale, or myth, let the students decorate your improvised stage with motifs that complement their story. They may enjoy a couple of basket floodlights, even unmasked, but turned away from the audience, to give them a real sense of participating in "theatre."

*Seventh Grade and Above*

Given an extra class period, you can now get into puppet heads molded of Plasticine and cast in papier-mâché. We don't recommend plastic wood because it is just too time-consuming for most classroom projects, and celastic has a debatable toxicity. If it spills, inhaling the acetone, even in a well-ventilated room, is like sniffing glue. For molded heads, follow guides given in the body of the text or, for more detail, see how-to books. A class that becomes interested in shadow puppets is quite capable at this level of producing an enthralling show. In fact, at junior high level shadow puppets may be one of the most useful of all forms of puppet theatre. Since the students have a horror of anything "babyish" and may equate the hand puppet with some poor efforts that they have seen or with children's toys, you may find them especially receptive to the ancient but probably new to them art of shadow theatre. Renting an exceptional film, especially one of Lotte Reiniger's, would be of great value in kindling interest. Happily, good puppet films are readily available. (If you choose to pursue hand puppets with junior high or above, show them some of Jiři Trinka's films; even though most of these are done in stop-motion, the crafting of the puppets is so sophisticated that it will catch even the most jaded student's interest.)

Students of junior high age and above will enjoy crafting shadow puppets of inexpensive acetate—and the fact that all aspects of a finished production are well within their grasp and any classroom budget is not a small consideration. It is often the case at this level in schooling that students are encountering for the first time a different teacher for each subject. If you are the drama teacher, you may need to enlist the cooperation of the art teacher, or vice versa. Such scheduling gets to be a real problem when all students do not take the same classes; then you can realistically consider a performance puppet theatre project only as an after-school activity, where it often finds its place in clubs and little theatres.

Junior high and high school children are often captivated by creating a kind of "street theatre" in which live actors, masked or not, appear on a full stage with many varieties of puppets whose operators are concealed in ways of the students' devising. Again, even at this age, an expensive and complicated "puppet stage" is not required. Students are very likely to enjoy figuring out how to stage a production, given budget, space, and time. You will undoubtedly be surprised at the inventiveness and professionalism of their results.

We can somewhat mitigate our opposition to hastily assembled marionettes when we consider the older student, who is fascinated with *how* things are done. The "quick marionette" made of folded paper or cardboard is rarely going to satisfy these students, but if they craft a marionette of wood, even without stopped joints, or of cloth, so long as the figures are well weighted and strung, they may be able to create a production for their peers and younger children which is truly "theatre." When a child or children perform for other young people, the criteria for judging what is "theatre" adjust themselves. It is not that we do not wish for the best performance possible or decline to encourage excellence, but we cannot expect the beginning teenager to perform professionally. But we should not discourage the desire to experiment and to try. Children will lay aside their disbelief when they know a young person is performing, and be understanding and accepting of flaws that they would deride in an adult. And this is as it should be; they are conscious, somehow, that they are all learning together. If the performer truly believes in what he is doing, so will the audience. They will forgive an arm that bends the wrong way. Most often, marionette efforts will be solo ventures or at most a production by two or three students; rarely is it a successful classroom experience. The technical problems are just too many.

Whatever the type of puppet play produced by a class of young people, the prime goal should be involvement in the production. You will want a short construction period and enough time for rehearsal (you will be able to gauge what is enough by the age of the young people and the complexity of the script). Your best audience is one of parents and/or of peers and younger children. Yes, making puppet theatre a part of the schoolchild's experience introduces some new problems for you as the teacher, but aren't the tremendous benefits of learned cooperation, give and take of criticism, excitement in the subject matter—to say nothing of the fun of learning the craft techniques—well worth your effort? Here in puppet theatre is a potent tool with which to kindle the imagination of children glassy-eyed from hours of television, introducing them to a medium that requires the imaginative participation of every dark recess and incandescent fantasy of their complex and curious selves.

# Appendix B
## The Puppet in Therapy

Very little has been documented on the use of the puppet in the many forms of therapy, yet it has been widely used and is more and more an acceptable tool. Here we have space only to give a cursory look at the application of the puppet to therapies, but at least let us examine some of the areas in which this potent mode of theatre can be useful.

### Speech Therapy

The puppet in speech therapy has received the most attention; usually the therapist animates a puppet, producing the sound the patient needs to learn to reproduce, as for example, a snake hissing a sibilant *s*. If it is a likeable snake, the child is very apt to try harder to make the desired sound than he or she would try for a mere person requesting the same result. Why? We must go back to the same reasons why a puppet is successful in performance at all; it is not human, and yet it is alive. It has no conscience, nor can it punish us if we make a mistake, so we won't feel foolish if we flub in front of it. In fact, if the therapist-puppeteer is at all clever, the puppet will often make mistakes, too, and require correcting. One can easily imagine a range of characters constructed to fit various problem-causing sounds and enlisting the child's cooperation in learning. It works.

Less has been done with the child operating the puppets. It is more work for the therapist. But think a moment; if you can get a child to act out a very simple story with puppets on hand (crafted by you or purchased, but ones that move easily and well), you can accomplish much more if you suggest to the puppet character that he correct a sound because you (the audience) cannot understand than you can if you directly correct the child. The displacement of the correction to the personality of the puppet relieves the child of the often threatening one-to-one therapy. Do not be surprised if the puppet refuses correction, makes his speech defect worse in performance (do make sure the child is behind a masking and only the puppet is seen), and then at the end of a session or sessions (not many) speaks quite naturally. Do not call the child's attention to the fact that the speech impediment has vanished. Usually the change is quite permanent and the child is convinced that it is transferred to the puppet. The child does not see this as magic, nor does he feel guilty for foisting some impediment upon the puppet. In future sessions for some other speech problem the child may even coax the puppet out of the defect. It is not always this simple, of course, but it often is. This is a type of therapy that merits a lot more attention than it has been so far given.

### Therapy for the Emotionally Disturbed

Emotional therapy is the next most obvious area, the most powerful, and the most neglected. Doll play has been widely used for many years to enable a child to act out fears and the complexities of his problems. For some reason, puppets have rarely been included. What more potent mode is there for getting a child to reveal his well-protected (even from himself) inner self than to have him act out, behind the mask of the puppet and safely hidden by a screen, some simple story that involves whatever is suspected of troubling him? The beauty of this treatment is that when the child puts down the puppet he seems to lay aside any guilt he may feel about what it said or did as well; almost with the efficacy of hypnosis, we have glimpsed the inner child.

There are two pleas we make here to those interested in emotional therapy with puppets; one plea is to the practicing professional and the other is to the puppeteer who wishes to experience this area of work. To the professional we appeal concerning the quality of the puppet he or she gives the child. Many are stiff and will not move; others are too identified with a certain well-known character. We have found the most effective therapeutic puppet to be a simple glove, plain or patterned, with a very stylized male or female face. The top of the head is bald and covered with Velcro. A variety of wigs backed with Velcro is supplied the child, as well as a box of costume pieces and props. Thus, the child personalizes the puppet, making it whomever he or she wishes it to represent. The eyes are simple and round. The female head is quite round with a small nose; the male head has a square jaw, aquiline nose, and little detail. The facial color could represent any race, being a neutral tan. The simple glove moves easily and does not impede what the child wants to *do* with the puppet, which after all is the point, isn't it? The important difference from doll play is that the other puppet (usually representing the child or one parent) must react. If the puppet doesn't react, you will know why. Astonishingly, the child in therapy is very capable of acting with two puppets at once and many in sequence. It takes months, even years, for a budding puppeteer to master this feat. But the troubled child seems impelled by inner forces, and he is eminently capable. He gets applause for his performance, which then can be discussed to the degree the therapist chooses at an immediately following or later session.

Our second plea is to the puppeteer who wishes to dabble in therapy. Please, be aware of the power of the medium. *Never* approach any type of therapy, with a child or an adult, without the aid of a competent psychologist or psychiatrist who is able to treat immediately any problems that may arise. Even in performing yourself for a group of emotionally disturbed persons, you run the risk of uncovering emotional problems that, once laid bare, you are not competent to deal with; nor is it fair to send these people away with scabs pulled off, bare tissue exposed, and no one to treat the wound. *Never* dabble here. The puppet, with his intense involvement with the human psyche, reaches too close to that which we protect so dearly for you to lay it bare and walk away. Tread carefully. Working with competent medical advisers you can be invaluable. Working alone, you can unwittingly destroy an already disturbed psyche. These are people you deal with, not puppets; they cannot be repaired the next day.

## Prehospital Orientation

Some work has been done in this area which is quite valuable and can be expanded, even by professionally guided amateurs. The child who is to undergo surgery, especially if it is major, is under great tension. If he or she sees a puppet play about mice or rabbits (there was a time when fantasy was out of fashion, and everything had to be *just as it is*; happily we have outgrown this, and an appreciation of the once-removed value of fantasy is again in good repute) undergoing the same sort of surgery the young patient anticipates and coming out of it fine, the effect is indeed encouraging. The best results seem to come when the characters are animals and the hospital setting is as accurate as possible. No attempt should be made to sugarcoat the facts or to mislead the child into believing that he will not feel pain; it is reassuring later, when you do feel pain, to remember what you were told you would feel. You have not been lied to. Children like to be familiarized with the places they will visit and the equipment they will see. One only wishes that the persons composing these puppet performances for groups of preoperative children would not be so shy of including some of the basic fears of all children, such as mutilation and castration or the fear that they will emerge from the operation as a different person. A puppet character could easily fight to retain his (or her) pajama bottom and be reassured that all the doctors were interested in was his heart or lung or ear. The message need not be spelled out so that parents would be offended; children will understand. A sympathetic puppet who expresses fears like the child's allows the child to feel more comfortable with his own fears and gives him a chance to discover, along with the puppet hero, that his fears, though real to him, are groundless. There is much in this preoperative treatment of fears that has not been explored; and it is certainly a worthy and useful area for you to pursue with your puppet.

There are so many areas where puppets can be used to convey messages or dispel fears. In this function, the puppet is truly performing puppet theatre, even if it is a theatre for one, for that one has a complete suspension of disbelief during the performance and in that sweet passage of time a life may change.

# Bibliography for Puppeteers

Note: The books are separated into categories according to their predominant subject, though many puppet books do treat several types of puppets. We have italicized areas of additional interest in our comments. Those books not in print are often to be found in public and university libraries or can be borrowed on inter-library loan. Local puppet guilds often maintain libraries. Many of the British books can be ordered directly; ·he large British book houses, such as Foyles in London, can be depended upon to find you just about anything that was ever in print! Most of the more recent books, plus the pamphlets, can be obtained from:

> The Puppetry Store
> Attn: Mrs. Marie Samanisky
> 3500 Tyler, N.E.
> Minneapolis, Minnesota 55418

The Puppetry Store is a function of the Puppeteers of America (see the list of puppetry organizations at end of Bibliography). No prices for books or pamphlets are given, since they are subject to change.

## General Puppet Books

Arnott, Peter D. *Plays Without People*. Bloomington, Indiana: University of Indiana Press, 1964. Intelligent discussion of the puppet, especially of *marionette* in *serious drama*. Rather stuffy, however, and presents a one-sided view with much discussion of the author's own work and biased criticism of professional puppeteers abroad.

Baird, Bil. *The Art of the Puppet*. New York: The Ridge Press, Macmillan, Inc., 1965. Brief text provides interesting, readable *history* of each type of puppet. *Beautifully* illustrated with many fine color and black-and-white plates.

Batchelder (McPharlin), Marjorie. *The Puppet Theatre Handbook*. New York: Harper and Brothers, 1947. Still the bible of how-to books, covering *every aspect of puppetry.* Illustrated with helpful line drawings. Several good stage plans with clear specifications for building. Highly recommended.

Beaumont, Cyril. *Puppets and Puppetry.* New York: The Studio Publications, 1958. Brief, well-meaning but not very well-documented text. Profusely illustrated with photographs from all over the world.

Bedman, Kamil. *Contes et Marionnettes.* Prague: Maison d'Édition. Technique à Prague, 1958. Inspiring but hard to find picture book of Czechoslovakian puppetry: hand, rod, string, and shadow; plus stop-motion film. Text in French tells stories of plays and films.

Benegal, Som, ed. *Puppet Theatre Around the World.* India: The Caxton Press, 1960. Comprehensive review for International Theatre Institute. Profusely illustrated.

Bussell, Jan. *The Puppets and I.* London: Faber and Faber, n.d. Autobiographical account of author's travels and recollections. Highly readable. The author and Ann Hogarth, his partner, remain major forces in British puppetry today.

————. *The Puppet Theatre.* London: Faber and Faber, 1947. A somewhat cursory puppet craft book.

Efimova, Nina. *Adventures of a Russian Puppet Theatre.* Birmingham, Michigan: Puppetry Imprints, 1935. Invaluable, highly readable. Efimova's personal insights into every aspect of her art. Through this book one becomes acquainted with Russian puppetry just after the Revolution, as well as with the work of a very individual artist.

Hanford, Robert Ten Eyck. *The Complete Book of Puppets and Puppeteering.* New York: Drake Publishers, Inc., 1975. Though one can mistrust anything purporting to be "The Complete . . .", the book is at least recent and includes several interviews with contemporary puppeteers.

Inverarity, R. Bruce. *A Manual of Puppetry.* Portland, Oregon: Binfords and Mort, 1975. Like Batchelder's, the other *highly recommended handbook,* covers *every aspect of puppetry* and especially good for beginning *marionette* work.

Joseph, Helen Haiman. *A Book of Marionettes.* New York: B. W. Huebsch, 1920. Readable, with reasonable accuracy. Covers not just marionettes but hand and shadow as well. Note: Watch out for the author's original scripts. Very long and talky.

Keene, Donald. *Bunraku.* Tokyo: Kodansha International, 1965. An incredible work, beautifully written and documented. The splendid illustrations include tipped-in color plates. A recording accompanies the text.

Magnin, Charles. *Histoire des Marionnettes en Europe depuis l'Antiquité jusqu'à nos jours.* Paris: Michel Lèvy Frères, 12th ed., revised, 1862. This is the granddaddy of all puppet history books. It is hard to find, as you might guess by its publication date; but if you are doing any serious work in puppet history, it is necessary for you to consult this prime source, even if you have to have it translated. Suggest a microfilm of the copy in the Rare Book Room at Harvard. The line of descent in puppet histories appears to be Magnin to Maindron to Von Boëhn to Beaumont and McPharlin (Paul). Unfortunately, each repeated the errors of his predecessors. One has to applaud Joseph, who, despite some lack of scholarly documentation, at least appears to have gone back to Magnin.

Magon, Jero. *Staging the Puppet Show.* Coral Gables, Fla.: University of Miami Press, 1976. Soft cover. An intelligent puppet book that views puppetry as theatre and contributes much from the author's rich background in theatre craft for puppets.

Malik, Dr. Jan. *Puppetry in Czechoslovakia.* Prague: Orbis, after 1947 and before 1958. Soft cover. Not as obscure as it sounds; quite a number of copies are around. Text in English. Black-and-white photographs of quality.

McKechnie, Samuel. *Popular Entertainments through the Ages.* London: Sampson, Low, Marston, Ltd., n.d. Accounts of fairs, *Punch and Judy,* wonderful Victorian illustrations, black and white.

McPharlin, Paul. *The Puppet Theatre in America.* New York: Harper and Brothers, 1949. Definitive. Contains list of American puppeteers, 1524–1948.

————. *Puppets in America.* (with an account of the first American Puppetry Conference). Detroit: Puppetry Imprints, 1936. Brief text, numerous black-and-white photographs.

Niculescu, Margarita. *The Puppet Theatre of the Modern World.* Boston: Plays, Inc., 1967. Profuse illustrations offer inspiration. Short commentaries by the Editorial Board of UNIMA, including Sergei Obraztsov, Harro Seigel, and Henryk Jurkowski.

Philpott, A. P. *Dictionary of Puppetry.* Boston: Plays, Inc., 1969. This really is a dictionary, alphabetized and cross-referenced and covering not only individual artists but just about *every aspect of puppetry and puppet theatre* ever thought of. Both accurate and scholarly.

Phipott, Violet, and McNeil, Mary Jean. *The How Book of Puppets.* Bristol, England: Purnell and Sons, Ltd., 1957. Elementary, but reasonable.

Purschke, Hans R. *Puppenspiel in Deutschland.* Darmstadt; Neue Darmstadter Verlagsanstalt, 1957. Soft cover. Text in German. Black-and-white and a few color plates. Definitive selection of the work of many puppeteers of Germany.

————. *Liebens Verte Puppenswelt.* Hamburg: Marion von Schröder Verlag, 1962. Black-and-white photographs. Extensive collection of puppet pictures.

Speight, George. *The History of the English Puppet Theatre.* New York: John de Graff, n.d. (c. 1955). Extremely well documented by a true scholar.

————. *Punch and Judy.* Boston: Plays, Inc., 1970. As good as the above.

*Theatre Crafts,* Vol. 9, No. 2, Mar/April, 1975. New York: Rodale Press, Inc., 1975. Contains solid articles on numerous aspects of puppetry by contemporary puppeteers. Especially notable is Tom Tichnor's cloth marionette.

Von Boëhn, Max. *Dolls and Puppets.* Boston: Charles T. Branford Company, Revised ed., 1956. Complete, scholarly, and with fewer errors than most.

————. *Puppets and Automata.* New York: Dover Publications, Inc., 1972. Soft cover. (Contains the volume dealing with puppets from the above at a fraction of the price.)

## Hand Puppets

Bramall, Eric, and Somerville, Christopher C. *Expert Puppet Technique.* Boston: Plays, Inc., 1966. A somewhat tedious, mostly theoretical book. Does not have exercises but does give interesting striplighting patterns.

Emberley, Ed. *Punch and Judy, a Play for Puppets.* Boston: Little, Brown and Co., 1965. Good clear edition of the *play,* but listed here for its bright, happy illustrations and the inspiration they give toward design.

Fijan, Carol and Engler. *Making Puppets Come Alive.* New York: Taplinger Publishing Co., 1973. Very basic, but shows puppet positions cleverly and clearly. Concentrates on teaching individual gestures to express emotions.

Lee, Miles. *Puppet Theatre.* Fair Lawn, New Jersey: Essential Books, 1958. Very good exercises plus discussions of movement, grouping, and handling the rehearsal period. Silhouette positions of puppets in illustrations by Olivia Hopkins are especially effective.

Mahlmann, Lewis, and Schubert, Lettie Connell. *Patterns for Machine-Sewn Felt Puppets.* Excellent. Available from Puppetry Store or from Mahlmann at 700 E. 24th Street, Oakland, California 94606.

Merton, George. *The Hand Puppets.* New York: Thomas Nelson and Sons, 1957. Soft cover. Excellent step-by-step casting illustrations with black-and-white photographs.

Russell, Joan. *The Woman's Day Book of Soft Toys and Dolls.* New York: Simon and Schuster, 1975. Many cloth animal patterns adaptable to puppets.

Schubert, Lettie Connell. *A Handbook of Hand Puppet Manipulation.* Xerox or similar copy pamphlet available through the Puppetry Store. Clear, concise, very workable, many exercises.

## Rod Puppets

Batchelder (McPharlin), Marjorie, and Michael, Vivan. *Hand-and-Rod Puppets.* Adventures in Education, Fine and Applied Arts, Series No. 1; Ohio State College, Columbus, Ohio, 1947. Clear and very helpful. Does not include any of the complex European controls.

Coad Canada Puppets. *Rod Puppets.* Self-printed excellent pamphlet. Many hints and step-by-step help plus illustrations of European controls. Available from the Puppetry Store.

————. *Black Theatre.* As fine as the above and similarly available.

Fettis, Hansjuergen. *Glove and Rod Puppets.* Trans. John Wright and Susanne Foster. London: Harrap, 1973. Invaluable.

## Marionettes

Beaton, Mabel and Les. *Marionettes.* New York: Thomas Y. Crowell Company, 1948. Intelligent with step-by-step casting processes illustrated in black-and-white photographs. Instruction given for wooden marionettes but also for the most workable of cloth string puppets.

Lanchester, Waldo S. *Hand Puppets and String Puppets.* Leichester: Dryad Press, 1949. Soft cover. Offers instruction of high quality on string puppets, of less note on hand puppets. Contains pattern sheet for the Lanchester marionette.

Merton, George. *The Marionette.* Toronto: Thomas Nelson and Sons, 1957. Better than the volume on the Hand Puppet, in fact, very clearly illustrates the author's methods of designing and crafting the marionette. Illustrates vertical control.

Rose, Rufus and Margo. *Making and Operating Marionettes.* Self-printed pamphlet, 1975. Concise and clear summary of the famous Rose Method. Try the Puppetry Store.

Whanslaw, H. W. *Everybody's Marionette Book.* London: Wells, Gardner, Darton and Co., Ltd., n.d. Belongs in every marionette puppeteer's library. Imaginative and informative. Line drawing illustrations.

————. *Animal Puppetry.* Redhill, Surrey: Wells, Darton and Co., Ltd., 1948. Really excellent. Helps you translate the animal anatomy into working marionettes.

———— and Hotchkins, Victor. *Specialized Puppetry.* Redhill, Surrey: Wells, Darton and Co., Ltd., 1948. The book every marionette person needs to make those *trick marionettes*!

## Shadow Puppets

Reiniger, Lotte. *Shadow Theatres and Shadow Films*. Boston: Plays, Inc., 1975. A beautiful and instructive book by a master of the shadow theatre in all its forms.

Schönewolf, Herta. *Play with Light and Shadow*. New York: Reinhold Book Corp., 1968. Interesting departures in the use of shadows, stress on use of projectors.

Siyayusgil, Sabri Esat. *Karagöz*. Ankara: Turkish Press, Broadcasting and Tourist Department (Toraman Basimevi), 1955. Hard to find, but this is the definitive work on the Turkish shadow theatre.

## Acting

Boleslavsky, Richard. *Acting; the First Six Lessons*. New York: Theatre Arts Books, 1949. A witty little book which provides delightful reading and much help in the profession.

Obraztsov, Sergei. *My Profession*. Moscow: Foreign Languages Publishing House, 1950. In English. If one book could be chosen for the beginning puppeteer, this would win our nomination. An inspired narrative telling of the author's growth in his profession as a puppeteer; the book should probably fall into *every category of this bibliography,* excepting only craft information.

Stanislavski, Constantin. *An Actor Prepares*. New York: Theatre Arts Books, 1950. Make this book your constant companion.

———. *Building a Character*. New York: Theatre Arts Books, 1949. Read this one second; it will be of inestimable help.

## Playwriting

Kerr, Walter. *How Not to Write a Play*. Boston: Writer, Inc., 1955. Delightful and most helpful.

Williams, Jesse Lynch et al. *The Art of Playwriting*. Freeport, New York: Books for Libraries Press, 1967. Has the virtue of availability; not as basic as Kerr.

## Puppet Plays

Note: If you *must* use a fully scripted show written by someone other than yourself, here are some of the better ones available. They may also give you ideas for original work of your own.

Baker, Frank. *Playing with Punch*. New York: T. V. Boardman and Co., Ltd., 1944. Contains "Mr. Payne Collier's transcription of the Immortal Drama of Punch and Judy." This will probably be your earliest source and most reliable *historically*.

Mahlmann, Lewis, and Jones, David Cadwalader. *Puppet Plays for Young Players*. Boston: Plays, Inc., 1974. The best of the lot; the authors really understand a child audience and have a witty humor as well.

Shaw, Bernard. *Shakes versus Shaw*. Stratford-upon-Avon: Waldo Lanchester, n.d. Shaw's tribute to puppetry. A very brief satirical conversational exchange between Shakespeare and Shaw represented as puppets.

Swortzell, Lowell, ed. *All the World's a Stage*. (Gr. 7 and up). New York: Delacorte Press, 1972. Contains a fascinating collection of plays, including "The Billy-club Puppets" by Federico García Lorca. Generally very elaborate productions for puppets to attempt, but wonderful springboards for ideas.

## Directing

Cole, Toby, and Chinoy, Helen Krich. *Directing the Play*. Indianapolis: The Bobbs Merrill Company, Inc., 1953. Observations of professional directors from George II to Harold Clurman.

Dean, Alexander. *Fundamentals of Play Directing*. New York: Holt, Rinehart and Winston, 3rd ed., 1974. Dogmatic, but it all works. Another bible.

## Costume

Barton, Lucy. *Historic Costume for the Stage*. Boston: Revised ed., 1971. The costumier's bible. Complete, concise, helpful in every way.

Boulard, Constance, and Doten, Hazel R. *Costume Drawing*. New York: Pitman Publishing Corporation, 1967. Soft cover. Brief. Helpful for the beginner in isolating the basic line of a given period.

Laver, James. *Costume in the Theatre*. New York: Hill and Wang, 1964. This and *numerous* other costume books by the author all exhaustive and excellent.

Wilcox, R. Turner. *The Mode in Costume*. New York: Charles Scribner's Sons, 1942. Especially valuable for motifs given from each period.

## Stage Lighting and Design

Craig, Edward Gordon. *Scene*. New York: Benjamin Bloom, 1923, 1968. This devotee of the puppet, who revitalized theatre design, sets forth his theories.

———. *On the Art of the Theatre*. New York: Theatre Arts Books, 1957. More of the above and contains the famous "Übermarionette" essay.

Finch, Christopher. *The Art of Walt Disney*. New York: Harry N. Abrams, Inc., 1973. Much is to be learned from the beautiful animation backdrops by Disney.

McCandless, Stanley. *A Method of Lighting the Stage*. New York: Theatre Arts Books, Inc., 1954. Another one of those trustworthy bibles.

Parker, Oren, and Smith, Harvey. *Scene Design and Stage Lighting*. New York: Holt, Rinehart and Winston, Inc., 1968. Detailed, complicated, but accurate *practical help*. Highly recommended.

Pecktal, Lynn. *Designing and Painting for the Theatre*. New York: Holt, Rinehart and Winston, 1975. Up to date!

Polus, Betty. *Why and How to Light the Puppet Stage*. Xerox pamphlet available from the author; 2 Bar Creek Road, Boulder Creek, California 95006. Has good, practical advice, though tends to emphasize home-built devices.

Selden, Samuel, and Sellman, Hunton D. *Stage Scenery and Lighting*. New York: Appleton-Century-Crofts, Inc., 3rd ed., 1959. Really fine and reliable practical training advice in every aspect of light and design and stage craft.

Thomajan, P. K. *Handbook of Designs and Motifs*. New York: Tudor Publishing Company, 1950. Invaluable; contains an endless series of designs without text.


## Puppetry in Education


Anderson, Benny E. *Let's Start a Puppet Theatre*. New York: Van Nostrand Reinhold Co., 1971. Innovative materials for children to use. Also novel ideas for sound effects.

Batchelder, Marjorie, and Comer, Virginia Lee. *Puppets and Plays, a Creative Approach*. New York: Harper and Brothers, 1956. Many good ideas and a very sound approach. Probably the most helpful book in this category.

Beresford, Margaret. *How to Make Puppets and Teach Puppetry*. New York: Taplinger Publishing Co., 1966. Basically sound with tips for incorporating puppetry into the curriculum.

Chessé, Bruce, and Armstrong, Beverly. *Sponge-ees*. Independent Printing Co., Early Stages, P. O. Box 5027, Walnut Creek, California. Order directly or try The Puppetry Store. A novel and well-detailed quick method for working with children creating puppets from foam rubber. Recommended.

Cummings, Richard. *101 Hand Puppets*. New York: David McKay Co., 1962. Really does illustrate 101 different puppets; a good idea source.

Fling, Helen. *Marionettes; How to Make and Work Them.* New York: Dover Publications, Inc., 1973. Explicit simple advice, good illustrations of joints; the best of the simple marionette books.

Hansen, Steve. *The Family Creative Workshop—Puppetry.* New York: Plenary Publications International, Inc., 1975. Pop-up, finger, and junk puppets by a charismatic street puppeteer.

Lesser, Gerald S. *Children and Television, Lessons from Sesame Street.* New York: Random House, 1974. Personal, planning, and broadcasting lessons learned from *Sesame Street;* includes analysis of what the child can assimilate at different ages.

Roth, Charlene Davis. *The Art of Making Puppets and Marionettes.* Radnor, Pennsylvania: Chilton Book Co., 1975. Many patterns for very simple puppets.


## Puppetry Organizations

*The Puppeteers of America.* Adult membership $12.00, junior $6.00, group $20.00. Bimonthly journal. Holds annual week-long festival of shows and workshops at a college campus in summer. For information write: Olga Stevens, Executive Secretary, The Puppeteers of America, P. O. Box 1061, Ojai, California 93023. The "P of A" also has numerous chartered local guilds.

*UNIMA* (Union Internationale des Marionnettes). Adult membership $10.00. International puppeteers organization. *Appropo,* journal published in U.S.A. by Mollie Falkenstein. Adult membership $10.00 per year. Inquire: Allelu Kurten, Executive Secretary, UNIMA, Browning Road, Hyde Park, New York 10024.

# Index